MANUSCRIPTS AND READERS
IN FIFTEENTH-CENTURY ENGLAND

Manuscripts and Readers in Fifteenth-Century England

THE LITERARY IMPLICATIONS OF MANUSCRIPT STUDY

Essays from the 1981 Conference at the University of York

Edited by Derek Pearsall

D. S. BREWER   BIBLIO

First published in 1983 by
D. S. Brewer, 240 Hills Road, Cambridge
an imprint of Boydell & Brewer Ltd
P. O. Box 9, Woodbridge, Suffolk IP12 3DF
and by Biblio Distribution Services
81 Adams Drive, Totowa, NJ 07512, U.S.A.

British Library Cataloguing in Publication Data

Manuscripts and readers in fifteenth century England.
  1. Manuscripts — Congresses
  I. Pearsall, Derek
  091   Z6602
  ISBN 0-85991-148-9

Library of Congress Cataloging in Publication Data
Main entry under title:

Manuscripts and readers in fifteenth-century England.

  Bibliography: p.
  Includes index.
  1. English literature -- Middle English, 1100-1500 --
Criticism, Textual -- Congresses. 2. Manuscripts,
English (Middle) -- Editing -- Congresses. I. Pearsall,
Derek Albert.
PR275.T45M35 1983   820'.9'002   83-9223
ISBN 0-85991-148-9
Printed and bound in Great Britain by
Short Run Press Ltd, Exeter

CONTENTS

LIST OF ILLUSTRATIONS

The Contributors

Julia Boffey Department of English, Queen Mary College, University of London

Dr A. I. Doyle University Library, Durham

Professor A. S. G. Edwards Department of English, University of Victoria, British Columbia

Kate Harris New Hall, Cambridge

Dr Lesley Lawton Centre for Medieval Studies, University of York

Dr C. W. Marx Department of English, St David's University College, Lampeter

Mrs Carole M. Meale Centre for Medieval Studies, University of York

Jeremy J. Smith Department of English, University of Glasgow

John J. Thompson Department of English, Queen's University, Belfast

Dr Thorlac Turville-Petre Department of English, University of Nottingham

INTRODUCTION

Derek Pearsall

The essays collected in the present volume are versions, revised for publication, of the papers presented at the conference held at the University of York, 10-12 July, 1981, on 'The study of fifteenth-century manuscripts and the study of late medieval English literature'. Nine of the twelve papers given then are represented here, and Dr Doyle, whose own opening address has been published elsewhere, has contributed a concluding 'Retrospect and Prospect'.

The idea for and subject matter of the conference were suggested to me partly by the direction that my own work has taken in the last few years, partly by the work I have been doing in the field with quite a large number of research students. With many of these I had worked in collaboration with the late Elizabeth Salter. But, in a wider sense, it seemed and seems important to recognise that palaeography, codicology and manuscript studies generally are now more than ever before to be seen as an integral part of the study of literature and literary history, and vice versa. The fact of their interdependence becomes clearer and clearer as research advances, and the nature of that interdependence needs to be similarly clarified. The days are gone when a palaeographer could be dismissed as soon as his job of dating a manuscript was done, or a manuscript dismissed as soon as it was discerned to be of little value to 'the critical edition'. All this is changing, and literary scholars are beginning to learn the importance of close attention to the primary materials of their study. The tyranny exerted by 'the critical edition' is now recognised, and scholars are learning the value of 'bad manuscripts': how in the work of interfering and meddling scribes, for instance, can be seen the activities of our first literary critics. The methods of compilers and manuscript editors of all kinds, whether professional or amateur, need to be studied, if we are to understand the reception and readership assumed for the literary works contained in their collections. The manuscript context of particular works needs to be understood in detail; matters of layout and format give an insight into the ways in which medieval poems were understood to exist; changes in handwriting, ink, or paper are often clues to the nature of the exemplars, even the authors' copies, with which scribes were working; the excerpting, abridging and paraphrasing of certain major works give unrivalled access to the modes of thought within which such works were first read and used; and the pictures provided by early illustrators always promise a glimpse of an authentic primary response to a text. In a broader context, there are particular modes of approach to the study of groups of manuscripts which have proved to be of special value: the cross-section, for instance, taken through the literary culture of the period in studying the manuscripts of a particular work, or the work of a particular writer; or another kind of cross-section which concentrates on manuscript production, on the makers and readers of manuscripts, in a specific localised area. As an indispensable accessory to all these kinds of study, there is also, of course, the close attention to the dialect of texts as they appear in individual manuscripts, and to the minutiae of scribal spelling, which provides not only a means of localisation but also an insight into the way literary texts were received and communicated by scribes. All of these matters are tackled, at more or less length, in the papers at present collected.

If it be argued that these are matters of merely historical concern, of interest only to the historian of taste or book-production, and of no essential importance to our consideration of the intentions that we presume to exist in the author's act of composition, then one would have to retort that no work of literature exists in a state of such pure being, and that reading is always an act in which we share with the writer in the making of meaning. Attention to the activities of the scribes, compilers, editors, decorators and illustrators of our fifteenth-century manuscripts helps to ensure that the reader's share is fairly apportioned.

I should like to conclude by thanking the contributors for originally agreeing to accept the invitation to speak at the Conference, for their care in preparing their papers for publication, and for their patience in the interim. I should like to thank Dr Doyle for his contribution, and for his support and advice at all times. The costs of the present publication have been partly borne by a grant from the F. R. Leavis Fund, administered by the Department of English at the University of York, and I am very grateful to the Committee responsible for the allocation of the Fund for their generosity.

THE MANUSCRIPTS OF ENGLISH COURTLY LOVE LYRICS IN THE FIFTEENTH CENTURY

Julia Boffey

The starting point for this paper is suggested by a remark made by Rosemary Woolf:

> The reading of lyrics in their manuscripts is a valuable exercise, for they often then give an impression very different from that which they give in modern anthologies. The manuscript context of the lyrics is one of the clearest indications of how they were regarded in the Middle Ages . . .[1]

I want to investigate the manuscript context of those fifteenth-century lyrics usually gathered together as 'courtly' love poems — short, essentially non-narrative compositions, in a refined and elevated style, which mostly concern the poet-lover's words to, or a description of, his mistress. At the same time I would like to consider some of the effects which anthologising can have on our reading of these poems. Modern editions of Middle English lyrics of all kinds must invariably 'uproot' the poems from their original contexts in some way,[2] but do they sometimes transplant them in new beds which are too neat, too ordered, and which imply rather too much homogeneity of genre and function? Different sorts of anthologies will of course suggest new and sometimes illuminating contexts for some of these lyrics, and in many respects their proliferation is stimulating and healthy[3] — chronological arrangement, or arrangement by subject, for example, may well suggest correspondences which might otherwise pass unnoticed; my purpose is not to quarrel with anthologisers, but merely to take the opportunity to look closely at the contexts of this particular group of lyrics to see if the evidence of the *manuscripts* suggests in any way that the poems were seen as serving similar purposes or fulfilling similar needs. My strategy will be to give a brief (and inevitably breathlessly sketchy) survey of the general manuscript situation,

---

[1] R. Woolf, *The English Religious Lyric in the Middle Ages* (Oxford, 1968), 376. For further interesting discussion of the contexts of lyrics, see J. A. Burrow, 'Poems Without Contexts', *Essays in Criticism* 29 (1979), 6-32.

[2] The exceptions here are the editions and facsimiles of complete manuscripts which are beginning to appear in greater numbers.

[3] R. H. Robbins, *Secular Lyrics of the Fourteenth and Fifteenth Centuries* (Oxford, 1952, rev. 1955), F. Sidgwick & E. K. Chambers, *Early English Lyrics* (London, 1907, repr. 1966), and R. L. Greene, *The Early English Carols* (Oxford, 1935, rev. 1977), for example, all adopt a 'subject' approach; R. T. Davies, *Medieval English Lyrics: a Critical Anthology* (London, 1963) opts for a chronological arrangement; T. Silverstein, *Medieval English Lyrics* (London, 1971) goes for a compromise between the two.

and then to go on to a comparison of the settings, in different manuscripts, of the same pair of lyrics.

In the preliminary general survey, I have confined myself to all the fifteenth-century[4] copies of courtly love lyrics which I have been able to trace, using *The Index of Middle English Verse* and its *Supplement*.[5] Most of these cluster in the second half of the century, interestingly enough, even those of Chaucer's shorter poems which fall into the courtly-love-lyric category. In total, they amount to over four hundred lyrics, contained in about one hundred manuscripts. A first glance at these manuscripts reveals nothing but bewildering diversity – the poems seem to be scattered in an enormous number of greatly differing collections – but a closer look suggests that this apparently negative evidence may after all have some positive use: it indicates, first of all, the comparative dearth of duplicate copies; secondly, it makes abundantly clear the fact that these poems do not survive generally in large, coherently planned and executed anthologies, but more often in unlikely places in ones and twos.[6] The largest collection, and the only one to concentrate on courtly love lyrics to the exclusion of everything else, is – ironically enough, but entirely typically – associated with a *French* poet: Charles d'Orléans. This is British Library MS Harley 682.[7] It contains English translations (or parallel versions, to put it more diplomatically) of a large number of French *ballades* and *chansons* contained in a manuscript which Charles himself owned, Bibliothèque Nationale MS f. fr. 25458,[8] together with some other English poems of a similar nature which have no surviving French equivalents.[9] The lyrics in the English collection are organised into a sort of pseudo-narrative sequence, linked by some longer explanatory passages, and they form a cycle of the kind which was seemingly particularly favoured by French poets.[10] It survives as

4 The boundaries which I have set myself here are inevitably arbitrary, as it is impossible to date the copies of many of these lyrics with any real precision. The situation is further complicated by the inclusion in the *Supplement* of lyrics from several early sixteenth-century collections (Bodleian MS Rawlinson c.813, for example, and the so-called 'Tudor song-books', British Library Additional MSS 5465 and 31922) on the grounds that they represent late copies of fifteenth-century poems. In the interests of consistency, I have taken account of all these in my total.
5 C. Brown & R. H. Robbins, *The Index of Middle English Verse* (New York, 1943); J. L. Cutler & R. H. Robbins, *A Supplement to the Index of Middle English Verse* (Lexington, Kentucky, 1965).
6 Oddly enough, the sixteenth-century manuscripts mentioned above in *note 4* account for a large proportion of these lyrics. MS Rawlinson c.813, especially, is one of the most substantial surviving collections; see F. M. Padelford & A. R. Benham, 'The Songs in MS Rawlinson c.813', *Anglia* 31 (1908), 309-97, and S. L. Jansen Jaech, 'A Late Middle English Literary Anthology: Rawlinson MS c.813', Ph.D. thesis, University of Washington, 1980. For the courtly lyrics in the Fayrfax Manuscript, BL Addit. 5465, see J. Stevens, *Early Tudor Songs and Carols, Musica Britannica* 36 (1965), and for those in Henry VIII's Book, BL Addit. 31922, J. Stevens, *Music at the Court of Henry VIII, Musica Britannica* 18 (1962). The texts alone, without music, are collected by the same author in *Music and Poetry in the Early Tudor Court* (London, 1961; Cambridge, 1979).
7 Ed. M. Day & R. Steele, *The English Poems of Charles d'Orléans*, EETS OS 201 (1941) and 220 (1946), repr. as one volume in 1970.
8 And in the copies deriving from it.
9 Steele and Day provide notes on the correspondences in their edition of the poems.
10 Examples of these are Froissart, *Le Livre du Tresor Amoureux*; Machaut, *Le Livre du*

something of a freak occurrence — the only thing of this nature in *English*, unless one includes works like *Troilus and Criseyde* or *The Temple of Glass* as examples of lyric 'chains'. Its right to be described as 'English' is, anyway, somewhat questionable; the manuscript may well have been prepared for Charles himself, like Bibliothèque Nationale MS f. fr. 25458, perhaps during his imprisonment,[11] and have been little publicised among English readers. There is certainly not otherwise a great deal of evidence to suggest that English versions of Charles's poems were particularly well-known. The most famous copy of his work in English hands during the fifteenth century, British Library Royal MS 16. F. ii, prepared for Arthur, prince of Wales, includes a specially arranged sequence of the *French* poems, carefully doctored to impress upon the recently betrothed prince the joys of married love.[12] Most English readers hungry for lyric cycles seem to have made for the French variety: Christine de Pisan's *Cent Balades d'Amant et de Dame* and *Le Livre du Duc des Vrais Amants*, included in the sumptuous British Library MS Harley 4431, passed successively through the hands of John, duke of Bedford, and of Richard Woodville;[13] Richard Beauchamp, earl of Warwick, owned a collection of Froissart's lyrics;[14] Thomas, duke of Clarence, was presented with a collection of Machaut's.[15]

Whatever impact the English versions of Charles's poems had seems to have been limited to his own particular circle. Part of Bodleian MS Fairfax 16, the large Chaucerian collection, is devoted to a series of English 'ballads', 'complaints', and 'letters' (so termed in the contemporary table of contents) which can plausibly be attributed to the French duke, or to whichever author produced the reworkings of his poems. One of them, a 'complaint' (*O thou fortune which has the governaunce*, *Index* 2567), also appears in Bibliothèque Nationale MS f. fr. 25458, Charles's personal collection, and it seems reasonable to suppose that its fellows in the Fairfax manuscript, all of which seem to have been copied together from a

---

Voir-Dit; Christine de Pisan, *Le Livre du Duc des Vrais Amants*, and René d'Anjou, *Le Livre du Cueur d'Amours Espris*.

[11] Steele and Day, *op. cit.* xxi, point out the close connections between MSS Harley 682 and Bibliothèque Nationale f. fr. 25458: 'the two manuscripts are of the same size, the arrangement of the verse on the page is the same, they are substantially identical in matter, and what is still more significant, in order — an order not found in any other manuscript'.

[12] Only three English lyrics crop up among the French ones here: *Go forth myn hert wyth my lady* (*Index* 922), *My hertly love is in your governans* (*Index* 2246), and *Ne were my trewe innocent hert* (*Index* 2289). For an examination of the order of the French poems, see J. Fox, *Charles d'Orléans: Choix de Poésies, ed. d'après le MS Royal 16. f. ii du British Museum* (Exeter, 1973).

[13] K. Varty, *Christine de Pisan: Ballades, Rondeaux & Virelais* (Leicester, 1965), xxxvii. The signatures of Jacquetta of Luxembourg and of her stepson Anthony Woodville appear on f.1r of the manuscript, together with that of Louis de Bruges, Sire de la Gruthuyse, friend and protector of Edward IV. It seems that John of Bedford, husband to Jacquetta, acquired the manuscript some time after his appointment as regent of France in 1425.

[14] Bibliothèque Nationale MSS f. fr. 830-31.

[15] Bibliothèque Nationale MS f. fr. 9221, presented to Clarence in 1412 by Jean de Berry. See H. Omont, *La Bibliothèque Nationale: Catalogue Générale des Manuscrits Français* I (Paris, 1895) 326; J. Porcher, *Les Manuscrits à Peinture en France du XIIIᵉ au XVIᵉ Siècle* (Paris, 1955) 72.

self-contained booklet, came from the same kind of source.[16] A further interesting link can be drawn between Charles and John Stanley, the probable commissioner of MS Fairfax 16. Stanley, Usher of the Chamber for a time under Henry VI, and Sergeant of the Armoury in the Tower, was responsible for guarding the Duke of Suffolk, Charles's friend and gaoler for a time, during his own confinement in 1450. Here is a possible route by which some of the English versions of Charles's poems may have reached an English reader. It seems to me entirely typical, though, that poems associated with a Frenchman should form the most substantial body of surviving English courtly love lyrics. It spells out the fact that English readers seem to have valued lyrics *as reading matter* only if they were either in French, or had strong French connections. John Shirley's manuscripts, as a further example, contain more courtly love lyrics in French than in English.[17]

No other English collections can match either the careful planning or the unanimity of tone which characterise these two collections associated with Charles. Humphrey Newton's commonplace book, Bodleian MS Lat. misc. c. 66,[18] while containing many lyrics, can hardly be said to represent the same impulse, for its poems survive in written form more by accident than by design. These are evidently Newton's own compositions (to judge from the numerous false starts and corrections which he makes) and they are copied haphazardly, almost as palimpsests, in one small section of his otherwise business-orientated commonplace book. The impression given is that this was the only spare paper he had to hand when composing the poems – not at all that he wanted to record them for posterity. The so-called Findern Manuscript, Cambridge University Library Ff. 1.6,[19] is another collection that contains many courtly love lyrics, but again it can hardly be called an organised anthology of them. It seems originally to have consisted of a number of booklets into which a variety of amateur (or possibly semi-professional) hands copied a selection of longer items. Most of the lyrics seem to have been inserted at different dates by later hands, perhaps after some of the booklets had been bound together. They function in this case rather like the poems in an autograph album – added to record the fact of the writer's association with the manuscript, rather than anything else. One interesting point which does emerge from this collection, though, is that some of the lyrics were definitely copied from *written*

---

[16] Information about MS Fairfax 16 is to be found in the very full introduction by J. Norton-Smith to the recent facsimile edition, *Bodleian MS Fairfax 16* (London, 1979).

[17] Trinity College Cambridge MS R. 3. 20, one of Shirley's autograph manuscripts, contains two large groups of courtly love lyrics in French; the majority of its English lyrics are on religious or moral themes. British Library Additional MS 34360, thought to have been compiled (with British Library MS Harley 2251) from a lost Shirley original, contains three of these same French poems. One of them, ascribed in both English manuscripts to the Duke of Suffolk, turns out to be by Alain Chartier; see J. Laidlaw, *The Poetical Works of Alain Chartier* (Cambridge, 1974) 140, 142.

[18] For a description of the manuscript, and editions of its lyrics, see R. H. Robbins, 'The Poems of Humphrey Newton Esq., 1466-1536', *PMLA* 65 (1950), 249-81.

[19] The Findern Manuscript is described by R. H. Robbins, 'The Findern Anthology', *PMLA* 69 (1954), 610-42, and by R. Beadle & A. E. B. Owen, *The Findern Manuscript* (London, 1977). A further note is provided by G. R. Keiser, 'MS Rawlinson A.393: Another Findern Manuscript', *Transactions of the Cambridge Bibliographical Society* 7 (1980), 445-48.

sources, not orally transmitted as 'songs', as is often supposed of this kind of thing. One hand has copied a group of three lyrics into the early part of the manuscript: Chaucer's *Pity*, and two anonymous *ballades*, *As oft as syghes ben in herte trewe*, *Index* 402, and *For lac of sighte gret cause I have to pleyne*, *Index* 828.[20] The same three lyrics appear, in exactly the same order, at the end of the first of the four booklets making up Bodleian MS Tanner 346.[21] The textual variants in the two copies are slight — almost solely orthographical — and it seems certain that both were copied from the same exemplar. The Tanner scribe, for instance, has difficulty with exactly the same portion of the first anonymous *ballade* as the Findern scribe; in Tanner it emerges jumbled, in Findern it is omitted entirely, as if the scribe realised that he could not make sense of it.[22]

Another collection which at first sight looks to be an anthology of lyrics is part of Trinity College Cambridge MS R. 3. 19,[23] one of the volumes described by R. H. Robbins in his introductory words on manuscripts in *Secular Lyrics of the Fourteenth and Fifteenth Centuries* as an 'aureate collection'.[24] Again, like Tanner 346 and the Findern Manuscript, this is a fascicular collection, with individual foliation, in a hand contemporary with those of the main scribes, marking off the different booklets. The first booklet, written entirely in one hand, contains thirteen love lyrics, many of them destined to be included in Stow's 1561 edition of Chaucer. Amongst these courtly love lyrics, though, are some other short poems of very different kinds. The booklet opens with a Christmas pageant — moral advice from seven philosophers (*Index* 3807) of a fairly conventional nature: 'Of elther men ye shall your myrrour make', 'Who that lakketh rest may nat long endure', and so on. It goes on to include three bits of Lydgate — extracts from *The Fall of Princes* extolling chastity (*Index* 1592),[25] *Bycorn and Chichevache*, and Parts II-IV of the *Testament*; a *ballade* against hypocritical women (*Index* 2661), and a longer piece, called (by a later hand) *The Craft of Lovers* (*Index* 3761). This last is a ludicrously aureate dialogue between an importunate lover and a coldly realistic lady who sees immediately the sordid motive behind his sugared words — 'carnal desidery', 'mans copulation' — but capitulates to his demands nonetheless.[26] It is almost as if the 'straight' courtly lyrics are there only to provide a butt for the satirical ones; their context here certainly

20 These lyrics occupy ff.15r-19v, at the beginning of the second main section of the manuscript.
21 For a description of MS Tanner 346, see P. Robinson, *Bodleian Library MS Tanner 346: a Facsimile* (Norman, Oklahoma, 1980).
22 H. N. MacCracken, 'Two Chaucerian *Ballades*', *Archiv* 127 (1911), 323-27, provides transcriptions (sometimes inaccurate) of the Tanner copies of the lyrics, and supplies variants from Findern.
23 For much detailed information on this manuscript, see B. Y. Fletcher, 'An Edition of MS R. 3. 19 in Trinity College, Cambridge, a Poetical Miscellany of c.1480', Ph.D. thesis, University of Chicago, 1973.
24 *op. cit.* xxiii-vi.
25 Bks iv 2374-87, iii 1373-1421, iii 78-84; see A. S. G. Edwards, 'Selections from Lydgate's *Fall of Princes*: a Checklist', *The Library* 26 (1971), 337-42.
26 A. K. Moore, 'Some Implications of the Middle English *Craft of Lovers*', *Neophilogus* 35 (1951), 231-8.

sheds a different light on them from that cast by a modern anthologised appearance (some of the lyrics are indeed included in Robbins's 'courtly' section[27]). The tenth booklet of this manuscript confirms the moral and essentially antifeminist tone of the whole collection: *O Mossy Quince* (*Index* 2524) and *The Describing of a Fair Lady* (*Index* 1300) — grotesque mock-panegyrics; a *ballade* warning the reader to 'beware of deceitful women' (*Index* 1944); Lydgate's *Horns Away* (against women's extravagance in dress); advice from a father to his son (*Index* 3502) and from a mother to her daughter (*Index* 671). So the whole collection hardly distils a quintessentially courtly tone; the love lyrics are effectively 'placed' by their context. The moral which emerges is this: make love to women, use to them all the extravagant terms you like — you can't conceal the baseness of your motives, and women will deceive you in the end.

This distinct lack of coherent collections or anthologies which I have been discussing so far seems to me to suggest that English courtly lyrics commanded little, if any, 'literary status'; they do not seem to have been thought of as a distinct genre, with a distinct flavour or a distinct function. The variety of different 'applied' and often very practical roles which they play in manuscripts exactly corroborates this, and I would like to go on now to consider some of these functions. Two of the most obvious are the most practical ones — courtly lyrics as *fillers*, and as *autographs*, left behind by readers as a mark of the fact that they have owned or perused particular collections. These are functions which courtly lyrics share with lyrics of all kinds, and I will not dwell on them here. A rather different function is that of 'lyric as biography', something which occurs in a variety of ways. It is often remarked that the fifteenth century witnessed a surge of interest in the idea of one author's 'collected works';[28] large Chaucer and Lydgate volumes provide the evidence for this, and the process culminates, I suppose, with Thynne's printed edition of Chaucer's works in 1532. Many of these manuscripts of collected works, while concentrating on assembling a poet's major pieces, make use of the lyrics associated with him (courtly or otherwise) as space-fillers, or as pseudo-biography, or even as diversions — like the short, slight pieces which intersperse a concert programme, allowing a pause for reflection and for the gathering of the faculties between the heavier, more demanding stuff. In Chaucer's case, all the minor poems, whether specifically courtly lyrics or not, tend to be copied in groups.[29] MS Fairfax 16 contains the largest collection of them (some running on from one another, undistinguished), with thirteen, including three of those classified by Robinson as 'of doubtful authorship'; several other manuscripts (Magdalene College Cambridge MS Pepys 2006, British Library MS Harley 7333, for instance) contain between four and eight.[30] The interest

[27] *Index* 2311, Robbins p.139; *Index* 1238, Robbins p.192; *Index* 267, Robbins p.162, for example.
[28] See, for instance, R. Woolf, *op. cit.* 375.
[29] J. Norton-Smith, *op. cit.* viii, lends some support to Brusendorff's theory that the minor poems were originally published in a set of six booklets.
[30] Fairfax 16 contains *An ABC*, *The Complaint unto Pity*, *The Complaint of Mars*, *Fortune*, *Truth*, *Lak of Stedfastnesse*, *The Complaint of Venus*, *Lenvoy de Chaucer a Scogan*, *Lenvoy*

that these poems are seen to have for the reader lies almost solely in their connection with Chaucer, I think. Shirley heads the first copy of *Truth* in Trinity College Cambridge MS R. 3. 20 (p.144) as 'Balade þat Chaucier made on his deeth bedde', giving it a similar immediately autobiographical attraction. One of the most interesting uses of a courtly lyric in this connection comes in Bodleian MS Rawlinson Poet. 163. This is a copy of *Troilus and Criseyde*, made by one main scribe and three others, in the late fifteenth century.[31] At the end of the work the main scribe has written, in a formal *textura*, the colophon 'heer endith the book of / Troylus and of Cresseyde' (f.113v). Bracketing together the two lines which make this up, he adds in an informal secretary-style hand on the left-hand side 'Tregentyll' and on the right-hand side 'Chaucer'. Skeat and Robinson took 'Tregentyll' to be the scribe's name,[32] but it surely seems more probable that it was intended as a compliment to the noble poet, at the end of this most 'gentil' of his works. *Troilus* ends on the verso of the last folio of the final quire, but one extra singleton follows, and on the recto of this the scribe who was responsible for the conclusion of *Troilus* has inserted the three stanzas of the lyric now known as *To Rosemounde*, separating the stanzas with the same faint ink line he had used in the major work. At the end of the lyric is written 'Tregentil – Chaucer' in a clumsy hand which does not closely resemble either of those used in the *Troilus* colophon, but which does seem to have used the same ink. Skeat and Robinson both accept this attribution as genuine, presumably taking it to be written by the *Troilus* scribe. Brusendorff argues that the colophon to *Rosemounde* is in fact merely a mindless copy of the *Troilus* colophon on the facing verso, and allows it no authority.[33] But none of the scribblers' hands on the flyleaf matches the *Rosemounde* colophon, and it seems to me more likely that it *is* the hand of the main scribe, perhaps in a bad moment – it is hardly impressively consistent at the best of times, earlier in the manuscript. The use of the lyric here is most interesting. It functions as a sort of *encore* to *Troilus*, giving the reader just an extra taste of 'gentil' poet, and offering a sort of graceful farewell.

As I have said, the large printed 'collected works' of the sixteenth century represent the culmination of this kind of process. Tottel, too, in his miscellany of *Songs and Sonettes* (first edition 1557)[34] makes great play of the biographical associations of the poems he includes. For a start, the full title of the volume is

de Chaucer a Bukton, *The Complaint of Chaucer to his Purse*, [*Against Women Unconstant*], [*Complaynt d'Amours*], and [*Proverbs*]; Pepys 2006 includes *An ABC*, *The Complaint of Mars* (twice), *The Complaint of Venus* (twice), *Fortune*, *Truth*, *Scogan*, *Purse*, and [*Merciles Beaute*]; Harley 7333 contains *Gentilesse*, *Truth*, *The Complaint of Mars*, *Lak of Stedfastnesse*, *Purse*, and [*Complaynt d'Amours*].

31 For descriptions, and reproductions of the hands, see W. W. Skeat, *Twelve Facsimiles of Old English Manuscripts* (Oxford, 1892), 36, and R. K. Root, *The Manuscripts of Chaucer's Troilus* (London, 1914), 37-42.

32 W. W. Skeat, *The Complete Works of Geoffrey Chaucer*, 7 vols (Oxford, 1894, rev. 1899) i, 81; F. N. Robinson, *The Works of Geoffrey Chaucer* (2nd edn Boston, Mass. 1957) 858. See also H. Kökeritz, 'Chaucer's *Rosemounde*', *MLN* 63 (1948), 310-18.

33 A. Brusendorff, *The Chaucer Tradition* (Copenhagen, 1925), 439ff.

34 STC 13860; I have used the Scolar Press facsimile, *Songes and Sonettes (Tottel's Miscellany) 1557* (Leeds, 1966).

not merely *Songs and Sonettes*, but *Songs and Sonettes written by the right honorable Lorde Henry Howarde late Erle of Surrey, and other*, with an emphasis on the fame and nobility of the best-known contributor. Tottel's own preface, while ostensibly highlighting his promotion of 'the honour of the English tongue', does not miss the opportunity of repeating the name of 'the noble Earle of Surrey', and of dropping a reference to 'the depewitted Sir Thomas Wyatt' — Tottel follows exactly in John Shirley's footsteps. Significantly, too, the poems are arranged in groups according to their authors: poems by Surrey, by Wyatt, by Nicholas Grimald, and by 'uncertain authors'. They also have long, descriptive titles which, in the case of the love lyrics, link the sentiments expressed with a 'lover', whose continued, albeit shadowy presence acts as a unifying factor and makes the poems into something approaching a cycle. So Wyatt's sonnet *My galey charged is with forgetfulnesse* is headed 'The Lover compareth his state to a shippe in perilous storme tossed on the sea', while *My lute awake* is entitled 'The Lover complayneth of the unkindness of his love'.[35] Tottel effectively combines two possible functions of these courtly lyrics: he both associates them with noble authors (presumably for the spicy cachet thereby gained), and links them up, with his rubrics, into a cycle which has a semi-narrative thread.

Instances like these, in which lyrics are used for peculiarly biographical purposes, lend a certain amount of authority to the supposition that all these poems are merely the written records of 'moves' in a courtly 'game of love', piquant but essentially occasional pieces whose tantalising significance is lost once they are removed from the social circumstances which inspired their composition. This is an attractive theory, certainly, made even more enticing by the opportunities for biographical speculation which it permits, and it is obviously to some extent supported by the contexts of one or two lyrics. MS Fairfax 16, for example, contains two obscure pieces designed to accompany real courtly games of some kind — *Ragman Roll* (*Index* 2251) and *The Chance of the Dice* (*Index* 803) — which suggest a definite social connection for its lyrics. British Library MS Sloane 1212, too — a copy of Hoccleve's *Regiment of Princes* enclosed in six odd leaves which seem to come from a dismembered Lydgate manuscript — contains some love lyrics surrounded by names and mottoes: 'Scales', 'Morley', 'Felbrigg', 'Fortune allas', 'Ʒouris allone', 'Sans mwer' (f.1v), to name only a few, seem to relate the poems to a specific milieu and suggest an 'occasional' significance for them at which we can hardly guess.[36]

Related to the idea of these lyrics enjoying a social role is their connection with music, often put forward as the key which unlocks all secrets. Many critics, lured I suspect by C. S. Lewis's powerfully attractive evocation of a suitable socio-musical milieu for courtly lyrics of the early sixteenth century,[37] see all

---

[35] H. E. Rollins, *Tottel's Miscellany* (2nd edn Cambridge, Mass. 1966) 38, 62.

[36] Some suggestions are made by H. N. MacCracken, 'Additional Light on *The Temple of Glass*', *PMLA*, 23 (1908), 128-40.

[37] C. S. Lewis, *English Literature in the Sixteenth Century, Excluding Drama* (London, 1954), 230.

these poems essentially as 'songs', with the texts recorded in manuscripts purely for mnemonic purposes. The survival of two large songbooks from Henry VIII's court (British Library Additional MSS 5465 and 31922), and of one late fifteenth-century choir repertory (British Library Additional MS 5665), all three containing courtly lyrics among their varied contents, does in part support this theory, although to contradict it one may advance the fact that hardly any other English courtly lyric manuscripts contain musical notation. There is too the detail that I mentioned in connection with the lyrics in the Findern Manuscript and in MS Tanner 346 — copied from a written exemplar for presentation as poems, seemingly, rather than remembered just as songs. One thing about this musical theory which I do think important, though, is its association of courtly love-songs with *clerks* — something which by the fifteenth and sixteenth centuries is usually overlooked in favour of the more colourful secular court context. Even the songbooks associated with Henry VIII's court were probably designed more for the use of the singing-men of the Chapel Royal — clerks — than for that of illustrious courtiers, or of the king himself. A very large proportion of surviving courtly love lyrics are contained in manuscripts compiled by clergy, monastic and lay. As an example, I would like to give a brief description of British Library MS Sloane 1584.[38] This is a small volume of paper and parchment, compiled and mostly copied by one John Gysborn, who signs his name on f.12r: 'Scriptum per me Johannes Gysborn/Canonicus de Couerham'. The connection with the Premonstratensian abbey of Coverham in Yorkshire is confirmed by the inclusion of some model letters later in the collection which refer to Newbo, another Premonstratensian house in Lincolnshire (f.80v). Gysborn's personal anthology is pretty much as one would expect: it includes prayers, in Latin and English; drawings and notes on Christ's wounds; a collection of model questions for asking at confession, and a collection of model letters; medicinal recipes and recipes for making ink and preparing parchment, and a variety of other notes and miscellaneous items of information. Sandwiched between all these are a convivial carol (*Index* 2654), and a courtly love lyric, *Grevus is my sorow/Both evyne and morow* (*Index* 1018), in fourteen eight-line stanzas, including one long section modelled on the 'Wo worth' passage in *Troilus*.[39] Whether Gysborn copied in his lyric because he knew it as a song, or becuase it seemed to him a good example of a fashionable literary form, its context is worth recording, I think. It is a good corrective to the notion that courtly love lyrics were the concern of a privileged, aristocratic élite.

So far I have been pointing out the multiplicity of contexts for these poems, giving examples of social, musical, literary, biographical, and purely practical functions which they can fulfil; there are doubtless many more which can be added to my list. To conclude, I should like to look briefly at a pair of lyrics

---

[38] For brief notes on this manuscript, see R. L. Greene, *The Early English Carols* (2nd edn Oxford, 1977), 306, and N. R. Ker, *Medieval Libraries of Great Britain* (2nd edn London, 1964), 55.
[39] *Troilus and Criseyde*, ii. 344ff.

which crop up in two different manuscripts, and by comparing their contexts, to suggest two very different readings of them. The two poems appear in various modern anthologies,[40] and have probably become best-known by their titles of *De Amico ad Amicam* (*Index* 16) and *Responsio* (*Index* 19). They are clever macaronic lyrics, unique examples of their particular form, with regular alternation of French, English, and Latin lines in six-line stanzas:

> A celuy que plus eyme en mounde
> Of alle þo þat I haue founde
>   carissima
> Saluez od treye amour
> With grace & ioye & alle honour
>   dulcissima[41]

The earlier of the two copies to survive appears in Cambridge University Library MS Gg. 4. 27, part 1a (ff.10v-11v), the well-known Chaucerian collection which has been described, with MS Fairfax 16, as one of 'the most beautifully produced and textually responsible' examples of 'the fifteenth century's desire to collect Chaucer and his poetic disciples'.[42] The manuscript dates from the first quarter of the fifteenth century, written mainly in one clear and attractive hand, but with a brief stint by a collaborator from ff.508r-510v and 514r-v.[43] *De Amico ad Amicam* and *Responsio* here, along with the poems associated with Charles d'Orléans in MS Fairfax 16, must be amongst the most carefully presented of all surviving courtly love lyrics. In the Cambridge manuscript, the initial letter of each piece is flourished, with the flourishing extending out into the margins, where tiny human heads are incorporated into it. The lyrics occur near the beginning of the collection, after Chaucer's *ABC*, his *Envoy to Scogan*, and a pseudo-Chaucerian piece (largely modelled on *The Parliament of Fowls*) which, although unheaded in the manuscript, has since been given the title of *A Parliament of Birds*.[44] This work picks up references to French song in the 'real' Chaucerian *Parliament*: each stanza ends with a line of French, and in the case of the fourth stanza this is the proverb 'Qui bien aime a tard oublie', which in some *Parliament* manuscripts (although not MS Gg. 4. 27) is inserted above the position of the concluding roundel.[45] It may well be that each of the French lines in *A Parliament of Birds* in fact refers to a French lyric. 'Qui bien aime a tard oublie', as critics since Skeat have noted,[46] is the first line of Machaut's *Lay de Plour* (even though the music for this will not fit the English song); other lines in *A Parliament of*

[40] F. Sidgwick & E. K. Chambers, *op. cit.*, 15-19; R. T. Davies, *op. cit.*, 159-60 (only the first of the pair). For other editions, see the *Index* and *Supplement* entries.
[41] Cambridge University Library MS Gg. 4. 27, f.10v.
[42] J. Norton-Smith, *op. cit.*, p.ix.
[43] See *Geoffrey Chaucer: Poetical Works. A Facsimile of CUL MS Gg. 4. 27, with Introduction by M. B. Parkes and Richard Beadle*, 3 vols (Cambridge, 1979-80), iii, 6 and 44-46.
[44] E. P. Hammond, 'A Parliament of Birds', *JEGP* 7 (1907-8), 105-109.
[45] In Trinity College Cambridge MS R. 3. 19, and Bodleian MSS Fairfax 16 and Bodley 638.
[46] Skeat, *op. cit.* i, 525-6.

Birds, like 'Amour me fait souvent penser' (line 16) certainly seem to suggest quotation from elsewhere. In this sort of context the two courtly lyrics, with their graceful French, take on a superbly cosmopolitan and precious flavour — international court culture at its most rarified. They are followed (with a gap of two missing leaves, perhaps originally bearing miniatures) by *Troilus and Criseyde*, which serves to confirm their tone. They take the form of a snatch of correspondence between a lover and his mistress — his letter to her, and her reply — and tie in nicely with the epistolary theme in *Troilus* itself: Pandarus's advice on the writing of love-letters, and the letters between Troilus and Criseyde which appear later in the poem.[47]

The later copy of these lyrics appears in British Library MS Harley 3362, a very different sort of volume. It is smaller and much less impressive than MS Gg. 4. 27, less lavish in its format, and closely written throughout, mostly in one tiny *anglicana* hand, although one gathering in the middle of the manuscript has been copied by another scribe, and there are various inscriptions in the hands of later owners or readers. The main part of the manuscript is composed almost entirely of snatches of Latin — proverbs, pithy sayings, epigrams, jokes, riddles — interspersed with some longer pieces such as the Latin advice on behaviour, headed *Ut Te Geras ad Mensam*.[48] There is also a lengthy technical section on Latin vocabulary and grammar which gives examples of correct usages, some of them glossed with English translations. Some translations of whole proverbs are given, too: in English — 'ȝoung seynt old deuyl' (f.2r), and in French — the familiar 'qi bien aime tart le oblie' (f.17v) again. Perhaps most interesting, in comparison with MS Gg. 4. 27, are the several macaronic poems here. There is one on 'fleas, flies, and friars' (f.24r), another on death (f.36r), and still another, this time a lumberingly humorous piece of anti-fraternal nonsense:

> ffratres carmeli nauigant in a bothe apud Eli . . .
> . . . Omnes drencherunt quia sterisman non habuerunt . . . (f.24r)[49]

The English lyrics are right at the end of the manuscript, copied in a later hand, of the end or turn of the fifteenth century, into the blank space which remains at the end of the notes on grammar and vocabulary. The *Responsio* is unfinished, ending here after only ten lines. It seems that a later owner of the Latin collections saw fit to write these lyrics into his book. But what are we to make of this sort of context? The Latin, the tiny practised hand, the informal layout of the manu-

[47] *Troilus and Criseyde*, ii. 1023-43, v. 1317-421, v. 1590-631.
[48] Often attributed to Grosseteste, and sometimes known as the *Liber Urbanitatis* or the *Liber Facessie*. In essence, it is the forerunner of Lydgate's English poem, *Stans Puer ad Mensam*. See S. Gieben O.F.M., 'Robert Grosseteste and Medieval Courtesy Books', *Vivarium* 5 (1967), 47-74. The Latin version from MS Harley 3362 is printed by F. J. Furnivall, *The Babees Book*, EETS OS 32 (1868), 26-8.
[49] The lines on fleas and friars, and on 'fratres Carmeli', are printed from this manuscript by T. Wright & J. R. Halliwell, *Reliquiae Antiquae* 2 vols (London, 1841), i, 91. They print a similar version of the song on death, from Cambridge University Library MS Ee. 6. 29, on pp.138-9.

script, and, most of all, the subject-matter of its contents, suggest a clerical provenance of some sort. The English translations and the notes on vocabulary suggest perhaps a volume designed for teaching purposes. The later owner or reader of the volume who copied in the so-called 'courtly' lyrics may well have seen links between *De Amico ad Amicam* and *Responsio* and the other macaronic pieces in his collection. What seemed exquisitely courtly in the context of MS Gg. 4. 27 here seems exquisitely clerkly, and essentially comic; the gracefully turned sentiments here become exuberant learned play. The differences suggested by two such manuscript contexts can only confirm the chameleon-like nature of these lyrics.

LYDGATE MANUSCRIPTS:
SOME DIRECTIONS FOR FUTURE RESEARCH

A. S. G. Edwards

In recent years there has been some growth in interest in the verse of John Lydgate. Such interest has been diversified in its forms — at times eccentrically so. We lack, in consequence, any overall sense of Lydgate's importance in English medieval cultural history. Certain aspects have been admirably dealt with in Derek Pearsall's *John Lydgate* (1970) — a work that will almost certainly remain a standard critical study for some time. Indeed, the lucid authority of its conclusions largely disposes of the need for further discussion of the intrinsic merits of Lydgate's verse. But some of the related questions it poses have yet to receive satisfactory answers. The most urgent of these have to do with Lydgate's manuscripts, which have been subjected to little systematic study. This neglect is particularly regrettable since, as I will try to suggest, these manuscripts constitute in their bulk a source that can enrich our understanding of late medieval English literature from a variety of perspectives: literary history, palaeography, textual criticism, codicology and art history.

All these different scholarly activities focus around a common concern: the manuscripts, manuscripts which in number and kind represent what remains of the late medieval response to the extraordinary range and diversity of Lydgate writings. If the number of surviving manuscripts is a fair indicator then we must credit the remarkable popularity of many of his works for contemporary audiences: twenty-two of the large *Troy Book*, twenty-nine of the *Siege of Thebes*, twenty of his pseudo-Aristotle, twenty-four of the courtesy poem *Stans Puer ad Mensam*, nearly forty of the various forms of the *Verses on the Kings of England*, at least thirty-seven of the massive (over 36,000 lines) *Fall of Princes*, together with roughly the same number including selections from it, and, topping everything in popularity, the fifty-five manuscripts of Lydgate's *Dietary*. (I say nothing of those represented only by independently derived prints.)[1] What we have here is a vast mass of data — and I have only mentioned the most frequently copied texts — capable of shedding light on a diverse range of issues to do with manuscript production, audience and the range and nature of Lydgate's popularity

---

[1] These figures are generally drawn from the listings of Lydgate manuscripts by Alain Renoir and David C. Benson in the revised *Manual of the Writings in Middle English*, general ed. A. E. Hartung (New Haven: Connecticut Academy of Arts and Sciences, 1980), VI, 2073-2175; I have occasionally corrected their findings.

and influence. I would like to very briefly suggest some avenues of enquiry and some of the questions that might usefully be asked.

One might begin with the manuscripts as they exist as the products of decorators and scribes. Very little work has been done on the identification of those who decorated Lydgate manuscripts, even though some of these — particularly those of the *Life of St Edmund* and the *Troy Book* — are among the most sumptuous of the period for vernacular poems. I will discuss the former work in a moment. But the *Troy Book* is an obvious focus of interest for those interested in the circulation of *de luxe* manuscripts in the first half of the fifteenth century. A number contain numerous miniatures and elaborate decoration, clearly the product of expert shops or ateliers. For example, Gereth Spriggs has linked Rawlinson C. 446, one such elaborately produced manuscript, with the so called Johannes atelier of the school of Scheere.[2] Jonathan Alexander has identified two sumptuously illustrated manuscripts of Lydgate: Rylands English 1 of the *Troy Book* (with sixty-nine miniatures) and Cotton Tiberius A. VII of the *Pilgrimage of the Life of Man* (with fifty-three miniatures) as the work of William Abel and one of his followers.[3] And Kathleen Scott has linked two Lydgate manuscripts of the *Troy Book* and *Life of Our Lady* to the 'owl' atelier.[4] These are helpful beginnings, but a systematic survey of the decoration of all Lydgate manuscripts would be invaluable for the light it would shed on the circumstances of fifteenth-century book production. It would also be of interest for what it might tell us about contemporary responses to these works. Why, for example, are some works generally decorated and illuminated elaborately and others, apparently equally popular, often not decorated at all? For example, of the thirty-seven manuscripts of the *Fall of Princes*, only five contain any miniatures and only two any number. I doubt whether this can be explained solely in terms of the availabilty of decorative models or programmes for certain works (like the *Life of St Edmund* and the *Troy Book*), but not for others. Decorated versions of Laurent de Premierfait's *Des cas des nobles hommes*, Lydgate's prose source, for example, had an extensive circulation.[5] What were the factors, aesthetic, economic and practical, at work in making decisions to decorate? What efforts were made to integrate miniatures and text and how were they constrained by existing models? These obvious but important questions would fruitfully repay enquiry. For preliminary, extremely interesting answers, the curious are referred to Lesley Lawton's paper elsewhere in this volume and to Kathleen Scott's researches discussed below.

We also need to know a great deal more about the scribes. At the very least it

[2] G. M. Spriggs, 'Unnoticed Bodleian Manuscripts Illuminated by Herman Scheere and his School', *Bodleian Library Record*, 7 (1964), 193-203.
[3] J. J. G. Alexander, 'William Abell "lymnour" and 15th-Century English Illumination', in *Kunsthistorische Forschungen*, ed. A. Rosenauer and G. Weber (Salzburg, 1972), 166-72.
[4] K. L. Scott, 'A Mid-Fifteenth-Century English Illuminating Shop and its Customers', *Journal of the Warburg and Courtauld Institutes*, 31 (1968), 170-96.
[5] See, for example, C. Bozzolo, *Manuscrits des Traductions françaises d'oeuvres de Boccace* (Padova, 1973), esp. 136-40. Lesley Lawton, in an unpublished study she was kind enough to allow me to read in draft, demonstrates that some of the decorators of Lydgate's *Fall* took details from Laurent and incorporated them into their pictures.

would be invaluable to have some identification of scribes who seem to have been characteristically engaged in the copying of Lydgate manuscripts or scribes who copied Lydgate who can be related to an identifiable corpus of material. Into the latter category fall such figures as John Asloan or William Ebesham.[6] But I would like to briefly illustrate this point by reference to the activities of a hitherto unnamed scribe, whom I propose to term 'the Lydgate scribe'.

The work of this scribe has been identified by various scholars: Dr Doyle, Dr Scott and myself.[7] Between us we have identified nine manuscripts, written in the same hand, all containing works by Lydgate: four of the *Life of St Edmund* (Yates Thompson 47, Ashmole 46, Harley 4826 and the Arundel Castle manuscript), three of the pseudo-Aristotle (Laud misc. 673, Sloane 2464 and Harley 4826), two of the *Fall of Princes* (Harley 1766 and McGill 143) and one of the *Troy Book* (Arundel 99). In itself this is interesting evidence of a degree of specialised activity by an able scribe – only one manuscript, Harley 4826, contains a non-Lydgate text (Hoccleve's *Regement of Princes*). But it has larger implications.

The first of these is the question of decoration I have already touched on. A number of these manuscripts have elaborate programmes of miniatures: of the *St Edmund* ones, Yates Thompson 47 has fifty-three and Arundel Castle has fifty; Harley 1766 of the *Fall of Princes* has a hundred and fifty-three. In addition, two of the other *St Edmund* manuscripts (Harley 4826 and Ashmole 46) each have single miniatures. Taking the *St Edmund* ones as a group, there are clear stylistic links between them, which suggest they derive from a common original. Mrs Scott, in her study in *Viator* (see fn. 7), has argued convincingly that this model was Harley 2278 of Lydgate's *Life of St Edmund*, often acclaimed as one of the most notable of all fifteenth-century English manuscripts and generally held to have been produced at Bury St Edmunds.[8] But if this is the model, then it was made available to a number of different artists, whose work can be distinguished in the various copies of this poem. We have, then, clear evidence of a co-ordinating scribe capable of drawing upon the services of a number of proficient artists and decorators to adorn his work.

[6] On Asloan see C. van Buuren Veenenbos, 'John Asloan, an Edinburgh Scribe', *English Studies*, 47 (1966), 365-72; on Ebesham see A. I. Doyle, 'The Work of a late Fifteenth-Century Scribe, William Ebesham', *Bulletin of the John Rylands Library*, 39 (1957), 298-325.
[7] The first person to suggest a relationship between some of the manuscripts in this group appears to have been Margaret Rickert in her examination of illumination in *The Text of the Canterbury Tales* (Chicago, 1940), I, 561-605. There (579-80) she draws attention to the 'similarities' between Harley 4826, Sloane 2464 and Harley 1766. Her comments are very brief and it is not clear whether she sees similarities in script or in decoration, or both. Dr Doyle discussed the similarities in script in several of the manuscripts of this group in his 1966 Lyell lectures. I discussed some others in 'The McGill Fragment of Lydgate's *Fall of Princes*', in *Scriptorium*, 28 (1974), 75-77. The fullest and most authoritative account of this group appears in Kathleen Scott's, 'Lydgate's Lives of SS Edmund and Fremund: A Newly Discovered Manuscript in Arundel Castle', *Viator*, 13 (1982), 335-366. I am greatly indebted to Dr Scott for permitting me to read her article in typescript and for much helpful conversation.
[8] The claim that Harley 2278 was produced at Bury is made by several authorities (e.g. M. Rickert, *Painting in Britain: The Middle Ages* (London, [1954]), 198). It must be stressed that the likelihood is based on circumstantial evidence alone. Mrs Scott's researches provide the most compelling case for a Bury provenance.

Such evidence of high class commercial traffic in Lydgate manuscripts is noteworthy. But when we turn to Harley 1766 of the *Fall of Princes* matters become more complex. Not simply is the degree and kind of its decoration extremely unusual — I am not aware of any English poetic text of the fifteenth century containing so many miniatures nor in such a striking style.[9] But textually, the poem is equally unusual. The text is highly aberrant, reducing the poem to barely three-fifths of its original length (twenty thousand odd lines), compressing it from nine books into eight and inserting some new material.[10] It is interesting that the aberrations of the text are confirmed by the fragmentary McGill 143, which also seems likely, in its original form, to have been as elaborately decorated.[11]

Such an apparent discrepancy between elaborateness of format and textual aberrancy is not easy to account for. It seems unlikely that the scribe himself would have undertaken such changes; there is no other evidence that he was interested in making large scale adjustments to his exemplars. We have, then, to consider the possibility that the changes could be Lydgate's own and that they represent either an early version or a later 'compact' version for presentation to some patron. This unambitious hypothesis fits most economically with the *de luxe* format and the intricacy of the textual changes.[12]

If this hypothesis has any force, it has some affect on our perception of this scribe and his activities. It changes his status from high class entrepreneur to that of Lydgate's personal publisher, working in proximity to his author. And if one gives credence to such an assumption, it seems reasonable to localise his activities to Bury St Edmunds, where Lydgate was a monk in the latter part of his life.[13] It was probably only at Bury that the scribe would have had access to Harley 2278. And Bury is an obvious focus for the veneration of St Edmund reflected in the elaborate copies of the *Life of St Edmund* made by the Lydgate scribe and his associates. Moreover, evidence of ownership inscriptions places several manuscripts he copied within Suffolk boundaries in the fifteenth or early sixteenth centuries. Harley 1766 was certainly owned by a Suffolk native;[14] and Harley 4826 was owned by the Drury family whose tastes were sufficiently catholic to

---

9 For a full description of the manuscript, including accounts of all the miniatures see H. Bergen, ed. *Lydgate's Fall of Princes* (London, 1927), IV, 30-51. Most of the miniatures are unframed and appear in the margins of the manuscripts.

10 For full details, see Bergen, IV, 30-37.

11 See further, 'The McGill Fragment of Lydgate's *Fall of Princes*'.

12 The problem of dating the activities of the Lydgate scribe is relevant here. Certain manuscripts could not have been produced earlier than the 1450s, such as the copies of the pseudo-Aristotle (Laud. misc. 673, Harley 4826 and Sloane 2464). The other manuscripts of the *Life of St Edmund* (Arundel, Yates Thompson 47 and Ashmole 46) can be dated after 1461, since allusions in the text to Henry VI have been changed to Edward IV. There is no evidence to date the *Fall of Princes*, but my arguments would, of course, push this scribe's activities back well into the 1440s and could suggest that his work spanned several decades.

13 For an account of Lydgate's later years and his return to Bury see W. F. Schirmer, *John Lydgate* (London, 1961), 206-54 *passim*.

14 John Walker of Willisham, Suffolk wrote his name in the manuscript in the sixteenth century — see C. E. Wright, *Fontes Harleianae* (London, 1972), 340.

include the possession of two copies of the *Fall of Princes* and the Ellesmere Chaucer.[15] And we know that Suffolk was a major centre of literary activity during this period.[16] It seems reasonable to suppose that there was a commercial infrastructure capable of sustaining the demand for manuscript copies it must have created. But if the evidence means what it appears to, we have to assume a degree of sophistication and affluence within a provincial milieu that is noteworthy even when directed to the products of a local author. And such an assumption challenges, moreover, generally held views about the relative sophistication of provincial centres of book production in the fifteenth century.[17]

I have discussed the activities of this scribe at some length because it provides a case history that demonstrates the way in which different interests in manuscripts of this period — palaeographical, textual and art historical — can fruitfully interact to provide us with a clearer understanding of the circumstances surrounding the production of particular works and of fifteenth-century book production. Other studies, working outward as it were from scribal identifications, might prove equally illuminating. It is already possible to identify certain hands. Morgan 4 and Pepys 2011 of the *Siege of Thebes* are both in the same hand, for example, as are Digby 230 and Rawlinson C446 of the *Troy Book*.[18] There are a number of manuscripts of the *Fall of Princes* in the hand of the 'hooked g' scribe.[19] And, perhaps most interestingly, University of Illinois 84, of the *Fall*, appears to be in the same hand as Harley 7335, a manuscript of the *Canterbury Tales* of Suffolk provenance.[20] By building on such identifications it should be possible to define more precisely the circumstances surrounding the dissemination of Lydgate manuscripts.

The activities of John Shirley provide further confirmation of the importance of the study of scribal activity in connection with Lydgate's poems. Collections written by Shirley include Trinity College Cambridge R. 3.20, Ashmole 59 and British Library Additional 16165. Further collections seem to derive from ones he compiled which are no longer extant — for example, Harley 2251, Harley 7333, British Library Additional 29729 and 34360.[21] Shirley seems an important figure in the dissemination of Lydgate's poems, because, among other reasons,

---

[15] See further H. C. Schulz, *The Ellesmere Manuscript of Chaucer's Canterbury Tales* (San Marino, California, 1966), 18-22.
[16] See S. Moore, 'Patrons of Letters in Norfolk and Suffolk, c.1450', *PMLA*, 27 (1912), 188-207.
[17] As formulated most substantially by A. I. Doyle and M. B. Parkes in 'The Production of Copies of the *Canterbury Tales* and the *Confessio Amantis* in the early fifteenth century', in *Medieval Scribes, Manuscripts and Libraries: Essays Presented to N. R. Ker* (London, 1978), 163-210.
[18] See Doyle/Parkes, 'The Production of Copies of the *Canterbury Tales*...', 201-fn.99.
[19] I had independently identified Hatton 2, B. L. Add. 21410 and Plimpton 255 as the work of this scribe, when Professor T. Takamiya gave me a much more extensive list of manuscripts with which he could be associated — including some non-Lydgate ones. It is to be hoped he will publish his conclusions shortly.
[20] I am indebted to the University of Illinois library for xeroxes of leaves of Illinois 84.
[21] We lack a definitive account of Shirley; but see A. I. Doyle, 'More Light on John Shirley', *Medium Aevum*, 30 (1961), 93-101 and references cited there.

he may represent a contemporary attempt to drum up commercial interest in Lydgate in fifteenth-century London, an attempt which has led to his designation as 'one of England's earliest publishers'.[22]

Recently, however, this view has been challenged by Richard Green, who has suggested that Shirley's scribal activity may have been prompted by 'a love of courtly literature and an antiquarian's concern to rescue it from obscurity'.[23] Whatever truth there may be in such a view it does not extend to Lydgate, who was one of Shirley's chief interests. The traditional view that he was a 'publisher' has yet to be seriously challenged. A crucial point is the verse prefaces to British Library Additional 16165 and 29729. Hammond has suggested that they indicate Shirley was operating a sort of 'lending library'[24] in addition to his publishing house — 'sende þis boke ageyne home to Shirley' is an instruction that appears more than once. But Shirley's so-called lending library may, I suspect, be more accurately seen as a case of samples, and his verse prefaces as an enumeration of his wares to potential clients. It seems likely that he combined with the function of publisher that of literary agent, especially for Lydgate. His prefaces stress in Lydgate's case both his versatility and his poverty:

> Lydegate the Munk cloþed in blacke
> In his makyng þer is no lacke
> And thankeþe daun Johan for his peyne
> Þat to plese gentyles is right feyne
> Boþe with his laboure and his goode
> God wolde of nobles he hade ful his hoode   (81-86)[25]

Or again:

> Suche as he [i.e. Lydgate] is haue we no mo
> yet for all his much konnynge
> which were gret tresore to a kynge
> I meane this lidgate munke dame John
> his nobles bene spent I leue ychon
> And eke his shylinges nyghe by
> his thred bare coule woll not ly
> ellas ye lordis why nill ye se
> and reward his pouerte   (36-44)[26]

The notion that Lydgate was involved, directly or indirectly, in such apparently commercial speculations, plying his pen to provide Shirley with vendible books, remains a plausible basis for his relationship with Shirley. But Shirley remains something of a problem. If he was seriously concerned to transcribe manuscripts for profit, it is not easy to be sure what market there was for manuscripts so

---

22 The designation is Eleanor Hammond's in her *English Verse between Chaucer and Surrey* (Durham, N.C., 1927), 191.
23 R. F. Green, *Poets and Princepleasers* (Toronto, 1980), 132.
24 Hammond, 191.   25 Hammond, 196.
26 Hammond, 197.

poorly produced. And, unless one assumes simple ineptitude or the infirmities of age,[27] it is difficult to see why his texts should appear in such slipshod transcriptions. And yet the scale of his transcriptional activities is not easily compatible with purely private or 'antiquarian' enthusiasm. Moreover, his anecdotal and highly circumstantial rubrics suggest a knowledge of the occasions of particular poems that imply some personal acquaintance with Lydgate. Yet it is not easy to credit that some, at least, of his exemplars derive at all directly from the poet. Shirley's activities merit much more definition to resolve their ambiguities and seeming contradictions. We need to know much more about the derivation of his texts, his reliability as a scribe and attributor, and the audience for which his manuscripts were intended.

The problem of Shirley is but one among a host of questions about scribal activity and book production that have a wider relevance than to Lydgate alone, but which the volume of copying of his works helps to focus. What were the mechanics of the relationship between author, 'publisher' and reader? Did scriptoria keep exemplars in stock to be copied as the need arose? To what extent was a common *ordinatio* established for copies of the same poem? What links can be established between scribes and patrons? A study of Lydgate's manuscripts would provide data to answer these and related questions, clarifying many issues that are still virtually unexamined.

Such issues can be helpfully considered in relation to the question of the audience (or audiences) for Lydgate's poetry. Such consideration as has been made of this question has tended to focus on Lydgate's patrons,[28] the list of which reads like a *Who's Who* of fifteenth-century England: Henry V, Henry VI, Humphrey, duke of Gloucester, John, duke of Bedford, Richard of Warwick, Alice, countess of Suffolk, Abbot John Whethamstede, Abbot William Curteys, to say nothing of a host of lesser nobility. It is not, of course, surprising that Lydgate's patrons should have been, in the main, from the wealthy nobility. It is clear that Lydgate was an adaptable and ubiquitous versifier, willing to reflect the sensibilities or enthusiasms of those who hired him.[29]

But his audience was not simply restricted to those who hired him. I stress the obvious in partial reaction to the recent stimulating arguments advanced by Richard Green. He has argued that there was no 'new reading public' in the fifteenth century, because the main impulses to literary activity came from the 'life and attitudes of the court'.[30] Insofar as this argument is held to encompass Lydgate's works, I confess that I find it unconvincing. It seems to presuppose

---

[27] This may be a factor; for example, Ashmole 59 was copied when Shirley was well into his eighties.

[28] There is no full account of Lydgate's patrons; see however Moore (fn.16 above).

[29] See, for example, E. P. Hammond, 'Poet and Patron in the *Fall of Princes*', *Anglia*, 38 (1914), 121-36; J. W. McKenna, 'Henry VI and the Dual Monarchy: Aspects of Royal Political Propaganda', *Journal of the Warburg and Courtauld Institutes*, 28 (1965), 145-62 and A. S. G. Edwards, 'A Note on Lydgate's Attitudes to Women', *English Studies*, 51 (1970), 436-7, for various demonstrations of Lydgate's adaptability.

[30] Green, 211.

that the circumstances that inspired the production of a literary work in fifteenth-century England necessarily and inevitably defined its readership. Lydgate, like others of his contemporaries, was clearly encouraged and, in part at least sustained by a courtly milieu. But his 'public' does not seem to have been restricted to such a milieu, as (among other things) the activities of the Lydgate scribe and Shirley make clear. One of the interesting things about the Lydgate scribe is the fact that none of his manuscripts can be certainly said to have been commissioned by the nobility; they have no coats of arms or other indications of provenance to suggest a noble provenance.[31] They seem to have been commissioned by the (presumably affluent) bourgeoisie or clergy. Nor does Lydgate seem to have felt it invariably necessary to undertake solely on commission. His very popular *Siege of Thebes* seems to have been undertaken without such support. And other works lack certain patrons.

It would be an instructive exercise, as a counter statement to Green's arguments, to construct a list of early owners of Lydgate manuscripts. My own very limited efforts with the manuscripts of Lydgate's *Fall of Princes* suggest that the range of such owners greatly extends beyond the social range of Lydgate's initial patrons. It suggests that his audience encompassed the nobility, bourgeoisie, religious institutions and individual clerics — in fact a full spectrum of potential fifteenth-century readership.[32] A full picture of the readership and audience of Lydgate's writings would add to our understanding of late medieval taste and patronage. It would also quite probably establish Lydgate as possessing a much broader appeal than any other medieval English writer — including Chaucer.

In anticipating the possible outcome of such enquiries it is necessary to confront the — for us — often perplexing question of Lydgate's popularity with fifteenth-and sixteenth-century readers. The manuscripts can help to shed some light on the nature of and reasons for such popularity. They support, for example, the contemporary view that Lydgate was the equal of Chaucer. Manuscripts place the two in conjunction with no sense of incongruity in such fifteenth-century anthologies as Fairfax 16, Pepys 2006, Rawlinson C. 86 or Bodley 686 — in the Rawlinson manuscript Lydgate is credited with the authorship of the *Legend of Good Women* and in the Bodley manuscript with the authorship of the *Manciple's Tale* — or, most obviously in the conjunction of Lydgate's *Siege of Thebes* with the *Canterbury Tales* in some manuscripts.[33] Contemporary compilers saw no incongruity in joining the *Monk's Tale* with selections from the *Fall of Princes* in Trinity Cambridge R. 3. 19 or, elsewhere, joining stanzas from the *Troilus* with

[31] One possible exception is Harley 4826 which may have been owned by Alice, countess of Suffolk; see Wright, *Fontes Harleianae*, 242.
[32] See 'The Influence of Lydgate's *Fall of Princes*, c.1440-1555: A Survey', *Medieval Studies*, 39 (1977), 428-30 for a discussion of Lydgate's audience.
[33] Thebes appears with the *Canterbury Tales* in the following manuscripts: BL Add. 5140, the Cardigan manuscript (now in the University of Texas Library), Egerton 2864, Christ Church College, Oxford 152 and Longleat 257.

the *Fall*.[34] The Naples manuscript of the *Clerk's Tale* concludes with a stanza from Lydgate's *Doublenesse*.[35]

The manuscripts also suggest that Lydgate and Chaucer were viewed as hagiographers of equal merit. For example, in Chetham 6709, Chaucer's *Second Nun's Tale* and *Prioress' Tale* appear conjoined with an anthology of Lydgate's saints' lives. Chaucer's saints' lives also appear linked to Lydgate's devotional works, this time the *Life of Our Lady* and the *Testament* in Harley 2382. Lydgate's *Life of St Edmund* appears with Chaucer's *Man of Law's Tale* in Cambridge University Library Ee. 2. 15 and the same work of Lydgate's stands out oddly in Harley 7333 'a library of secular literature in 7 "books"',[36] a collection which contains the *Canterbury Tales* together with largely political and historical writings. There are other indications of connections between Chaucer and Lydgate's devotional writings.[37] A study of the *compilatio* of manuscripts containing the works of the two might prove an illuminating exercise.

There are other ways in which the manuscripts can shed light on Lydgate's contemporary popularity. A study of the manuscript selections from his works is one such. I have made a partial attempt in this respect for manuscripts of the *Fall of Princes*. There are numerous selections from it, affording insight into the way it was valued by contemporary readers. Almost invariably they show no interest in the *de casibus* tragedies that Lydgate translated so relentlessly from Boccaccio. What seems to have mattered to them was the sententious, didactic content of the Envoys he added to the work, his reduction of human tragedies to generalities or gnomic wordplay.[38] At least one stanza seems to have achieved an oral tradition, surviving scribbled on the flyleaves of a number of manuscripts.[39] Equally interesting is other evidence of contemporary engagement with the text in the form of annotation; this appears most strikingly in the series of antifeminist extracts in Harley 2251, which someone, possibly Shirley, has annotated with vehement disagreements.[40]

These are not the only indications of an active participation by Lydgate's readers in this text. More study of the actual manuscript text of his poems would be of considerable value in reminding us of the extraordinary intimacy readers seem to have achieved with his poems, so much so that they were capable of adapting stanzas or even lines for new purposes. Thus we find separate poems

---

[34] See further 'Selections from Lydgate's *Fall of Princes*: A Checklist', *The Library*, 5th series, 26 (1971), 337-42.
[35] See J. Manly and E. Rickert, *The Text of the Canterbury Tales* (Chicago, 1940), I, 378.
[36] Manly/Rickert, I, 207.
[37] For example, the Devonshire manuscript of the *Canterbury Tales* contains also Lydgate's *Life of St Margaret*; and Harley 2251 includes the *Prioress's Tale* among an anthology of Lydgate's poems – for a full description of the latter manuscript see E. P. Hammond, 'Two British Museum Manuscripts (Harley 2251 and Adds. 34360) . . .', *Anglia*, 28 (1905), 1-28.
[38] See above, fn. 34; to the selections listed there may be added the stanzas in Me LM 1 in Nottingham University Library – see A. I. Doyle and G. B. Pace, 'Further Texts of Chaucer's Minor Poems', *Studies in Bibliography*, 28 (1975), 46 and n. 25.
[39] For details see Edwards, 'Selections . . .', 338.
[40] I have transcribed and discussed these extracts in *Annuale Medievale*, 13 (1972), 32-44.

made up from stanzas from the *Fall of Princes*, each stanza coming from a separate book separated by thousands of lines in the original.[41] Or, one may recall the adaptations by 'Lucas' in Sloane 1212 of lines from the *Temple of Glas*, which were carefully retooled to form two smaller, distinct poems.[42] And recently David Fallows has traced a single phrase from the *Temple of Glas* to a fifteenth-century Escorial chansonnnier and to Skelton's *Garland of Laurel*. With respect to Skelton he might have noted the appearance of the phrase in the margin of a leaf of Harley 7335 of the *Canterbury Tales*, a manuscript probably owned by the dukes of Norfolk in the sixteenth century.[43] It is interesting to note that when Skelton addressed lines to the daughter of the duke of Norfolk, Anne Dacres, in the *Garland of Laurel* he uses (as Fallows notes) the phrase as a refrain.

Such studies of texts in context can prove highly illuminating. Henry Hargreaves has demonstrated this by subjecting the variant versions of Lydgate's *A Ram's Horn* to analysis to show how the poem changed as it was transferred from a courtly to a bourgeois audience.[44] I suspect that a study of the numerous versions of the *Verses on the Kings of England* would be especially interesting. The examination of its various revisions and additions could shed light on the ways such a text was adapted and re-worked to reflect divergent sensibilities and changing times, showing how Lydgate could be used as a kind of literary portmanteau, to be stuffed with the prejudices and preconceptions of his readers.[45]

Such textual studies would be salutary in a larger sense, in that they might remind us that much of Lydgate needs to be re-edited and the affiliations of existing manuscripts more accurately defined. But before undertaking any extensive study of the dissemination of Lydgate's poems, it might be worthwhile to determine which, in fact, are Lydgate's. We need to go back to the manuscripts to clarify the fundamental issue of the canon. It is sobering to reflect how insecure is our belief of the authorship of many of the works traditionally ascribed to Lydgate. The standard work on the canon remains H. N. MacCracken's 1910 study.[46] Since then, it has been subject to attack by a number of disintegrationist termites. The latest account of the canon, in the revised Wells *Manual*, includes at least thirty-five items among the two hundred under Lydgate about the authorship of which it has doubt.[47] The number could be added to. It would in any case include such major works as *Reason and Sensuality*, generally claimed as

[41] See, for example, the 'poem' in Harley 2202, ff. 71-72^v which has the following sequence of stanzas: II, 2542-8; VIII, 1660-80; I, 1331-7; I, 5125-31; I, 3998-4004; II, 2535-41.
[42] For discussion see E. Seaton, *Sir Richard Roos* (London, 1961), 376.
[43] D. Fallows, 'Words and Music in two English Songs of the mid-15th Century: Charles d'Orléans and John Lydgate', *Early Music*, 2 (1977), 40-42; for discussion of the Harley manuscript and its provenance Manly/Rickert, I, 236.
[44] See H. Hargreaves, 'Lydgate's "A Ram's Horn"', *Chaucer Review*, 10 (1976), 255-9.
[45] The various versions of the *Kings of England* have never been systematically studied; see, however, A. Renoir, 'A Note on the Third Redaction of John Lydgate's Verses on the Kings of England', *Archiv*, 216 (1979), 347-8.
[46] Reprinted most accessibly in his edition of *The Minor Poems of John Lydgate* (EETS, ES 107, 191), v-lviii.
[47] See e.g. *Manual* . . ., VI, nos. 7, 12, 17, 25, 31, 32, 37, 53, 60, 62, 69, 73, 82, 89, 98, 99, 113, 114, 127, 135, 139, 144, 148, 150, 153, 154, 158, 161, 168, 175, 183, 184, 190, 191, 194.

Lydgate's on no substantial grounds,[48] and the translation of Deguileville's *Pelerinage*, about which doubt exists, as well as a number of shorter poems.[49]

Such a reappraisal of the canon would have to resist the impatient demands of those who would either claim the best bits of Lydgate for someone else, or add implausibly to his oeuvre. In the former respect it is impossible to avoid mentioning the work of Ethel Seaton, whose book, *Sir Richard Roos* (1961) would claim for her eponymous hero vast chunks not only of Lydgate, but also Chaucer, Wyatt and Surrey among others on the very dubious criterion of manuscript cryptograms. Even if one believes, as I do, that her work is largely a combination of critical myopia and misapplied acuity, her remarkable knowledge of the manuscripts does command respect and suggests the uncertain basis of at least some Lydgate attributions. At the other extreme we have the recent attempt by Gail Gibson to add to the Lydgate canon the N Town plays on grounds that seem very doubtful.[50]

A fresh survey of the manuscript evidence for the canon is overdue. It must include, among much else, some reassessment of the reliability of various early attributors, particularly of the indefatigable and ubiquitous John Stow, a figure whose involvement in Lydgate manuscripts deserves a full study in its own right.[51]

One final area of enquiry in which Lydgate's manuscripts can serve a useful purpose is in an assessment of his influence on Scottish literature. For example, Gregory Kratzmann's very interesting recent book on Anglo-Scottish literary relations denies Lydgate any influence on Scottish medieval literature.[52] But there are sufficient indications of such influence to invite the mustering of a counter statement. Kratzmann himself points to the appearance of Lydgate in the Bannatyne manuscript in the form of extracts from the *Black Knight* and the *Temple of Glas*.[53] In addition there are a number of extracts from manuscripts of Scottish provenance.[54] It is not strictly true that there are 'no surviving

---

[48] The only copies are in Fairfax 16 and B.L. Add. 29729, the latter a sixteenth-century copy by John Stow. And Stow provides the only authority for the attribution to Lydgate in the Fairfax manuscript.

[49] See K. Walls, 'Did Lydgate Translate the Pelerinage de la Vie Humaine?', *Notes & Queries*, 222 (1977), 103-5, and the response of R. F. Green, 'Lydgate and Deguileville Once More', Ibid., 223 (1978), 105-6.

[50] Gail Gibson, 'Bury St Edmunds, Lydgate and the *N. Town Cycle*', *Speculum*, 56 (1981), 56-90. Part of her argument for Lydgate's connection with the N Town Cycle is based on a belief that he is the author of the pageants on the Entry of Queen Margaret of Anjou in 1445; but Professor Gordon Kipling has pointed out that there is no evidence that Lydgate is the author of this work, the sole authority for attribution being John Stow. See his 'The London Pageants for Margaret of Anjou: A Medieval Script Restored', *Medieval English Theatre*, 4 (1982), 5-27, esp. 8-13.

[51] For a preliminary study see J. I. Miller and A. S. G. Edwards, 'Stow and Lydgate's St Edmund', *Notes & Queries*, 218 (1973), 365-9.

[52] G. G. Kratzmann, *Anglo-Scottish Literary Relations, 1430-1550* (Cambridge, 1980).

[53] Kratzmann, 14-15.

[54] Copies of Lydgate's minor poems appear in the Maitland and MakCulloch manuscripts and there is a Scottish version of *Cristes Passioun* in a manuscript in the Pepys Library; see further P. H. Nichols, 'William Dunbar as a Scottish Lydgatian', *PMLA*, 46 (1931), 220-1; a stanza from the *Fall of Princes* appears in Advocates MS I. I. 6, f.75[v].

manuscripts, in Scots or English, of Lydgate's long historico-moral works'.[55] One thinks, for example, of the scribe of the Asloan manuscript who copied out missing portions of the *Troy Book* into Douce 148 and the links noted by Bergen between that manuscript and Cambridge University Library Kk. V. 30.[56] One might also cite the copy of the *Siege of Thebes* owned by the Campbells of Glenorquay which was in Scotland from at least the middle of the sixteenth century.[57] These indications, together with the frequent indications of knowledge of and borrowing from Lydgate's poems by Scottish poets may prompt some reassessment of his Caledonian presence.

Lydgate's manuscripts merit much more systematic study than they have received, not because he is a great poet, but because of his great popularity and influence. His manuscripts can provide a mass of information which can increase our understanding of literary activity in the fifteenth and sixteenth centuries. It may not seem as fair a field as some for the medievalist; but, with patience, it could well yield fruit of surprising richness.[58]

[55] Kratzmann, 15.
[56] See van Buuren Veenenbos (fn. 6 above) and H. Bergen, Lydgate's *Troy Book* (EETS, ES 126, 1935), IV, 46-50.
[57] This manuscript is now Boston Public Library MS 94.
[58] I am particularly grateful to Dr A. I. Doyle and Mrs Felicity Riddy for their efforts to save me from error.

JOHN GOWER'S 'CONFESSIO AMANTIS': THE VIRTUES OF BAD TEXTS

Kate Harris

It is an unfortunate poem which survives in a vacuum[1] and it seems especially necessary when dealing with medieval texts to establish, in the absence of the fuller records available to the modernist, the ways in which such texts were read and understood by their early audiences, to establish an authentic contemporary, or near contemporary, commentary.

For Gower's *Confessio Amantis* such a commentary may be supplied from the evidence of manuscript provenance (including the evidence of recorded copies, annotation in the manuscripts and, for that matter, in the early printed copies[2]), from allusion to, and imitation of Gower by other medieval writers, from illustration of the poem, from its appearance in manuscript collections with other works not by Gower and, lastly and most importantly, from the detailed consideration of the bad texts of the poem. The whole process[3] is, in effect, an exercise in historical semantics, an attempt to deduce what the *Confessio* meant to its first readers in their own time — meaning is, after all, usage.

In dealing with this body of evidence it is necessary to be strictly evaluative; a single form of the evidence will be discussed here, that which might be judged to be of the highest value, bringing the issue into the sharpest focus — the bad texts.

The phrase 'bad text' is given, for the present purpose, a very specific meaning, referring not just to any text showing the scars of transmission or of late production but to those usually given the shortest shrift by the modern editor, those in which the intrusions of the medieval manuscript compiler or editor (or both)

---

[1] Daniel S. Silvia 'Some Fifteenth-century Manuscripts of the *Canterbury Tales*', *Chaucer and Middle English Studies: in Honour of Rossell Hope Robbins*, ed. Beryl Rowland (London, 1974), 158 ['One regrets the vacuum in which, say, *Beowulf* has reached the present: one MS, dating from a time far removed from the date of composition of the poem. Unlike a work that has come to us in a solitary form, in the case of the *Tales* there is some slight variety. The context for a work provided by its inclusion in an anthology can provide a useful adjunct to the naked text in helping to determine meaning, intent, and significance.'] The research behind the present paper shares the basic premise of this essay (an essay dealing with the occurrence of extracts from the *Canterbury Tales* and presenting a more detailed account of the context of the extracts in two manuscripts) but differs in method of work and in the conclusions drawn.
[2] Study of some few of the surviving copies of Caxton's edition of 1483 (*STC* 12142) has suggested that there are significant parallels in the forms of readers' annotation most commonly found in the manuscripts and the printed version.
[3] My thesis for the University of York will attempt to describe this 'whole process'.

are most obvious. I refer to the texts appearing in the form of extracts – this occurs in eight manuscripts each supplying evidence of specific interests in the *Confessio* and placing it in a particular literary context. I refer also to the two manuscripts containing an abridged text.[4] Such texts, deliberately breaking with the integrity of the poem's transmission, are here regarded as virtuous in so far as they offer insight into the kind of reading given to the *Confessio* by its medieval audience.

After trying to give some idea of the general picture I shall attempt to describe three sets of extracts which have undergone thorough revision by medieval editors, that is to suggest the virtues of very bad texts and demonstrate the uses of textual criticism not, as is customary, to determine a text but rather to determine a medieval criticism, or rather *at best* to determine a medieval criticism. Such discussion is, of course, very much dependent on a large corpus of textual variants and this gives rise to a difficulty; this is not the place to supply such an extended corpus of variants. The discussion will have to be largely restricted to results divorced from the bulk of the textual evidence lying behind them. It is hoped that this will not cloud the issue and make possible the suspicion that the evidence presented for deliberate programmes of editorial revision of Gower's text is in actual fact merely the evidence of spasmodic scribal interference.[5]

An abridged version of the *Confessio Amantis* appears in two manuscripts widely separated as to date, Princeton University Library, Garrett 136,[6] dating from the earlier fifteenth century, and, dating from the first half of the sixteenth century, Manchester, Chetham's Library $\frac{A.7.38}{6696}$.[7] It is quite clear that both are copies of the same version; they not only omit the same passages but offer the same cosmetic rewriting to 'bridge' the omissions; this latter process suggests the deliberateness of the procedure of abridgement. The two copies differ in their presentation of Gower's Latin apparatus to the *Confessio*; the Garrett manuscript omits the Latin notes entirely whilst the Chetham copy replaces most of this apparatus with a simplified English substitute. Such notes as remain in their Latin form and the form of some of the English notes in the Chetham manuscript

---

4 Full descriptions of all the manuscripts will be available in Jeremy Griffiths, Kate Harris and Derek Pearsall, *A Descriptive Catalogue of the Manuscripts of the Works of John Gower* (in preparation).

5 Compare the difficulties encountered in Dr Windeatt's treatment of some variants in *Troilus* manuscripts (B. A. Windeatt, 'The Scribes as Chaucer's Early Critics', *Studies in the Age of Chaucer*, I, 1979, 119-141) where the distinction between scribal and editorial activity is not formulated.

6 See G. C. Macaulay, *The English Works of John Gower*, EETS ES 81 and 82, 1900-1901 (henceforward Macaulay), volume I, *Introduction* p.cxli (*olim* Phillipps 2298). Seymour de Ricci, *Census of Medieval and Renaissance Manuscripts in the United States and Canada* (New York, 1935) (The Library of Robert Garrett . . . Baltimore, Maryland), volume I, 892.

7 Macaulay, cxli. Macaulay dates the manuscript too early and is inaccurate in ascribing the abridgement to the writer of the manuscript ['there are many omissions, apparently because the copyist got tired of his work,']. The scribe usually copies the notes in a bolder script (compare Macaulay 'perhaps by later hand'). The first of these errors was corrected by Heinrich Spies (following Max Foerster), 'Goweriana', *Englische Studien*, 34 (1904), 175, offering a date of the first half of the sixteenth century.

suggest access to a copy preserving the author's apparatus, or at least a considerable portion of it.

C. A. Luttrell[8] has shown that the Manchester manuscript was copied by Thomas Chetham of Nuthurst in Lancashire (c.1490-1546) who also copied Glasgow, Hunterian V. 2. 8 (388); Chetham was in the service of the second and third Earls of Derby.[9] The Hunterian volume is the unique manuscript of the alliterative *Destruction of Troy* (*IMEV* 2129).[10] On the basis of comparison with dated documents in Thomas Chetham's hand amongst the Clowes deeds (these include a rental roll 1520-1546) in the John Rylands Library in Manchester, Luttrell judges that the copy of the *Confessio* was produced between 1533 and 1537.[11] The origin of the Garrett manuscript remains obscure.

The aim of the abridgement appears to be straightforward enough; the procedure seeks to enhance the nature of the poem as a collection of stories; the passages dropped are almost exclusively from the frame. This abridged version also has an 'incidental' usefulness; it contributes to the understanding of the text of the *Canterbury Tales* in Cambridge, Fitzwilliam Museum, McClean 181, a manuscript omitting a considerable number of passages. It was thought by Edith Rickert to preserve early drafts of some of Chaucer's tales.[12] The Garrett and Chetham copies of the *Confessio* offer a precedent tending to confirm that the Fitzwilliam manuscript presents rather a later abridged version of no authority.

Of the eight manuscripts containing extracts from Gower's poem four show a basic similarity in procedure. These are British Library, Harley 7333, a manuscript coming from St Mary's Abbey in Leicester, having access to Shirley-derived texts and well known as containing a copy of the *Canterbury Tales* which has been subjected to some ideological retouching, Oxford, Balliol College 354, Richard Hill's commonplace book, Tokyo, Toshiyuki Takamiya 32 (the Delamere Chaucer) and Cambridge University Library, Ee. ii. 15, a manuscript also contain-

---

[8] C. A. Luttrell, 'Three North-West Midland Manuscripts', *Neophilologus*, 42 (1958), 38-50. Luttrell identifies the scribe, p.43, and writes emphatically, p.46, 'There can be no doubt that the person with whose writings we are concerned is Thomas Chetham himself.' (I should like to thank Mrs Elizabeth Urquhart for drawing my attention to this article.)

[9] Luttrell gives a brief account, *op. cit.*, 46-47. See also Ernest Axon, *Genealogy of the Chetham Family*, an appendix (separately paginated) in the second volume of Frederick Robert Raines and Charles W. Sutton, *Life of Humphrey Chetham*, Chetham Society, NS 49, 50 (1903), 20-21.

[10] ed. G. A. Panton and D. Donaldson, *The 'Gest Hystoriale' of the Destruction of Troy*, EETS OS 39 and 56 (1869 and 1874), *Preface*, liii-lv. John Young and P. Henderson Aitken, *A Catalogue of the Manuscripts in the Library of the Hunterian Museum in the University of Glasgow* (Glasgow, 1908), 309-310. Both give confused accounts of the origin of the manuscript. See also *A Manual of the Writings in Middle English 1050-1500*, general editor J. Burke Severs (New Haven, 1967), I, 115-116, 275; this does not notice Luttrell's article and dates the manuscript considerably too early (c.1450).

[11] *op. cit.*, 46. Luttrell dates the Hunterian manuscript 1538-1546. Reduced facsimiles of the Hunterian manuscript and the rental roll are given facing p.48 in Luttrell's article.

[12] Edith Rickert and J. M. Manly, *The Text of the Canterbury Tales* (Chicago, 1940) (henceforward Manly and Rickert), II, 502-518 and for a description of Fitzwilliam, McClean 181, I, 160-169, where the manuscript is dated 1450-1468/9.

ing an extract from the *Canterbury Tales*, the *Man of Law's Tale*.[13] In all four the extracts are formed from the narrative material in the *Confessio*, the intention being to create separate, self-contained, short narratives. This frequently entails editing at beginning and end to disengage the story from the frame, to retain a single narrative voice. Three of these manuscripts, Balliol, Takamiya and Ee, show editorial programmes going far beyond this; they are the subject of the second part of this paper.

The procedure behind the texts in Cambridge, University Library Ff. i. 6, the so-called Findern anthology, is rather different. On two occasions extensive passages from the frame are included; the story of Rosiphelee from Book IV is preceded by the Lover's account of his 'besischippe', his defence against the accusation of idleness in love (IV 1114-1466, omitting 1328, ff 5^r-10^v). The manuscript also includes the passage on the Lover's wakefulness from the same book (IV 2745-2926, omitting 2876, ff 81^r-84^r).[14] Material from the frame further appears in Oxford, Bodleian Library Rawlinson D 82; the manuscript seems to have been early in the possession of John Keme, mercer and alderman of London (d.1528). Hitherto unnoticed, the name appears in the lower margin of f 14^r; it is decipherable with the aid of an ultra-violet lamp. The manuscript once formed part of a larger collection now dismembered and surviving as eight distinct volumes; it gives the account of the court of love, companies of lovers and the dismissal of the Lover in Book VIII.[15]

Cambridge, Gonville and Caius 176/97 seeks to excise a 'lyric' from the *Confessio*. Caius is a predominantly vernacular, predominantly medical collection. Here twelve lines from Book IV (1623-1634, p.23 in the manuscript) appear amongst a group of later additions in a single hand by which the collection is diverted from its original purpose towards the uses of a commonplace book. The

13 See Macaulay, clxv-clxvi (omitting the Delamere manuscript). Harley 7333 is described by Manly and Rickert I, 207-218. Balliol 354 is described in ed. R. Dyboski, *Songs, Carols and other Miscellaneous Poems from the Balliol MS. 354*, EETS ES 101 (1908), xiii-lix and briefly by R. A. B. Mynors, *Catalogue of the Manuscripts of Balliol College Oxford* (Oxford, 1963), 352-354. See also ed. R. L. Greene, *The Early English Carols* (revised and enlarged, Oxford, 1977), 320-321. Takamiya 32 (*olim* Delamere, *olim* Boies Penrose 6) is described by Manly and Rickert I, 108-116. (Professor Takamiya very kindly allowed me to study the manuscript when it was in the hands of Bernard Quaritch, booksellers.) Ee. ii. 15 is described by Manly and Rickert I, 126-129.

14 Macaulay, clxvi. For this manuscript see especially the facsimile edition, *The Findern Manuscript: Cambridge University Library MS. Ff. i. 6* (London, 1978), Introduction by Richard Beadle and A. E. B. Owen. This treats the extract IV. 1114-1466 as two distinct items (numbers 2 and 3); the manuscript does not endorse this division. See also R. H. Robbins, 'The Findern Anthology', *Publications of the Modern Language Association of America*, 69 (1954), 610-642, an article perhaps needing to be treated with some reservation.

15 Macaulay, clxvi. *SC* 12900. An account of the whole collection was published by Kathleen Scott, 'A Fifteenth-Century Vernacular Manuscript Reconstructed', *Bodleian Library Record*, 7 (1966), 234-41. See also Pamela Robinson, *A Study of some Aspects of the Transmission of English Verse Texts in late Medieval Manuscripts*, unpublished Oxford B. Litt. thesis (1972), 231-5. For John Keme see ed. Laetitia Lyell and Frank D. Watney, *Acts of Court of the Mercers Company 1453-1527* (Cambridge, 1936), *passim*, the entries falling between the years 1501-1527. See also A. B. Beaven, *The Aldermen of the City of London* (London, 1908-13), volume II, 24 and *passim*. The eighth volume (Sloane 3489) has only recently been identified by Dr Doyle.

lines are on the duties of a knight and are headed rather inappropriately as to matter and form 'A pure balade of love'.[16]

The last of the eight manuscripts, Oxford, Trinity D 29, is the least known and probably the least understood.[17] It presents the most complex case and will therefore have to be treated at somewhat greater length. The extracts, mostly paraphrased, are inserted in a prose history beginning with Adam and ending defectively with Hannibal. The manuscript is copied in the same hand as San Marino, Huntington HM 144,[18] a volume which also includes two extracts from the *Canterbury Tales* (*Melibee* and the *Monk's Tale*), as well as such texts as Burgh's *Cato*, the *Gospel of Nicodemus*[19] and part of Lydgate's *Life of Our Lady*. The second manuscript is perhaps the most suggestive about the origins of the two volumes. In this manuscript the paper quires (both manuscripts are of paper) are reinforced by parchment sewing strips. The strip at the centre of the sixth quire has the names of several who professed at the Priory of Bisham Montague in Berkshire, a house of Augustinian canons. This evidence was not known to Manly and Rickert when they sought to establish the provenance of the manuscript; however, they associate one of the names in the volume, that of John Skinner, with the 'John Skinner gentleman' who was seneschal of the Court of Augustinian canons at Tandridge in Surrey not far from Bisham.[20] Clerical origin, particularly origin in an Augustinian house, would be fully in accord with the temper of both manuscripts. Such an origin would also offer explanation of the number and, to some extent, the nature of the sources used in the Trinity history. This is a peculiarly repetitious, sometimes a bizarre compilation. The compiler frequently repeats the same information from different sources, some-

[16] Not noticed by Macaulay, not in *IMEV*. The lines are mentioned by Ethel Seaton, *Sir Richard Roos* (London, 1961), 458 and by J. A. W. Bennett ed., *Selections from John Gower* (Oxford, 1968), 152, note to IV 1632ff. The twelve lines were printed as a separate lyric unique to the manuscript by H. A. Person ed., *Cambridge Middle English Lyrics* (Seattle, 1953), 38. For a description of the manuscript see M. R. James, *Descriptive Catalogue of the Manuscripts in the Library of Gonville and Caius College* (Cambridge, 1907), 201-203. See also Dr Linda E. Voigt's forthcoming edition of the Middle English phlebotomy treatise in this manuscript.

[17] No accurate, full account of this manuscript has been published though misleading references to it have appeared; see Margaret Deanesly, *The Lollard Bible and other Mediaeval Biblical Versions* (Cambridge, 1920), 332 'a history of the Old Testament from Adam to Ptomely Philopator, chiefly from Comestor and Josephus about 1450' and, deriving from this source, Saralyn Ruth Daly, 'The Historye of the Patriarchs', *Ohio State University Abstracts of Dissertations*, 1950-1951, no. 64; both name one of the sixteenth-century annotators of the manuscript, Henry Hawkins, as the compiler of the history. (The information appears to derive ultimately from Coxe's catalogue rather than directly from the manuscript).

[18] This is not noticed by Manly and Rickert in their description of the Huntington manuscript, I, 289-294.

[19] See Jeanne Ferrary Drennan and C. W. Marx, *The Middle English Prose Complaint of Our Lady and Gospel of Nicodemus*, forthcoming edition, Middle English Texts.

[20] The indications of provenance in the Trinity manuscript itself include references to Tillingham, Maldon, Great Dunmow and Little Dunmow in Essex. I note that Jeremy Smith's first analysis of a questionnaire on the language of the Trinity manuscript secured the answer 'Berkshire (?)'.

times even from the same source. The history is a patchwork and, as is the nature of patchwork, the seams are clearly visible.

If any single text could be said to form the framework of the whole it is probably Trevisa's translation of the *Polychronicon*; Caxton's edition is used, extracts from the same source appear in the Huntington manuscript.[21] The compiler also draws on Mandeville's *Travels*; a printed edition is not the source in this case. Many details in the history derive from Petrus Pictavensis' *Compendium historiae in genealogia christi*. The *Compendium* supplies the single illustration in the manuscript, a plan of Jerusalem (f 211[r]).[22] The compiler incorporates a Holy Cross Legend; his version is independent of the only other version in Middle English prose previously recognised, that appearing in Worcester Cathedral F 172.[23] He also includes the better part of Jacques Legrand's *Livre des bonnes Moeurs*. There are a number of distinct translations of this text extant; versions appear in British Library, Harley 149 and Additional 5467, the latter by John Shirley (a copy of the French text belonging to Shirley survives in Cambridge University Library, Ff. i. 33, ff38[r]-106[v]); another appears in two manuscripts, one formerly at Beaumont College and now in the Huntington Library, the second Glasgow, Hunterian T. 3. 16 (78), and another was printed by Caxton in 1487 (*STC* 15394). My analysis of the texts has shown that the Trinity copy contains the same version as Harley 149.[24] The compiler further incorporates a translation of one of the Latin pilgrimages in Wynkyn de Worde's print *Infor-*

[21] The appearance of extracts from the *Polychronicon* in the Trinity manuscript, but not their precise source, was noticed by Professor A. S. G. Edwards (following Ralph Hanna III) in 'The Influence and Audience of the *Polychronicon*; some Observations', *Proceedings of the Leeds Philosophical and Literary Society*, (Literary and Historical Section), 17 (1980), 117, n. 2.

[22] *M. Petri Pictavensis Galli Genealogia et chronoligia sanctorum patrum*, Ulrich Zwingli the younger (Basel, 1592). Hans Vollmer, *Deutsche Bibelauszüge des Mittelalters zum Stammbaum Christi* (Potsdam, 1931), prints the Latin text from Hamburg Staatsbibliothek Theol. 2029, pp.127-187; for the plan of Jerusalem see fig. X and Plate 7. See also Philip S. Moore, *The Works of Peter of Poitiers Master in Theology and Chancellor of Paris (1193-1205)*, Publications in Medieval Studies, the University of Notre Dame, I (Notre Dame, 1936); for the *Compendium* see chapter V, and especially pp.111-117 where Moore notices the use of this text in four universal chronicles. For the manuscripts containing the work see F. Stegmüller, *Repertorium Biblicum Medii Aevi* (Madrid, 1954), IV, 362-365, no. 6778; this cites no. 6779,1 the English translation in British Library, Additional 30509 (a fifteenth-century parchment roll); see also Oxford, Corpus Christi College 207.

[23] For the version in the Worcester Cathedral manuscript see Betty Hill, 'The Fifteenth-century Prose *Legend of the Cross before Christ*', *Medium Aevum*, 34 (1965), 203-222.

[24] I should like to thank Dr R. Lyall for comparing some passages from the Trinity manuscript with the version in the Hunterian collection. For the identity of the version in the Hunterian manuscript and the volume formerly at Beaumont College with notice of the present location of this copy in the Huntington Library see B. Lindström's letter in *The Library*, VI, 2 (1980), 225. For the second manuscript see also Maurice F. Bond, 'Some Early Books at Beaumont College', *The Berkshire Archaeological Journal*, 54 (1954-5), 54. See further B. Lindström, 'Some Remarks on two English Translations of Jacques Legrand's *Livre de Bonnes Meurs*', *English Studies*, 58 (1977), 304-311, and the same author's 'The English Versions of Jacques Legrand's *Livre de Bonnes Meurs*', *The Library*, VI, 1 (1979), 247-254. See also Otto Gaertner's dissertation, *John Shirley sein Leben und Werken* (Halle, 1904) (Gaertner prints a chapter from the Additional and Harleian manuscripts and from Caxton's edition, pp.70-79, and gives a general account of *The boke of gode maners*, pp. 45-49).

macion for pylgrymes vnto the holy londe (*STC* 14081). This suggests a *terminus post quem* of 1500.[25] Most notably the compiler incorporates several short extracts from the *Canterbury Tales*; the extracts, previously unrecognised, are from *Melibee* and the *Parson's Tale*. Comparison of the former with the *Melibee* in HM 144 clearly shows that the texts are derived from the same source. A case might also be made for the compiler as an independent biblical translator (this is an area of the text on which I am still working); it also needs to be said that the compiler seems to be one and the same as the scribe. The manuscript is not a 'fair copy'; signs of disjunction in the process of copying appear to preserve evidence of the compiler's moments of indecision as to which of his sources to follow next.[26]

The extracts from the *Confessio* in the Trinity manuscript usually appear in prose form. The one exception is *Nebuchadnezzar's Dream*, excerpted from the Prologue; this preserves its verse form; it is the only extract from the *Confessio* in the manuscript which has previously been noticed.[27] On three further occasions the compiler uses Gower's poem as a narrative source; he extracts *Gideon*, the *Folly of Rehoboam* and *Constantine and Silvester*. The compiler, uniquely among medieval extractors of the poem, is also responsive to the discursive material in the *Confessio*; the many extracts (sometimes indebtedness is a matter only of a phrase or two, or even of a couple of words) include much of the discursive material on the religions of the world and on idolatry from Books V and VII.[28]

Out of the diversity of interest discernible in the eight manuscripts a single issue might be raised. At first sight the manuscripts could be said to show a considerable community of interest: the *Tale of the Three Questions* appears in extract form five times, *Tereus* three times, *Nebuchadnezzar's Dream*, *Nebuchadnezzar's Punishment*, *Apollonius*, *Adrian and Bardus*, *Constance*, *Demetrius and Perseus* and *Constantine and Silvester* all appear twice. I would like to suggest that such statistics on the survivors of a sort of obstacle race of medieval taste and manuscript survival are of very limited utility; on closer inspection apparent community of interest disperses into variety; it is with this variety, with the extracts in their settings in the individual manuscripts that the 'archaeologist of

[25] Further editions appeared in 1515 and 1524, *STC* 14082-14083.
[26] The editing of the history in the Trinity manuscript presents some problems; it would perhaps be inappropriate, given the nature of the compilation, to edit the text as a whole. I have prepared a separate edition of the Chaucer extracts ('Huntington MS HM 144, Trinity Oxford MS 29 and the "Canterbury Tales"', forthcoming article) and am preparing editions of the extracts from Mandeville, the Holy Cross Legend and the translation from de Worde's print. Unfortunately it would be premature to produce this rather eccentric version of the *Livre des Bonnes Moeurs* since no complete modern edition of the other texts is available.
[27] See *IMEV* 2662.
[28] In this the compiler is perhaps most nearly comparable with a much later extractor of the *Confessio*: Elias Ashmole gives an account of the Philosopher's Stone from Book IV of Gower's poem in his *Theatrum Chemicum Britannicum* (London, 1652) (a facsimile appeared 1928), pp.368-373. A full account of the lines extracted will appear in the *Descriptive Catalogue* (*op. cit.* note 4); the texts themselves, and those of all the *Confessio* extracts, will appear in my thesis; the issue demands a protracted account and is too complex to be treated intelligibly in the small space here.

reading'[29] must be concerned. Precise information is to be gathered only from the acceptance of diversity and the explication of the minutiae of each individual case.

I move on to such minutiae, to three manuscripts, Balliol, Takamiya and Ee. ii. 15, containing heavily edited texts. Here a genuine and remarkable community of taste can be discovered.

At first Takamiya and Ee will be treated as a pair; close analysis of the *Confessio* text they have in common, the *Tale of the Three Questions*, shows the clearest signs of textual affiliation. There are many agreements in variant readings, most notably in additions to the text, the sort of agreements, in fact, which can hardly be the result of coincidence. However, it is equally clear that Ee (this is the later manuscript) is not copied from Takamiya; it preserves some original readings where Takamiya departs from them — this is a matter which will be taken up again later. The two manuscripts descend from a common ancestor; it seems unnecessary to complicate the situation with further hypothetical intermediaries. The nature and extent of the editorial process as it is discernible in Takamiya and Ee make it likely that this common ancestor was a series of extracts rather than a complete copy of Gower's poem. Thus it may be quite possible that heavily edited extracts from the *Confessio* were in circulation before the middle of the fifteenth century (the date of Takamiya) and still available in the late fifteenth century (the date of Ee).

The independent programme of revision in the Balliol manuscript is carried out according to the same canons to be discovered in Takamiya and Ee. It appears likely that the editor was Richard Hill himself as the editor's second thoughts are embedded in the text in the form of deletions and rewriting. Balliol differs from the others in presenting a series of texts which are also slightly abridged but in two strands of editorial policy the manuscripts are precisely similar.

I refer firstly to the inroads the medieval editors make into the chief means by which Gower builds poetry out of the short line, the enjambement by which he secures the lucid and extended verse paragraph typical of the *Confessio* and which he uses frequently to be precisely descriptive of his sense as at the beginning of book I (1-3) —

> I may noght strecche up to the hevene
> Min hand, ne setten al in evene
> This world, which evere is in balance:

where the break of the line reflects the impossibility of the attainment and yet the extremity of the desire, or when describing Tantalus (V 384-8) where the verse like the water vanishes away —

[29] This useful phrase is borrowed from Lee W. Patterson's article, 'Ambiguity and Interpret ation: A Fifteenth-Century Reading of *Troilus and Criseyde*', *Speculum*, 54 (1979), 299. The article contains a discussion of the appearance of *Troilus* I 400-406 in the treatise *Disce mori*, suggesting that the writer's aim was 'not to disarm the text but to arm the reader' (p.330) and so countering the view that medieval readers (like some medievalists) were innoculated against the 'sweetness of the letter' of the *Troilus* (p.328).

> thogh him thurste sore
> And to the water bowe a doun,
> The flod in such condicioun
> Avaleth, that his drinke areche
> He mai noght.

or when describing predatory violence and fearful stasis in the rape of Philomene (V 5642-6) —

> sche ne myhte noght arise,
> Bot lay oppressed and desesed,
> As if a goshauk hadde sesed
> A brid, which dorste noght for fere
> Remue.

The medieval editors consistently degrade the fluent continuity of Gower's syntax to produce peculiarly rebarbative versions where continuous semantic units are broken down by the insertion of extra verbs, subjects and objects. A kind of semantic end-stopping is sought. Familiar enough as a feature of scribal practice, or malpractice — the copyist losing his nerve before the end of a line, finding no main verb — in the three manuscripts this becomes a systematic editorial policy.[30] Indeed in Takamiya the policy is so consistent that the impression is given that the editor's intention was no less than to alter Gower's metre, to produce a longer line; closer inspection reveals rather the general wreckage of that metre.

I begin with some examples from the latest manuscript, Balliol. The first (an example of the addition of a subject) is from Book III (1661-2) where[31]

> Whan he in haste his swerd outdrowh
> And on the point himselve slowh

is replaced by

> whan he in hast his sword owt drowgh
> & on þe poynt him self *he* slowgh

Next I give an example of the forestalling of an object from *Dives and Lazarus* (VI 1046-7); instead of

> Bot Habraham answerde thenne
> And seide to him in this wise

the lines read

> But abraham answered *hym* then
> & said to hym in this wise.

30 Compare Windeatt, *op. cit.*, 134-135 and 138.
31 The text of the lemma is that of Macaulay's edition (that is substantially Oxford, Bodleian Library, Fairfax 3); to avoid anachronism the punctuation has been excised. Italics are mine.

Lastly I give an example of the forestalling of a verb from *Apollonius* (VIII
982-3) —

> Wher as thei sen toward the londe
> A Schip sailende of gret array

becomes rather

> Wher as they sawe *com* toward þe londe
> a Schippe saylyng of gret arraye.

I follow this with an example of the addition of a subject from the Ee text of
the *Trump of Death* (an extract not in the Takamiya manuscript); here lines 2216-
2218 in Book I

> That thou art of so litel feith
> That only for a trompes soun
> Hast gon despuiled thurgh the toun

appear rather as

> That thowe art of so lytell feythe
> That only for a trompys soune
> *Thowe* hast gone dyspoyled thorowe þe toune.

From Takamiya I give first the version of the lines quoted earlier from *Tereus*
(V 5644-6); instead of

> As if a goshauk hadde sesed
> A brid which dorste noght for fere
> Remue

the lines read

> As yif a Goshawke *hiere* hadde sesed
> As a brid that durste nowght for fere
> Remeve.

The editor 'clarifies' the simile by the insertion of the object 'hiere' in the first
line, forestalling the 'brid' of the second line. I close this group of examples with
a very extreme case from the Takamiya manuscript; the medieval editor doubles
the number of verbs and subjects, altering line order *en passant*. The lines from
Nebuchadnezzar's Dream in the Prologue (851-5, the 'cause' in the first refers to
the reason why Rome's fame is blighted)

> The cause hath ben divisioun
> Which moder of confusioun
> Is wher sche cometh overal
> Noght only of the temporal
> Bot of the spirital also

are extensively altered to read rather

> Thee chef cavse hath been devysioun
> Thee wyche *is* moder of confusioun
> *Schee* ne *is* nowt only of thee temperall   854
> *Schee* is where schee comyht over all   853
> And of thee spirituall *schee is* also

Such readings reflect a desire for simplification; they provide an index to the sophistication of Gower's syntax.

Following a second procedure the medieval editors make inroads into the chief means by which Gower builds poetry out of the frequency of rhyme in the short couplet, his use of the whole gamut of kinds of rhyme.

Gower's poetic in this respect is closest to that formulated by the French writers on the Second Rhetoric. Thus one finds Jacques Legrand writing on the subject of rhyme —[32]

> La seconde reigle si est que les rymes de tant sont meilleurs quant les diccions finables s'entressemblent plus, et pour tant dit l'en communement que la meilleur ryme qui soit c'est par equivocques, pour ce que les diccions equivocques sont du tout semblables, non obstant qu'elles ayent diverses significacions.

or one reads in *L'Art de Rhetorique Vulgaire*, attributed by Langlois to Jean Molinet —[33]

> qui veult practiquier la science choisisse plaisans equivocques, riches termes et leonismes, et laisse les bregiers user de leur rhetorique rurale.

or in the anonymous *Traité de l'Art de Rhetorique* —[34]

> Rimer n'est autre chose que faire deux bastons finer par telle lettre ainsy bien l'un que l'autre. Et que plus resembleront l'un l'autre en la fin, milleur sera la rime.

Gower frequently uses 'rime riche' (rhyme on initial, stem and terminal), often to point his sense — I note particularly his rhyming on 'acord' and 'discord'. He uses identical rhyme, 'rime équivoque' (that is, rhyme on homonyms, some-times, indeed, a whole nexus of homonyms), less frequently he uses broken rhyme, 'rime contrefaite' (rhyme on homophones). The 'meilleurs rimes' also have a special function in the complete text of the *Confessio*; they act as a form of punctuation, frequently appearing as a bridge between speakers or at the end of sections of the poem.

To many of these rhymes the medieval editors register an objection; they object especially to Gower's rhyming on homonyms. They rewrite such couplets

[32] ed. Ernest Langlois, *Recueil d'Arts de Seconde Rhétorique* (Paris, 1902; reprinted in Geneva 1974), *Des Rimes*, p.3.
[33] *op. cit.*, 249.
[34] *op. cit.*, 201.

or omit them, excising such forms almost completely.[35] Here I shall have to
cease treating Takamiya and Ee as a pair; Ee frequently retains such forms where
Takamiya excises them. Ee shows only the beginnings of the process of excision;
both manuscripts give an altered reading of Book I lines 3163-4 involving the
replacement of the first line. The couplet

> Hire yhe mai noght be forbore
> Sche wissheth forto ben unbore

becomes in Takamiya

> Schee wyshieht here self to have been vn bore
> ffor sche leet here self full neer lore

and in Ee

> Sche wysshyd here selfe to ben vn borne
> ffor she lete here selfe full nere lorne

but in other cases of excision of the 'meilleurs rimes' in the Takamiya text of the
Three Questions Ee retains the original reading. In the *Trump of Death* extract,
in Ee but not in Takamiya, the couplet (I 2131-2)

> Hath in kepinge and therof serveth
> That whan a lord his deth deserveth

is destroyed by the omission of the second line. However, it would probably be
unwise to draw a firm conclusion from silence. The situation would seem to be
as follows: the breakdown of Gower's syntax into smaller units discernible equally
in the two manuscripts is the work of the editor of their common exemplar, the
excision of the rhyme forms is largely the responsibility of the Takamiya editor;
he intensifies a process only begun in the common exemplar.

I draw some examples from the Takamiya extracts where one finds, for instance,
instead of (I 3253-4)

> Als wel in wynter as in Maii
> The mannes hond doth what he mai

the reading

> As well in wynter as on somerys day
> Thee mannys hond dooh<t>what hee may

and instead of (I 2905-10)

---

[35] Occasionally I have observed the omission of these forms in complete copies of the
Confessio (compare incidentally some of the variants cited in Windeatt, *op. cit.*, 126, 127,
130); they represent, of course, a particularly 'vulnerable' area of the text, vulnerable to
homoeoteleuton. In these three manuscripts the excision is systematic and may be deduced
to be a matter of deliberate policy, editorial procedure; it is not explicable in terms of the
chances of transmission. My analysis of the texts of the *Canterbury Tales* in Takamiya and
Ee suggests that the same editorial procedures are also to be found in operation on Chaucer's
work.

> Thi regne schal ben overthrowe
> And thou despuiled for a throwe
> Bot that the Rote scholde stonde
> Be that thou schalt wel understonde
> Ther schal abyden of thi regne
> A time ayein whan thou schalt regne

the reading

> Thy Regne schall been over throwe
> And thow disspoyled and leyd full lowe
> But by thee Roote thow mayst vnderstonde
> That thow schall Regne ayeen kyng in londe
> Theer schall a tyme a byde & been seygne
> Of thee laste Eende of thy Reygne.

The same policy is also to be found in the Balliol manuscript; there one finds instead of (VIII 413-14)

> Of his ansuere and if he faile
> He schal be ded withoute faile

the reading

> Of his answere yf he ffayle
> he shall be dede for his travayle

instead of (I 3143-4, this is an example of 'rime contrefaite')

> And that was where he made his mone
> Withinne a Gardin al him one

the reading

> & þ^{t} was wher he made hys mone
> w^{t} in a gardayn on his own

and instead of (II 1483-4)

> And in his fader half besoghte
> As he which his lordschipe soghte

the reading

> and in his faders be half besowght
> with dewe Reverence as he owght.

For the earliest formal comment on Gower's rhyme one·has to wait for Puttenham's *Arte of English Poesie*.[36] Puttenham, of course, regards couplet as

---

[36] George Puttenham, *The Arte of English Poesie*, ed. Gladys Doidge Willcock and Alice Walker (Cambridge, 1936). The *Arte* was first published in 1589.

an inferior form, 'riding rhyme'; he is a true modern in giving preference to perfect rhyme (sound identity of stem and terminal if there is one, but not of initial) and censuring the use of 'rime riche' as 'licencious'. He writes (p.62) —

> Gower sauing for his good and graue moralities, had nothing in him highly to be commended, for his verse was homely and without good measure, his wordes strained much deale out of the French writers, his ryme wrested, and in his inuentions small subtillitie:

and later (pp.81-2) —

> a licentious maker is in truth but a bungler and not a Poet. Such men were in effect the most part of all your old rimers and specially Gower, who to make up his rime would for the most part write his terminant sillable with false orthographie, and many times not sticke to put in a plaine French word for an English,

Puttenham's comments are restricted to the quality of Gower's rhyme; his attitude can perhaps be seen as analogous to more recent analyses of fifteenth-century metre in which thwarted stress dogs the heels of the supposed iambic pentameter.

The medieval editors rather respond to the *kind* of rhyme used by Gower. Their procedures suggest that this aspect of his poetic was already unfamiliar, unfashionable some fifty years after the composition of the *Confessio*. They show the initial stages of the outlawing of the 'meilleurs rimes' from serious English poetry, a process very similar to that undergone later by the pun: to put the matter in a different way, they show the early stages of the process by which the poetic potential of the 'meilleurs rimes' was redirected from the production of such lines as (IV 1321-2) —

> The beaute faye upon her face
> Non erthly thing it may deface;

towards something rather of this order —[37]

> Father, my bride is gone, faire mistresse 'Luce',
> My soule's the fount of vengeance, mischiefes sluce.

In so far as the intrusions of the medieval editors in Gower's poetry are made on purely aesthetic grounds they can be said to provide the earliest true criticism of the *Confessio*. In this lies the chief virtue of bad texts. That they should also provide information on the history of poetics was a virtue hardly to be expected.

---

[37] The works of Barham, Gilbert or Ogden Nash perhaps come most readily to mind; these lines, however, are from Francis Beaumont's *Knight of the Burning Pestle*, general editor Fredson Bowers, *The Dramatic Works in the Beaumont and Fletcher Canon*, I (Cambridge, 1966), p. 78, V ll. 36-37.

THE ILLUSTRATION OF LATE MEDIEVAL SECULAR TEXTS, WITH SPECIAL REFERENCE TO LYDGATE'S 'TROY BOOK'

Lesley Lawton

An intriguing question for anyone working with medieval secular texts that receive illustration is: what purposes did the miniatures serve? Modern comments on the problem can be divided into three broad categories. Firstly, that they have little real significance: luxury manuscripts with numerous pictures were essentially *objets d'art*, intended to impress the viewer with their beauty.[1] Secondly, that miniatures provide a visual commentary on the text they illustrate and thus can provide one means of access to the way it was originally received and understood.[2] Thirdly, that illustrations were an essential part of the apparatus designed to guide the reader through the book and to help him find required passages.[3] The second

---

[1] A typically sceptical note is sounded by C. F. Bühler, *The Fifteenth Century Book: the Scribes, the Printers, the Decorators* (Philadelphia, 1960), 162 n.29: 'One may well speculate on whether or not the grand, de luxe, illuminated manuscripts are books at all. They may well be works of art — or furniture, as little to be used as furniture on display in a museum.'

[2] Specific studies will be discussed later. In general terms, the desire to see works of literature and works of art as proceeding from a unified sensibility has a venerable history. At the beginning of their paper, 'Pictorial Illustration of Late Medieval Poetic Texts: the Role of the Frontispiece or Prefatory Picture', *Medieval Iconography and Narrative: a Symposium*, ed. F. G. Andersen (Odense, 1980), 100-123, Elizabeth Salter and Derek Pearsall provide a useful outline of approaches that have proved influential. They rightly criticise the over-abstraction of this method of analysis. A sign of the importance that literary critics attribute to the visual arts of the middle ages can be seen in the provision of a chapter on 'Chaucer and the Visual Arts' in the Chaucer volume of the Writers and their Background Series, ed. Derek Brewer (London, 1974), and in Derek Pearsall, 'The Visual World of the Middle Ages', in *The New Pelican Guide to English Literature. 1. Medieval Literature. Part One. Chaucer and the Alliterative Tradition*, ed. Boris Ford (Harmondsworth, 1982), 290-317. Indeed, as J. V. Fleming observes, in Chaucer studies 'Recourse to pictorial sources has become a nearly routine feature of literary analysis' ('Chaucer and the Visual Arts of His Time', in *New Perspectives in Chaucer Criticism*, ed. D. M. Rose (Norman, 1981), 121-36 (p.121)). Manuscript scholars S. Hindman and J. D. Farquhar, *Pen to Press* (Baltimore, 1977), remark p.160: 'Pictures not only functioned as alternate rubrics, but also as visual glosses on a text, providing yet another level of meaning to text and commentary.'

[3] S. Hindman and J. D. Farquhar, *op. cit.*, 63-76, discuss the functional role of all decorative elements in dividing a text into its component sections and indicating their relative importance by providing a sense of hierarchy. The development of the organisation of manuscript layout for maximum efficiency and ease of reference is a complicated subject. M. B. Parkes, 'The Influence of the Concepts of *Ordinatio* and *Compilatio* on the Development of the Book', *Medieval Learning and Literature: Essays Presented to R. W. Hunt*, eds J. J. G. Alexander and M. T. Gibson (Oxford, 1976), 119-141, provides an account of the development of the *mise-en-page* to respond to the requirements of a scholastic rather than monastic *lectio*. 'Features of the apparatus can be found even in well-produced copies of vernacular texts which do not presuppose an academic readership', particularly in the Ellesmere manuscript of the

and third of these approaches assume that illustrated manuscripts were actually read and that some thought went into the positioning and composition of the miniatures. In the first half of this paper I hope, by analysing these viewpoints, to make some preliminary observations about the possible functions of miniatures in late medieval secular texts; in the second half I offer a case-study of a particular group of manuscripts, drawing on some of the theoretical issues raised.

The use of a book as in investment must be taken into account: as Mynors points out, books, like plate, were 'one of the recognized ways of holding capital in a portable and negotiable form'.[4] But, granted that an illuminated manuscript may not necessarily have been commissioned by a patron eager to enjoy an admired work in a sumptuous format, the fact of illustration can provide useful information about a particular text. Since an illustrated book involves a considerable capital outlay, it is a measure of the value accorded a certain work that it, rather than any other, was selected for embellishment in this way.[5] It betrays, at least, an interest in the physical form of the book. The point is whether the pictures ever provided a more direct commentary on the text they accompanied.

That they did is the assumption behind J. V. Fleming's study of the *Roman de la Rose*[6] in which he uses illustration to establish his contention that the lover's pursuit of the rose was viewed ironically by its first readers as the pursuit of *fole amour*. Rosemond Tuve[7] interprets the poem in a similar, though more subtle, way and she, too, uses detail from manuscript illustration to support her analysis. Like Fleming, she attributes to the artists a conscious participation in presenting the text to the reader. Her approach is more fruitful since she is concerned in general terms with changing attitudes towards the reading of allegorical texts. Critics as diverse as C. S. Lewis and D. W. Robertson agree that the fifteenth century neither read nor produced allegory with the vigorous purity of earlier

Canterbury Tales.

[4] *Catalogue of the Manuscripts of Balliol College Oxford* (Oxford, 1963), xi. See also Cecil Roth, 'Pledging a Book in Medieval England', *The Library*, 5th ser., 19 (1964), 196-200 (p.196).
[5] Millard Meiss, *French Painting in the Time of Jean de Berry: The Limbourgs and Their Contemporaries*, I (London, 1974) discusses the secular texts which were newly illustrated in fifteenth-century France. 'The subjects fall into four main categories: accounts of foreign travels, allegories, histories of the ancient world, and stories of eminent persons, chiefly of antiquity' (p.7). There seems to have been a sense of appropriateness, a concept of these texts as ones to be illustrated. For various economic and social reasons texts in English are not as extensively embellished. None the less there are distinct groups of texts which seem to have been viewed as illustrated books. These would include: John Gower's *Confessio Amantis*; Stephen Scrope's translation of the *Epître d'Othea* and the *Dicts and Sayings of the Philosophers*; Lydgate's *Troy Book*, *Fall of Princes* and *Life of St Edmund and St Fremund*; the English prose translation of Guillaume de Deguileville's *Pèlerinage de l'Âme*.
[6] *The Roman de la Rose: A Study in Allegory and Iconography*, (Princeton, 1969). Charles Dahlberg, *The Romance of the Rose* (Princeton, 1971), 22 endorses this approach: 'It is no accident that recent studies which emphasise the importance of the poem's ironic technique are also those that for the first time have revealed the importance of manuscript illustrations.' Claire Richter Sherman, 'Some Visual Definitions in the Illustrations of Aristotle's *Nicomachean Ethics* and *Politics* in the French Translations of Nicole Oresme', *Art Bulletin*, 59 (1977), 320-330 (p.321 n.33) refers approvingly to Fleming's discussion of miniatures as 'visual glosses' on the text.
[7] *Allegorical Imagery: Some Medieval Books and Their Posterity* (Princeton, 1966).

ages;[8] a poem like the *Roman*, composed in the thirteenth century and re-interpreted in the fifteenth,[9] offers ample scope for the charting of changes in sensibility. Moreover, the 'Querelle' involving Christine de Pizan, Jean Gerson, Jean de Montreuil, and Gontier and Pierre Col is one of the earliest collections of documents revealing disagreement about the meaning of a secular text.[10] It shows that, by the early fifteenth century, it was possible to miss the ironies and to concentrate upon the literal level of the poem.

Ideally, then, study of the relationship between text and image in these manuscripts would provide insights into the reading process and reflect the reader's changing perception of the text over the centuries.[11] In practice it is very difficult to find conceptual changes in method of illustration occurring in a chronological way. Some of Tuve's most fruitful examples of miniatures making explicit the ironic nature of the text are drawn from late fifteenth-century manuscripts. If anything, fifteenth-century illustrations, particularly those in Bodleian MS Douce 195 and BL MS Harley 4425, Tuve's most often quoted examples, are more lively and more detailed than are their earlier counterparts.[12] A readily accessible parallel is provided by Kuhn, who has published a complete schedule of pictures from Vienna, K.K. Hofbibliothek Cod. 2592, a representative French manuscript from the second half of the fourteenth century.[13] The generalised style of visual narration adopted by these miniatures relies heavily on simple groupings and stereotyped gesture. They provide the barest skeleton of events in the text: for example, fol. 26ʳ shows Venus interceding for the lover with Bel-Acceuil. The artist has chosen to depict the kindling of desire in Bel-Acceuil by symbolic means:

---

[8] C. S. Lewis, *The Allegory of Love* (Oxford, 1939 repr. 1979), 231 ff. analyses the 'weakening of the genuinely allegorical impulse'. See also D. W. Robertson, *A Preface to Chaucer: Studies in Medieval Perspective* (Princeton, 1962), 361 ff.

[9] From the end of the fifteenth century comes Jean Molinet's over-ingenious *Romant de la rose moralisie cler et net*.

[10] The documents of the 'Querelle' are edited by Eric Hicks, *Le Debat sur le Roman de la Rose* (Paris, 1977).

[11] P. Brieger, 'Pictorial Commentaries to the *Commedia*', in P. Brieger, M. Meiss and C. S. Singleton, *Illuminated Manuscripts of the Divine Comedy*, 1 (Princeton, 1969), 81-113, traces changes in the way Dante's poem was perceived by analysing illustrative cycles accompanying the poem. He, too, sees a difference between the fourteenth century and fifteenth century reception of the text. He traces three stages. During most of the fourteenth century Dante's poem is accepted as an authentic account of an other-world journey granted by God. During the second stage emphasis is not only on the poem but on the poet, 'now thought of not so much as a Christian who has received divine inspiration, but as a great genius relating his personal experiences' (p.89). In the third phase Dante is viewed as 'the scholar who spreads out for our intellectual and aesthetic enjoyment a vast repertory of philosophical, historical and political information' (p.90). This notion of enjoyment marks a crucial change in concepts of reading as Hindman and Farquhar, *op. cit.*, 158-9, point out.

[12] The most remarkable thing about the miniatures which Tuve reproduces from these manuscripts (see pp.254, 257, 277) is the considerable detail, unspecified by the text, that has gone into their construction. This may well be rather a result of formal advances – the technical resources of a more naturalistic style – than of a different approach to the text.

[13] 'Die Illustration des Rosenromans', *Jahrbuch der Kunsthistorischen Sammlungen der Allerhöchsten Kaiserhauses*, 31 (1913/1914), 1-66. The oldest illustrated manuscripts date from the last years of the thirteenth century (p.20) and the cycle, during the fourteenth century, is consistent (pp. 59 and 61).

the goddess holds flames in her left hand. Otherwise this miniature could be one of the many scenes of undifferentiated figures in colloquy with one another that appear in this manuscript. It would be perverse to claim that these miniatures present an interpretation of the text; they seem designed, since they are distributed throughout the manuscript, to break it into readily accessible units.[14]

Twentieth-century critics have used the evidence of manuscript illustration as a way of establishing a reading of a text; did medieval readers do so? There are indications that they were, on occasion, expected to look at it carefully. Some thought went into the construction of pictorial cycles and in the opinion of Hindman and Farquhar[15] 'almost every manuscript was the product of a carefully conceived plan'. Authors,[16] patrons,[17] learned commentators[18] and translators[19] can all be shown to have shared a concern for the provision of miniatures and their location in the text.[20] That pictures were considered to be a useful aid in the presentation of new concepts can be demonstrated by the carefully co-ordinated programmes in manuscripts of Oresme's translations of Aristotle. Claire Richter Sherman has shown that the illustrations were an important factor in

14   This is, however, an important function of miniatures. See below.
15   *Op, cit.*, 63.
16   Christine de Pizan is the author who has received most attention in this respect. There is no doubt that Christine supervised the production of the illuminations for some of her works. For further discussion see: L. Schaefer, 'Die Illustrationen zu den Handschriften der Christine de Pizan', *Marburger Jahrbuch für Kunstwissenschaft*, 10 (1930), 119-208; Charity Cannon Willard, 'An Autograph manuscript of Christine de Pizan?' *Studi Francesi*, 27 (1965), 452-457; Eric Hicks, 'The Second "Autograph" Edition of Christine de Pizan's Lesser Poetical Works', *Manuscripta*, 20 (1976), 14-15; Mary Anne Ignatius, 'Christine de Pizan's *Epistre Othea*: An Experiment in Literary Form', *Medievalia et Humanistica*, N.S. 9 (1979), 127-142. According to Ignatius it is Christine who provides the rubrics in BN fr. 606 and Harley 4431, presumed to have been prepared under her instructions, which provide iconographic explanation to aid the reader in interpreting certain of the pictures.
17   Hindman and Farquhar, *op. cit.*, 161, speculate that the patron may have issued specific instructions for the composition of the book's pictures and text. In the case of Charles V we have more solid evidence: autograph colophons in extant manuscripts show that he took a keen interest in all aspects of the production of the books he had commissioned. See L. V. Delisle, *Recherches sur la Librairie de Charles V Roi de France, 1337-1380*, I (Paris, 1907), 156, 218 and 229. For the Duke de Berry see Millard Meiss, *French Painting in the Time of Jean de Berry: The late XIV Century and the Patronage of the Duke*, 2 vols (London and New York, 1967).
18   The most famous example is that of Jean Lebègue's set of extraordinarily extensive instructions in the form of a brief treatise on how to illustrate Sallust's *Catalina* and *Jugurtha*, dating from the early fifteenth century. See J. Porcher, 'Un Amateur de Peinture sous Charles VI: Jean Lebègue', in *Mélanges d'Histoire du Livre et des Bibliothèques offerts à Monsieur Frantz Calot* (Paris, 1960), 35-41; J. Porcher, *Jean Lebègue, Les Histoires que l'on peut Raisonnablement Faire sur les Livres de Sallust* (Paris, 1962).
19   An example is Nicole Oresme, translator of Aristotle. See Claire Richter Sherman, *op. cit.*; Claire Richter Sherman, 'A Second Instruction to the Reader from Nicole Oresme, Translator of Aristotle's *Politics* and *Economics*', *Art Bulletin*, 61 (1979), 468-9.
20   Gilbert Ouy, 'Une Maquette de Manuscrit a Peintures (Paris, B.N. lat. 14643, ff. 269-283v°, Honoré Bouvet, *Somnium prioris de Sallono super materia Scismatis*, 1394)', in *Mélanges d'Histoire du Livre et des Bibliothèques offerts à Monsieur Frantz Calot* (Paris, 1960), 43-51 discusses a set of directions, written in part by Jean Gerson, which shows the utmost concern with *mise-en-page*: Gerson provides not only directions to the illustrator, but also a model, by displaying the text with spaces left at the relevant places.

making 'intelligible in contemporary terms the concepts, terminology and institutions essential to an understanding of the Aristotelian texts'.[21] The pictures
were actually used to supply visual definitions of difficult neologisms coined by
Oresme in his translations. Furthermore, he actually provides guidance to the
reader on relating the concepts in the text to the illustration.[22]

It is impossible to assume that all illustrative programmes received this kind
of attention. An additional problem for the modern critic wishing to lay particular
stress on the miniatures is the disjunction between the devisor and executor of
the programme. Ideas regarding appropriate illustration would have been mediated
to the reader by an artist who may not have read the text or properly understood
what he was required to portray. It is well known that medieval artists tended to
copy or to follow instructions either verbal, written or in the form of marginal
sketches,[23] rather than to invent for themselves on the basis of the text.[24] Even
a precise programme is likely to have been subjected to the conventional motifs
of the artist: he may have been told what to draw, but was free to choose his own
specific forms. He may well have evolved his images out of moduli: the stock of
motifs involving undifferentiated figures and simple gestures which could be
recombined at will.[25] These elements of a scene have their analogy in woodcuts.
As Hodnett points out, the early printers eked out their pictorial cycles by what
he calls 'factotum pictures': that is, small figures of men, women, trees and build-
ings.[26] Such motifs may provide a convenient way of elaborating a sequence or

21 'Some Visual Definitions', *op. cit.*, 323.
22 In this case, it must be stressed that there is a specific audience — Charles V — and a
specific problem — how to present a serious work of scholarship to a non-academic audience.
23 Samuel Berger and Paul Durrieu, *Les Notes pour l'Enlumineur dans les Manuscrits du
Moyen Age*, extracted from *Mémoirs de la Société Nationale des Antiquaires de France*, 53
(Paris, 1893); H. M. R. Martin, 'Les Esquisses des Miniatures', *Revue Archéologique*, 4 (1904),
17-45; E. G. Millar, 'Les Principaux Manuscrits à Peintures du Lambeth Palace à Londres',
Bulletin de la Société Française de Reproductions des Manuscrits à Peintures, 9e Année
(Paris, 1925), 17 discusses the directions in French in Lambeth Palace MS 6 to a Flemish
artist for the illustrations in an English text, a *Brut*; D. J. A. Ross, 'Methods of Book Production in a XIVth Century French Miscellany (London, B.M., MS. Royal 19 D. 1)', *Scriptorium*, 6 (1952), 63-75 (pp. 65 and 66); Millard Meiss, *The Late XIV Century*, *op. cit.*, where
the plate volume, *passim*, shows examples of marginal sketches; Robert Branner, *Manuscript
Painting in Paris during the Reign of Saint Louis: A Study of Style* (Berkeley, Los Angeles,
London, 1977), 12.
24 There is no guarantee that the artist would have followed his instructions precisely. 'On
pourrait multiplier à l'infini les examples de ce genre, qui montrent des enlumineurs traduisant
infidèlement la pensée de leur maître, soit parce qu'ils ne l'ont pas comprise, soit pour des
considérations diverses,' Martin, *op. cit.*, 26.
25 Moduli have been discussed by M. A. Stones, *The Illustration of the French Prose Lancelot
in Flanders, Belgium and Paris 1250-1340* (unpublished Ph.D. thesis, London, 1970), 29-30.
Collections of patterns and *aides mémoires* which could have served the artist as a guide
have been reproduced by M. R. James, 'An English Medieval Sketch Book', *The Walpole Society*, 13 (1925), 1-17; D. J. A. Ross, 'A Late Twelfth-Century Artist's Pattern Sheet', JWCI,
25 (1962), 119-128; R. W. Scheller, *A Survey of Medieval Model Books* (Harlem, 1963).
These elaborate figure-types, but they show that the tendency to abstract images from
context was prevalent throughout the middle ages.
26 *English Woodcuts 1480-1535* (Oxford, 1973), vii. For England, BL MS Harley 1766, a
manuscript of Lydgate's *Fall of Princes*, is a good example of the construction of an extensive

of adding seeming complexity to the composition of a particular miniature. If the cycle of pictures is not a new one, the artist might procure himself a visual exemplar, a copy of a text already illustrated, and copy it himself in his turn. This might lead to misunderstandings of what was depicted in the original.[27] This is not to suggest that a medieval artist never consulted the text; but he seems to have done so only in a local and sporadic way. Meiss[28] quotes the example of an associate of the Boucicaut Master attempting to depict the story of Polycrates from Laurent de Premierfait's *Des Cas des Nobles Hommes et Femmes*. This was a scene often included in illustrated manuscripts of this text: the salient action is of Polycrates throwing his ring into a river as a sop to Fortune. The ring was swallowed by a fish which was subsequently caught and thus the ring was returned to its owner. In the version by the Boucicaut associate, the king and attendants stand by the river bank while the fish, protruding its head above the water, disgorges a sheep. The artist has misunderstood the text, taking *annel* — ring — to be *anel* — lamb. The resulting composition is bizarre, distracting and certainly not useful in aiding the reader's comprehension of the text.

The conclusion to be drawn from this seems to be that people concerned in the making of medieval manuscripts were frequently convinced of the value to the medieval reader of pictures, but the finished product may not always reflect this.[29] It is thus difficult to propose with confidence a direct interplay between text and image. One must be particularly cautious in using the detail of illustrations as a way of making fine critical discriminations. To return to the *Roman de la Rose*: having noted the attention to detail in Douce 195, it is difficult to account for it in a way that would unequivocally indicate a considered response to the text. For example, Tuve remarks that the miniature on fol. 59^v of Douce 195:

> ... with its pair in the pastoral Golden Age-garden modelled nearly after the illustrations of the sin of Luxury, shows that at least the illustrator of MS. Douce 195 . . . would have smiled as he spoke of "free" love.[30]

It is quite true that if we compare the miniature on fol. 113^r showing Venus and Adonis, the positioning of the couple is very similar and, if anything, slightly more decorous. It is clear that the love of Venus for Adonis is not held up as an admirable model. Yet the miniature on fol. 59^v also contains sheep. Do they also

---

picture cycle from a few frequently repeated figure-types.

[27] D. J. A. Ross, 'Nectanebus in his Palace', JWCI, 15 (1952), 67-87, finds in one of the frontispieces to Bodleian MS Bodley 264, a 'confused and much altered derivative of a frontispiece found in certain manuscripts of the French prose Alexander'.

[28] *French Painting in the Time of Jean de Berry: The Boucicaut Master* (London and New York, 1968), 51.

[29] Such a hypothetical situation in which a keen interest in the contents of miniatures on the part of the commissioner of the manuscript is translated into the pictorial stereotypes of an artist might account for the illustrations in BL Cotton MS Nero A. X. It has often been noticed (see, for example, Jennifer A. Lee, 'The Illuminating Critic: the Illustrator of Cotton Nero A. X', *Studies in Iconography*, 3 (1977), 17-46) that the pictures pay scrupulous attention to the structure of the narrative; the details of the composition, however, are not equally scrupulous.

[30] *Op. cit.*, 254 n.13.

have a symbolic function to suggest the moral ambiguity of this Golden Age garden? Or, more likely, is the artist haphazardly combining various elements which the term 'Golden Age' suggested to him, with complete lack of regard for total effect? The repetition of the lovers on fols 59[v] and 113[r] suggests a detaching of motif from context. In other words, the artist was more concerned to find a suitable modulus from which to create his miniature than with interpreting the text.

The difficulty of interpreting correctly the significance of iconographic detail is demonstrated by manuscripts of Marco Polo's *Il Milione*. Rudolph Wittkower has a very interesting article[31] in which he notes that, judging from the illustrations in the well-known Paris, BN fonds. fr. 2810,[32] the book was received by its medieval readers in a way that was at variance with the intention of its original author. As he points out, Marco Polo is an objective and critical observer; although he was undoubtedly familiar with the fabulous Eastern material known to the Middle Ages from sources such as encyclopaedias and romances, on at least two occasions we see him referring his experience to traditional imagery and explicitly preferring direct observation. His work strips many of the marvels from the East. This was obviously thought unsatisfactory: Wittkower demonstrates extensively that the illustrator of the *Livre des Merveilles*[33] consistently tended to 'correct' the text where Polo scrupulously avoids the marvellous, so as to align it with the 'expected' and conventional imagery. He does not actually contravene the text; monsters such as acephali, sciapodes, and cyclopes are inserted only where lack of explicitness would give licence: a vague assertion that the inhabitants of Siberia are wild allows the artist to specify all three creatures.[34] He thus adds a further layer of meaning by presenting *Il Milione* as a stereotyped book of wonders. It would appear, therefore, that the illustrations offer access to a genuinely medieval reading of the book of which the modern reader would be unaware though both would describe it as 'factual'. This view of *Il Milione* would seem to be confirmed by its co-existence in the collection with *Mandeville's Travels* and by the explicit to the last text in the collection which pointedly speaks of 'les monstres et les merveilles'.

Wittkower's point can be extended: *Il Milione* is associated with romance rather than fabulous travel material in two illustrated manuscripts — BL Royal MS 19. D. 1, a fourteenth-century French manuscript containing an Alexander

---

[31] 'Marco Polo and the Pictorial Tradition of the Marvels of the East', *Oriente Poliano* (Rome, 1957), 155-172; reprinted in *Allegory and the Migration of Symbols* (London, 1977), 75-92.

[32] Reproduced in facsimile by Henri Omont, *Livre des Merveilles. Reproduction des 265 Miniatures du Manuscrit Français 2810 de la Bibliothèque Nationale*, 2 vols (Paris, 1907). This richly illustrated compendium of books of travel to Jerusalem and the Far East contains, apart from *Il Milione* with which it begins: Odoric de Pordenone's account of the East; Guillaume de Boldensele's description of the Holy land; the letter of the Grand Khan to Pope Benedict XII and the estate of the Grand Khan written by the Archbishop Saltensis; *Mandeville's Travels*; Hayton's *Fleurs des Histoires d'Orient*; and Ricold de Montcroix's journey to the east.

[33] Interestingly, in view of the illustration of the Polycrates episode, he was an associate of the Boucicaut master.

[34] Omont, Pl. 30.

romance followed by the travels of Marco Polo,[35] and Bodleian manuscript
Bodley 264, an early fifteenth-century codex produced in England consisting of
Alexander B and *Il Milione* added to a mid fourteenth-century French *Alexander
Romance*. In Bodley 264, in particular, the devisor of the programme of the
Marco Polo section, which bears little relationship to that in fr. 2810, shows a
similar interest in the fabulous races for which there is no textual warrant. On
fol. 260ʳ (see Pl. 1) the section concerned with India begins. The first chapter is
prefaced by a miniature containing a genially conceived collection of fur-covered
monsters: the cynocephalus; the acephalus; a cyclops; a sciapod. The next picture
in the series, that on fol. 262ʳ again exhibits a number of grotesque and fantastic
people. Although the text on this page is concerned with the country of Cianda
and the account of the siege which resulted in the payment of tribute to the Khan,
the miniature deals with the siege in a perfunctory way. To the right is a walled
city, over the ramparts of which look three helmeted soldiers; the rest of the
miniature is devoted to the portrayal of horned or tusked fur-covered men.
Ostensibly, then, the artist of Bodley 264 seems to be offering a similar interpretation of the text to that in fonds. fr. 2810. A closer inspection of fol. 260ʳ suggests
an alternate possibility. Above the miniature, the chapter heading reads:[36]

Ce dit le viiˣˣ. et xvii chapitre, le Commencem*ent* du livre dynde. et deuisera
toutes les m*er*ueilles qui y sont et les manieres des gens.

Below the miniature, the chapter which goes on to speak of the construction of
the merchants' ships, begins:

Or puis que vous auez oy*er* conter de tantes p*r*ouinces derraines nous vous
laisserons de ceste matiere si vous commencerons a entrer en ynde por
vous conter toutes les merueilles qui y sont.

The words 'merueilles' and 'ynde' occur twice in close proximity to the illustration.
It is possible that such words suggested aspects of India to the artist that he felt
were *de rigueur* to present in some form to the reader, no matter how irrelevant
to the text; it is equally possible that the words merely stimulated him to provide
the visual clichés available to him without any concern for overall effect. The
artist of Royal 19. D. 1 is more restrained: the miniature introducing the section
on India on fol. 118ʳ depicts on the left a crudely drawn cynocephalus and a
man in a tunic; on the right three figures look over the parapet of a castle. There
are no monsters in the siege miniature.[37] It is impossible to determine whether
we have, in the case of Bodley 264 and fr. 2810, a mechanical reliance on time-
honoured prototypes or whether the prototypes aided the formulation of the
particular kind of imaginative world that it was deemed appropriate to evoke for

[35] It also contains other travel texts. For full description see George F. Warner and Julius P.
Gibson, *British Museum Catalogue of Western Manuscripts in the Old Royal and King's
Collections, II, Royal MSS. 12 A. i to 20. E. X and APP. 1-89* (London, 1921), 339-341.
[36] There are indications that the frame, at least, was done after the rubrication.
[37] As we have seen, the iconography of Royal 19. D. i was familiar to at least one of the
fifteenth-century artists of Bodley 264.

Pl. 1   Oxford, Bodleian Library MS Bodley 264 fol. 260ʳ

Il Milione. Though the artist of fonds. fr. 2810 shows himself more discriminating in the choice of when to quote visually from conventional material, there is no guarantee that there was anything other than pragmatism behind his choice of subject-matter. Since *Mandeville's Travels* was also contained in the volume, he would have had to depict the usual repertory of monsters at some stage. His provision of them in the Marco Polo section may have been a result of creative economy rather than of active interpretation.

Though the miniatures in the Marco Polo manuscripts may not have expressed an interpretation of the text, they may have been instrumental in shaping a response to it. Only a careful reading of the work rather than an inspection of the pictures would reveal that Polo does *not* use the familiar imagery when describing his travels.[38]

Lebègue's detailed treatise on how to illustrate *Catalina* and *Jugurtha* suggests that the amount of detailed attention to be placed on the components of a miniature may have fluctuated within the space of a single manuscript. As one might have expected, the directions for the prefatory miniature[39] are particularly complex: Lebègue was obviously anticipating that it would be considered with some degree of attention. It is, at first sight, a conventional author portrait. It is to show Sallust seated in his study writing at a desk, dressed in a tunic under which may be seen a coat of mail. He is also to wear greaves and gold spurs and to have a coif on his head. The horse is to be half-hidden behind the study 'en signifient que le dit homme escripvant sera descendu de chevalerie a l'estude'. It can be seen that Lebègue puts considerable conceptual pressure on the components of what would otherwise seem a fairly simple miniature. Here the iconographic detail in the miniature is of crucial importance: the combination in his attire of the scholarly and the chivalric is designed to convey as much about his pattern of life as is the half-hidden horse. The function of this illustration is apparent: it supplements the text by providing information about its author. The remainder of Lebègue's instructions give no indication as to how the rest of the scenes should operate. Though they are precise, paying attention to the position of the miniatures in the text,[40] they address themselves to questions of composition rather than of interpretation. He does not theorise about why he went to such trouble to compose this meticulous cycle, or the kind of aid to the reader, if any he thought he was providing. Each scene to be depicted is described scrupulously; though the detail is not symbolically significant as it is in the frontispiece, great care has been taken to ensure accuracy to the text. It is possible, therefore, that their main purpose was to offer a parallel narrative and to emphasise its events by giving visual expression to the words on the page. Certainly, in some late medieval

---

[38] Millard Meiss points out the influential effects of visual material: 'Nowadays we recognise that the visual arts had a central place in the culture of the fourteenth and fifteenth centuries and that they were capable of a formative effect', Brieger, Meiss and Singleton, *op. cit.*, 43.

[39] This is the prefatory miniature to *Catalina*, but *Jugurtha* is associated with it in manuscript (see Porcher, *Les Histoires*, *op. cit.*, 15). The visual information offered about Sallust himself thus holds good for both texts.

[40] He makes a note of the phrase which the miniature is to precede.

romance manuscripts, illustrations with their lengthy rubrics summarising the events of the chapter to come,[41] provide an alternative way of gaining access to the narrative. They must have been much appreciated by those readers more interested in following the story from the pictures than from reading the text.[42] For those interested in a more meticulous reading, miniatures accurate to the text would provide a useful way of relocating favourite passages and a real aid to remembering the stages of the narrative.[43] The illustrations provided by Lebègue may thus possibly have been envisaged as part of the apparatus designed to guide the reader through the text. They would have been a genuine aid to the reader, but they would have aided the process of reading rather than of understanding.

Such a device would be of particular service in the case of works which are essentially compilations of stories. Manuscripts of Laurent de Premierfait's *Des Cas des Nobles Hommes et Femmes*, a translation of Boccaccio's *De Casibus Virorum Illustrium*[44] make extensive use of apparatus designed to subdivide and order the reading of the text. The work itself is a universal history of misfortune from Adam and Eve to King John of France taken prisoner at the battle of Poitiers in 1356. In both recensions, following Boccaccio, Laurent divides the text into nine books; he further subdivides each book into a number of chapters, each of which is supplied with a heading, usually written in red ink to attract the eye. In many manuscripts each book is prefaced by a table of contents supplying a transcript of the chapter headings which are to be used in the ensuing book; there is thus an elaborate system of cross-referencing. Furthermore, there seem to have been two distinct ways of illustrating *Des Cas* manuscripts; a short cycle involving nine or ten miniatures to the prologue and each of the books and a long cycle of some seventy plus miniatures marking the book and the majority of the chapter divisions.[45] These miniatures visually summarise the contents, or at least depict a major scene. At the end of Book I Laurent provides a theoretical rationale for dividing his work into books:

Mais nous divisons ceste oeuvre afin que nous facions selon la maniere des pelerins errans qui partent leur chemin par certainnes bournes aulcune foiz

[41] Cedric E. Pickford, 'An Arthurian Manuscript in the John Rylands Library', *Bulletin of the John Rylands Library*, 31 (1948), 318-344, discusses the lengthy rubrics that are found in prose romances of the later fourteenth and fifteenth centuries.

[42] An important aspect of Ignatius' article, *op. cit*, is the discussion of the development of reading as an 'eye-oriented medium' as opposed to the idea of oral performance.

[43] In the case of Dante illustrations Brieger views the miniatures as providing a parallel and complementary narrative. He is quite clear about illustrations as a visual aid and mentions their function as *aides mémoire*: 'The purpose of the illustrations was not to compete with the text or to be a substitute for it but to provide a visual aid to understanding and remembering all the steps along the soul's road to salvation', *op. cit.*, 84.

[44] De Premierfait translated his source twice. The first attempt was a fairly close transcription of the original and made little impact. In 1409 he revised his translation completely, expanding it into a veritable encyclopaedia of fact and anecdote, and dedicated it to Jean, Duke de Berry. This recension became one of the most popular secular texts of the time. Carla Bozzolo, *Manuscrits des Traductions Françaises d'Oeuvres de Boccace: XVᵉ Siècle* (Padova, 1973), provides the most recent list of manuscripts.

[45] See Bozzolo, *op. cit.*

par une belle pierre, aulcune foiz par un vieil chesne ou par aulcun moustier, ou par aulcune fontaine clere, afin qu'ilz mesurent plus legierement combien de chemin ilz ont fait, et combien ilz en ont a faire. Et affin aussi que les pelerins puissent plus clerement monstrer en racomptand leurs adventures, aussi nous partirons ceste oevre par neuf livres distinctez, combien que elle peust proceder par un mesme chemin sanz faire division.[46]

The two issues with which he is concerned here are those of pacing and of memory. It is worthy of particular note that he relates memory to the physical layout of the manuscript and that the physical layout of the book is related so precisely to physical objects. Such a device may remind us of the techniques of artificial memory current in the Middle Ages, particularly the placing of objects in a physical environment.[47] Some of the manuscripts with their lavish programme of synoptic illustrations may possibly be seen as an extension of this.

Since there is a range of functions which miniatures may have served, ranging from the merely decorative to the explicatory, it is clear that generalisations are inadequate. Specific case studies of individual manuscripts or groups of manuscripts are preferable, though the conclusions yielded will vary from case study to case study.

Lydgate's *Troy Book*, a translation into English of Guido de Columnis' *Historia Destructionis Troiae*, falls into the category of fashionable reading. The proportion of illustrated to unillustrated manuscripts is impressively high for an English text: of twenty-three extant manuscripts, including fragments, eight have or had miniatures;[48] of the remaining fifteen, six have been carefully provided with decorated borders or initials to mark major divisions in the text; and a seventh bears traces that a similar format was envisaged. Most of the *Troy Book* manuscripts are large, impressive volumes, whether or not they contain miniatures. They are not readily portable volumes and were evidently intended for ostentatious display. The *Troy Book* was commissioned from Lydgate in 1412 by Henry V while still Prince of Wales and was completed in 1420.[49] The issue of prestige seems very much to the forefront in the text itself: Lydgate begins with much self-consciousness with a highly rhetorical introduction, invoking the aid of Mars,

[46] P. M. Gathercole, *Laurent de Premierfait's Des Cas des Nobles Hommes et Femmes*, Studies in the Romance Languages and Literature No. 74 (Chapel Hill, 1968). This is an edition of Book I only; there is no modern edition of the complete text.

[47] The importance of visual data for these artificial memory systems has been discussed by Frances A. Yates, *The Art of Memory* (London, 1966).

[48] Manuscripts to receive illustration are: London, BL MSS Royal 18. D. ii and Cotton Augustus A. iv; Oxford, Bodleian MSS Rawl. C. 446 and Digby 232; Cambridge, Trinity College MS 0. 5. 2; Manchester, John Rylands Library MS English 1; New York, Pierpont Morgan Library MS M. 876; Bristol, Public Library MS 8. This last has been mutilated for the pictures. Manuscripts with illumination only are: BL MSS Arundel 99, Royal 18. D. vi; Oxford, Exeter College MS 129; St John's College MS 6; Bodleian MS Digby 230; olim Phillips 3113. Large spaces for illuminated initials were left at the beginning of the Prologue of each book of Bodleian MS Rawl. poet. 144 and smaller spaces elsewhere in the manuscript.

[49] H. Bergen, *Lydgate's Troy Book*, EETS ES 97, 103, 106 and 126 (London, 1906-1935), Prologue 121-146 and V. 3366-3369.

Othea (goddess of prudence) and Calliope, thus assembling a host of classical
references designed to elevate his style. The Troy story itself enjoyed an immense
vogue in most European countries in the Middle Ages. Since most nations in
Europe traced their ancestry back to a Trojan refugee, the Troy story gains its
influential narrative status partly as an account of national origin.[50] A conjunction
of subject, poet and patron conspires to make the *Troy Book* one of the most
prestigious of Lydgate's works.

Evidence in the form of coats of arms provides a good indication of the audience for illustrated manuscripts of the poem. From the visual impression of the
manuscripts alone, it is easy enough to deduce that the majority of *Troy Book*
owners were wealthy or at least prepared to divert a substantial proportion of
their wealth to the acquisition of expensive editions. Fortunately it is possible to
be more precise. Three of the manuscripts were owned by men of very similar
social standing, influential men who were all sheriffs, J.P.s and M.P.s. The coat
of arms in the first initial in BL Cotton Augustus A. iv is that of Sir Thomas
Chaworth and his second wife, Isabella de Ailesbury.[51] Cambridge, Trinity College
MS O. 5. 2 has coats of arms throughout the volume and as an integral part of
the pages which have decorative borders.[52] Almost all of them can be traced
to the Thwaites or Knevet families; the position of the Knevets in the late fifteenth century was similar to that of Sir Thomas Chaworth.[53] Fol. 173ʳ of
Manchester, John Rylands Library MS English 1 is the most impressive armorial

[50] Knowledge of the story derived not from Homer and Virgil but from the popular *Ephem-
eris de Historia Belli Trojani* written by 'Dictys Cretensis' in the fourth century A.D. and
De Excidio Trojae Historia by 'Dares Phrygius' written in the sixth century A.D. (see
Nathaniel Edward Griffin, *Dares and Dictys: An Introduction to the Study of Medieval
Versions of the Story of Troy* (Baltimore, 1907)). In about 1155-1170 a Benedictine monk,
Benoit de Sainte-Maure, blended together the material in the *Ephemeris* and *De Excidio* to
produce over 30,000 lines of Old French poetry (ed. L. Constans in 6 vols for the Société
des Anciens Textes Français (Paris, 1904-12)). A prose version of the *Roman* was incorporated
into the second (fourteenth-century) recension of the early thirteenth-century *Histoire
ancienne jusqu'à César*, thereby making Troy the principal subject of the chronicle as a whole
(see Hugo Buchthal, *Historia Troiana: Studies in the History of Medieval Secular Illustration*,
Studies of the Warburg Institute, 32 (London, 1971)). This confirmed the Troy story in all
its aspects as an essential part of the history of Europe. The Latin prose version of the *Roman*,
the *Historia Destructionis Troiae* of Guido de Columnis, was finished in 1287 (ed. Nathaniel
Edward Griffin, Medieval Academy of America Publications, 26 (Cambridge, Mass., 1936)).
Compared with the interest in translating works of classical scholarship in France, Henry's
choice of text might seem a little old-fashioned. But he seems to feel that England is lagging
behind in not having a vernacular version (see Prol. 111-117).
[51] Bergen, *op. cit.*, vol. 4, p. 2.
[52] In its present form the manuscript consists of *Generydes* (fols 1ʳ-37ᵛ), the *Troy Book*
(fols 38ʳ-190ᵛ) and Lydgate's *Siege of Thebes* (fols 191ʳ-211ᵛ). Only the *Troy Book* has
been supplied with decorative borders. Although fol. 191ʳ is part of the same quire as the
end of the *Troy Book*, the exemplar for the *Thebes* section was of a totally different kind
from the exemplar for the *Troy Book*. *Thebes* has running titles, chapter headings and marginal annotations giving topic headings; *Troy Book* has none of these. For a full analysis of
the escutcheons see D. A. Pearsall, 'Notes on the Manuscript of *Generydes*', *The Library*,
5th ser., 16 (1961), 205-209.
[53] See J. C. Wedgewood and Anne Holt, *History of Parliament: Biographies of the Members
of the Commons House 1439-1509* (London, 1936), 520-1.

statement of ownership yet encountered. It is a full-page miniature displaying a coat of arms complete with helmet, mantling and crest, surrounded by an elaborate border. These arms are those of the Carent family, and the manuscript itself was probably owned by either William Carent (1395-1476) or his brother John Carent (d.1478) or his son, John Carent (1425-83).[54] A fourth manuscript, BL Royal 18. D. ii, provides the only direct evidence we have of aristocratic ownership: it is associated with Sir William Herbert who became the first Earl of Pembroke in 1468 and his wife Anne Devereux whom he married c.1455.[55]

There is a consistency about the format of some of the *Troy Book* manuscripts which suggests that they were brought out in 'editions'. An apparently uniform sequence of miniatures seems to have evolved, linked closely to the structure Lydgate adopts for his narrative. Guido tells his story in thirty-five books, thus breaking down his tale into thirty-five constituent units. The *Troy Book* is a fairly close translation of Guido but Lydgate organises his material rather differently. Although he destroys the coherence of Guido's despairingly pessimistic view of history,[56] his grasp of narrative structure is more cogent. Including the Prologue to the whole, the *Troy Book* is divided into six parts.[57] Book I is by way of a preface to the main events and recounts the quest for the Golden Fleece and the first destruction of Troy. Book II is concerned with the rebuilding of Troy, the attempts to secure the return of Hesione, the abduction of Helen, and the encampment of the Greeks outside Troy. Books III and IV deal with the battles fought by the two armies; Book III ends climactically with the death and burial of Hector. Book V provides a coda, setting out the adventures of the Greeks as they leave Troy.

Of the eight illustrated manuscripts, four of them[58] have a sequence of six miniatures to designate the formal divisions of the narrative. A fifth, Digby 232, follows the normal pattern except that the beginning of Book V is marked, not

---

[54] J. J. G. Alexander, 'William Abell "Lymnour" and 15th Century English Illumination', in *Kunsthistorische Forschungen Otto Pächt zu seinem 70. Geburtstag*, ed. Artur Rosenauer and Gerold Weber (Salzburg, 1972), 166-172 (169 n.35).

[55] Warner and Gilson, *op. cit.*, 310. In its present form the manuscript consists of a codex from the third quarter of the fifteenth century bound up with items written at the beginning of the sixteenth century. The *Troy Book* begins on fol. 6^r, being preceded by a copy of 'The testament of John Lydgate, monke of Berry, whiche he made hymself by his lyfe days'. *Thebes* follows: although it begins on a fresh quire, it is written in a similar hand to that of the *Troy Book* and was thus presumably part of the original concept of the volume. Seven other items are appended, all of a moral or topical nature. (For details see Warner and Gilson, *ibid.*, 308-10.)

[56] C. David Benson, *The History of Troy in Middle English Literature* (Woodbridge, 1980), 119.

[57] This way of dividing the text would not have been suggested by any extant Guido manuscripts. Most importantly BL Harley 51 and Bodleian MS Holkham misc. 37, both of which were in the library of the monastery of Bury St Edmunds (Neil Ker, *Medieval Libraries of Great Britain: A List of Surviving Books* (2nd edn London, 1964), 20 and 21) and may have been seen by Lydgate, do not divide the work in this way.

[58] Cotton Augustus A. iv; Rawl. C. 446; Trinity College 0. 5. 2; the Bristol manuscript has pages missing at the crucial points, but it is evident that it was originally provided with a sequence of six.

by a miniature and partial border, but merely by an initial and partial border. The other three manuscripts represent an expansion of the basic scheme: the pictorial programme of Pierpont Morgan 876 did not get very close to completion but, from the position of the spaces left in the text, it is possible to reconstruct the proposed subjects; in Royal 18. D. ii and Eng. 1, the sequence of six still retains its importance, as will be seen. The content of the miniatures remains remarkably consistent and they are closely related, though there are differences in the detailed working out of the composition. They are all by different artists, though Digby 232 and Rawlinson C. 446 are both by the same scribe.[59] An element of standardisation is apparent. There is a slight disagreement about the placement of the miniature for Book II: the beginning is in the form of a prologue as Lydgate mourns the workings of Fortune, moralises over Laomedon's fall, and apologises for the deficiencies of his style. Four of the manuscripts mark the beginning of the Book as the recommencement of the narrative at 1.203; the other four place the miniature at the beginning of the Prologue with a conventional depiction of Fortune's wheel[60] though Morgan 876 has only a space for a miniature at the beginning of the narrative. The basic point remains unchanged: owners of the *Troy Book* were provided with a standard series, one of the functions of which was to mark in a visually arresting way the formal divisions of the text. Apart from the running titles in red giving the number of the book in Latin in Morgan 876 and the elaborate rubricated 'explicits' at the end of each book giving a reprise of its contents and the unique series of chapter headings in Royal 18. D. ii, there is, generally speaking, no apparatus in the form of running titles, tables of contents and chapter headings to guide the reader through the text. It is not presented for easy reference; Roy. and Eng. 1, as will be seen, are the exceptions.

Illustrated manuscripts of the *Troy Book*, apart from Royal 18. D. ii, begin with a presentation miniature showing Lydgate offering the completed volume to Henry V. Otherwise the illustrations have a narrative reference, but they do not provide a synopsis of the matter of the book; they merely allude to the first major incident. Thus the moments chosen for illustration are not necessarily germane to the story. It is not that the episode selected has any particular significance in itself; significance is conferred upon it by the structure of the work which places it as the beginning of a book. Lack of narrative importance can be seen in the case of the miniature which usually announces Book I, the replacement of Peleus' subjects by the metamorphosis of ants into Myrmidons. The composition does, however, show a scrupulous alertness to the detail of the text. Similarly, the squabble between Ulysses and Ajax, the first episode in Book V, does not really set the tone for the rest of the book, apart from the general theme of dis-

[59] A. I. Doyle and M. B. Parkes, 'The Production of Copies of the *Canterbury Tales* and the *Confessio Amantis* in the Early Fifteenth Century', *Medieval Scribes, Manuscripts and Libraries: Essays Presented to N. R. Ker*, ed. M. B. Parkes and Andrew G. Watson (London, 1978), 163-210 (201 n.100).
[60] Since the leaf has been cut out in the Bristol manuscript, one can only assume that this would have been the composition. For the other manuscripts apart from Eng. 1 see the table.

Table 1 A comparative list of the subjects of the pictures in all manuscripts, except Eng. 1, of the Troy Book

	DIGBY 1420-30	AUG. A. iv 1430s	RAWL. 1425-50	TRINITY 1440-60	M 876 1440-50	ROY. 1455-69
	Troy Book only	*Troy Book* only	*Troy Book* only	*Troy Book & Generydes*	*Troy Book & Generydes*	*Troy Book & Thebes*
PROLOGUE	Presentation miniature	Presentation miniature	Presentation miniature	Presentation miniature	Begins incomplete	'Presentation' miniature
BOOK I	Peleus praying: the creation of the Myrmidons ll 1 ff	Peleus praying: the creation of the Myrmidons ll 1 ff	Peleus praying: the creation of the Myrmidons ll 1 ff	Peleus praying: the creation of the Myrmidons ll 1 ff		
PROLOGUE	Illuminated border				Fortune and her wheel ll 1 ff	Fortune and her wheel ll 1 ff
BOOK II	Priam, besieging rebel city, receiving news of the destruction of Troy ll 203 ff	Priam, besieging rebel city, receiving news of the destruction of Troy ll 203 ff	Stereotyped siege picture ll 203 ff	Leaf cut out: according to Bergen it contained a miniature	Space left for miniature	
					Space left for miniature at the beginning of the reconstruction of Troy ll 479 ff	
BOOK III	Hector killing Patroclus (but inaccurate to	Hector killing Patroclus who has a wounded head	Hector killing Patroclus by cleaving him	Miniature of unusual type: contending	Space left for miniature	Hector killing Patroclus by cleaving him

text). Patroclus has been killed by a spear thrust ll 5757 ff	and a right arm practically severed at the shoulder ll 5757 ff	in half ll 5757 ff	forces? Hector leading out his division and Agamemnon assigning his troops into battalions? ?ll 565 ff?	in half ll 5757 ff
				Greek tents overthrown by tempest ll 3273 ff
				Troilus taking leave of Cressid ll 4077 ff
				Mourning over Hector ll 5423 ff
BOOK IV Hector lying in state; ?the Palladium ll 1 ff	Hector's tomb; Achilles lying wounded; Agamemnon in council ll 1 ff	Hector's tomb; Achilles lying wounded; Agamemnon in council ll 1 ff	Hector's tomb; Achilles wounded; Agamemnon in council ll 1 ff	Hector's statue? Achilles lying wounded; Agamemnon in council ll 1 ff
				Troilus surrounded ll 2712 ff
				Troilus executed ll 7256-7779

	DIGBY	AUG. A. iv.	RAWL.	TRINITY	M 876	ROY.
						Brazen horse and Calchas ll 6023 ff
						Brazen horse being dragged into Troy ll 6206 ff
BOOK V	Illuminated partial border and initial	Ulysses and Ajax before Agamemnon; the Greek ships ll 1 ff	According to Bergen there was originally a miniature, but the relevant page has been cut out	Agamemnon and ships; some puzzling aspects to composition ll 1 ff	Quarrel between Ulysses and Ajax; the Greek ships ll 1 ff	Quarrel between Ulysses and Ajax; the Greeks march away to ships ll 1 ff

integration and decay. The only exception is Hector killing Patroclus,[61] an incident which occurs towards the end of Book III. This is a major episode in the book, though one might argue that it is the death of Hector himself[62] that is the crucial event. Table 1 provides a comparative list of the subjects of the pictures in all manuscripts of the *Troy Book* apart from Eng. 1 which is separately considered below. It shows the strength of the tradition of illustrating the *Troy Book* and it is possible that behind the basic series of six miniatures lies a lost presentation copy.

In their stress on the formal divisions of the work, the illustrations are radically different from the other English text which is supplied with a constantly repeated sequence, John Gower's *Confessio Amantis*.[63] The two miniatures depicting Nebuchadnezzar's dream of the statue and Amans confessing to Genius do not address themselves to narrative incident as much as they provide a conceptual schema. They isolate the two elements which may be seen as the main intellectual interests of the poem, the end which the narratives serve. Man's individual love for woman is a microcosm for the larger schemes of order and affinity, particularly in the political sphere. The disordered individual is seen as an emblem for the

[61] The killing of Patroclus is explicit: following Benoit and Guido, Lydgate describes Hector:
> . . . with a swerd rood to Patroclus,
> Avised fully þat he schal be ded;
> And furiously gan hamen at his hed,
> And rof hym doun, þer was no maner lette,
> In-to þe brest þoruȝ his basenet,
> As seith Guydo, with so gret a peyne,
> þat with þe stroke he partid hym on tweyne   (III. 782-8)

The manner of rendering the slaying visually in Benoit and Guido manuscripts is more frequently like that in Digby than accurate to the text. In BN fr. 782 fol. 58ᵛ, for instance, the protagonists are labelled so there can be no mistake about interpreting them: Hector tilts at Patroclus with his lance and Patroclus falls backwards. A similar motif occurs in other Benoit manuscripts: BL Harley 4482 and Venice, Bibl. Marc. fr. 17; *Histoire ancienne* manuscripts: BN fr. 301 and BL Royal 20. D. i; it persists until 1495 in a manuscript of Raoul Lefèvre, BN fr. 2252. It is difficult to know if the Digby artist was following a tradition of illustration or was adopting the identical formulaic response that had occurred to other artists given the task of illustrating the story.

[62] In Digby Hector is lying on a bier, surrounded by mourners. In the foreground are three kneeling figures in various poses of dejection. On an altar on the right stands a small gold image carrying sword and spear. A close parallel to this composition can be found in BL Royal MS 16. F. ix, an early fifteenth-century manuscript containing a translation of Guido into French. This too shows Hector lying on a bier surrounded by mourners, though it does not have anything like the image on the altar, which Bergen suggests may be the Palladium. A comparison with the more traditional – in English terms – miniature in Roy. may provide some clues. English artists respond to the problems of depicting Hector's elaborate tomb by simplifying it, showing only the embalmed figure of Hector in armour, and incorporating it into a multiple composition. In Roy. the illustration shows the wounded Achilles in his tent while below, a tent forms the backdrop to a seated Agamemnon flanked on either side by two knights. These tents are linked vertically by a high Gothic column surmounted by a small, gilt, naked figure bearing a cusped shield and with a pennon over its shoulder. It looks remarkably like a pagan idol; the artist seems to have misunderstood the significance of Hector's statue in his model and translated it into a stereotype with which he was familiar. It is possible that the Digby artist may have done the same thing.

[63] For a list of manuscripts see G. C. Macaulay, *The English Works of John Gower*, EETS ES 81 (London, 1900), cxxxviii-clxvii.

disordered state. The visual motif of confession is related to the personal element while Nebuchadnezzar's dream provides Gower's political analysis with urgency. In the *Troy Book*, on the other hand, the illustrations are used as visual punctuation.

Eng. 1, from the middle of the fifteenth century, with sixty-nine miniatures, is the most lavish of the *Troy Book* manuscripts. The impression of luxury provided by its extensive series of pictures is intensified by the fact that each miniature is accompanied by a border which frames both columns of text so that the decoration is extremely elaborate. The majority of illustrations occur in the substantial margins either along the lower margin or up the side.[64] Though it might seem to have little to do with other manuscripts of the *Troy Book*, the profusion of miniatures being so much greater, the original sequence is still embedded in the fabric of the manuscript. Five miniatures are incorporated into the text space at the beginning of each book: there is a half-page presentation miniature for Book I (fol. 1ʳ), a Wheel of Fortune for Book II (fol. 28ᵛ); Book III commences with Hector killing Patroclus (fol. 78ᵛ), the beginning of Book IV (fol. 112ʳ) is denoted by Achilles lying wounded in his tent. These illustrations occupy both columns of the text space. Thus far they are closest to the miniatures which begin each book of Royal 18. D. ii. The picture to Book V (fol. 151ᵛ, see Pl. 2) is at first sight an exception: unlike the others, it has only one column allocated, and the subject matter is puzzling. In all the miniatures the major figures are labelled, usually in white, but occasionally in black ink. Thus on fol. 78ᵛ the relevant figures are marked 'Ector', 'Patroclus' and 'Rex Merion'. On fol. 151ᵛ the composition is divided into three by means of two stylised mountains in the middle ground. In the background between the two mountains, is a king with a group of soldiers to the left. In the foreground on the left is a tightly clustered group of three men in civilian dress, the two in front in profile seemingly caught in a moment of heated altercation while the figure behind shown full face is apparently listening. In the foreground on the right is a group of standing knights. The three figures on the left are labelled 'Daniell', 'Ezechiell' and 'Sedechie', an inexplicable subject to find in a *Troy Book* manuscript. It is, however, quite obvious what has happened. The illustration is in the second column; in the first column, parallel with the miniature, we have the moment at the end of Book IV where Lydgate tries to convey the enormity of the fall of Troy by suggesting that even the great Judaic prophets would have been inadequate properly to lament the destruction. It is, of course, a variation on the modesty topos. The following lines occur:

> . . . nor thou Ezechiel
> That were that tyme when that meschif fel
> Vnto the king called Sedechie
> In Babilone and for thi prophecye
> With stones were thou cruely slawe
> Nor he that was departed with a sawe

64 Bottom margin approx. 97mm; outer margin approx. 80-94mm.

    Ye bothe two that so coude compleyne
    Ne Daniel that felt so grete peyne . . .
        (IV 7063-7070 transcribed from the manuscript)

Iconographically the scene depicts the episode usual at the beginning of Book V: the dispute of Telamon Ajax and Ulysses over possession of the Palladium and its adjudication, but the labeller, unclear as to what the picture was meant to represent, cast his eyes over the page in search of clues and came across these three names conveniently close to the miniature.

In selecting the scenes for illustration, the devisor of the programme was not as much concerned with copying a cycle or providing images for the text as with responding to previous decisions as to how the manuscript should be set out. All of the *Troy Book* manuscripts, whether illustrated or not, are carefully sub-divided into sections by means of champ initials as a supplement to the large initials which mark book divisions. A decorative hierarchy is thus established. These initials are not arbitrarily placed: there is a good deal of consistency from manuscript to manuscript. An incidental effect of the liberal use of champ initials is that the decorative impression of the *mise-en-page* is considerably enhanced, but they also seem to represent genuine stages in the narrative. Moments of rhetorical intensity are also picked out, particularly seasonal descriptions couched in astrological terms. The three earliest manuscripts, Cotton Augustus, Digby and Rawlinson concur almost exactly as to what are the crucial moments to be given decorative notice; later manuscripts place initials to introduce the same sections but intensify the sense of division of the text by increasing the number of initials. It is clear that certain aspects of the narrative were perceived as important by all the manuscripts. Eng. 1 is quite consistent about preserving the hierarchy suggested by the earlier manuscripts. In almost every case where they have a champ initial, Eng. 1 supplies a border and miniature. It also has champ initials; but these are usually reserved for divisions in the text not indicated by Cotton, Digby and Rawlinson. The consequences of this for the pictorial programme in Eng. are interesting. There is evidently a strong sense of propriety behind the location of the miniatures, a sense of propriety which is conditioned by an idea of the structure of the work contained in the earliest manuscripts. On one level, at least, the illustrations reflect an expansion of the original decorative programme governed by earliest decisions as to how to present the text. The hierarchy of development seems to be rigidly graded. The original series of pictures is formally incorporated into the text-space itself; the old sequence of division appears in a new, lavish guise; and the text is further sub-divided by a number of fresh champ initials.

This view of the illustrations as an elaboration of the original process of division and thus having primarily a formal genesis, may help to explain one apparent anomaly in the cycle of miniatures. All the illustrations, apart from the presentation miniature, with one exception, are narrative; they attempt, on however rudimentary a level, to engage with the text and to present a visual equivalent of events on the page. This is not the case with the illustration on fol. 54^v which depicts Guido (labelled) seated inside a turret-like structure with a book on his

Pl. 2 Manchester, John Rylands Library English MS 1 fol. 151ᵛ

Pl. 3   Manchester, John Rylands Library English MS 1 fol. 53ʳ

knee, expounding to two disciples, seated on the floor, each with a book on his knee. This provision of an author/teaching picture is one solution of a technical problem. Very little is happening at this stage for the artist to depict: Lydgate discusses the fate of both Castor and Pollux after death — they were transformed into the constellation Gemini — and then cites Dares as an authority for the ensuing description of the chief protagonists of the war. Guido is also mentioned in the column adjacent to the miniature, and this was evidently the source of the labeller's information; to the artist, the authority figure may well have been intended for Dares. For someone constructing a programme with the content of the miniatures in mind, this is not the most logical page in the manuscript for which to supply an illustration. But for someone concerned to follow the decorative hierarchies of earlier manuscripts in a visually arresting way, there is a powerful precedent for marking this particular moment in the text as worthy of notice.

On another level, the miniatures are by way of visual chapter headings. Eng. 1, with its profusion of labelled miniatures, has the most elaborate apparatus designed to guide the reader through the book. By providing a visual synopsis they remove from the reader the onerous task of actually perusing the text. However, any reader relying on the pictures rather than the text is vulnerable to the care and competence of the labeller. It is ironic that an attempt to clarify the text by providing numerous pictures and to clarify the pictures by labelling them should be thwarted by sporadic failures of adequate supervision in the latter stages of production. The labeller is responsible for adding a couple of new knights to the *dramatis personae* of the Troy story. On fol. 53^r (see Pl. 3) is a composite miniature showing, in the top register, Menelaus receiving the news of Helen's abduction. Menelaus is swooning supported by two friends labelled 'Nestor' and 'Pira' and regarded anxiously by two others. Nestor is appropriate enough, but 'Pira' is a problem until one reads the lines of text in the second column above the miniature:

> To menelay the tydynges were brought
> Whiles he abode with Nestor at Pira
> (II 4276-7 transcribed from manuscript)

The same process occurs on fol. 83^v. Potentially this is a summary of the second battle, especially of the people killed by Hector, apart from the slaying of Patroclus which has been visually noted elsewhere. As with all the illustrations of battle scenes, the groups of armed figures are given significance by means of labelling. Among the dead is a corpse labelled 'Duke antro*pus*'. This grimly appropriate and ironically dead knight has been evolved in the usual way: in the second column of the folio appear the lines:

> But that he carf & brake atwo the threde
> And the knotte of cruel Antropos   (III 966-7)

A casual glance over the opening has led to the creation of a fresh knight. Though the labeller is sometimes arbitrary in his selection of names to correlate with figures, he is consistent about his incongruities. On fol. 131^r the supervisor of the manuscript has apparently made a mistake. The scene is one of generalised mounted combat, supplemented on either side by standing knights. A novel detail can be observed: the second figure on the right is wearing a female head-dress over her helmet. This is a clear visual allusion to the Amazons who do not, in fact, arrive to help the Trojans until the subsequent battle. The labeller was evidently puzzled by this detail and uncertain as to who the contenders were meant to represent. Two of the main figures have been labelled: the one is 'Rex Philomene', the other with the headdress is 'Quene pollidamus'. The genesis of these names is clear: they occur linked together in a line in the second column above the miniature:

Kyng Philymene and Pollydamas   (IV 3429)

Though the labeller has been casual in the names he has selected from the text, he is alert enough to the illustration to change Pollidamas' sex. He is also tenacious in the use of the name. Fol. 136[r] depicts the killing of Penthesilea by Pirrus. The queen of the Amazons lies semi-recumbent wearing a crown and long hair. She is also labelled 'Quene Pollidamas'. Having selected this as the name of the Amazon queen, the labeller does not relinquish it easily.[65]

The analysis of the illustrated *Troy Book* manuscripts so far has revealed that the miniatures were primarily used as visual indices, a means of dividing the text up into units in the manner suggested by Laurent de Premierfait. In the case of Eng. 1 the miniatures provided a ready reference system to portions of the text. The artist who executed the miniatures, probably an associate of William Abell who illustrated two other English vernacular manuscripts — Bodleian Library MS Laud. misc. 733, a chronicle of England to Henry V, and Edinburgh, National Library of Scotland, Adv. 18. 1. 7, Nicholas Love's *Mirror of the Blessed Life of Jesus Christ*[66] — had an extensive vocabulary of stereotyped figures. In his efforts to depict an incident suitable for what was considered a point of division in the text, his natural method of construction seems to be in the recombination of stylistic clichés. Whole groups of figures are duplicated and whole miniatures seem to be constructed *ad hoc* from elements conventional to the artist.[67] Such

[65] See also fol. 106[v], a scene of Andromache in bed dreaming and her beseeching of Hector not to go into battle, which is disconcertingly turned into a scene between Cressid and Diomede. It is Diomede who implores Cressid's favours; ardent kneeling is inappropriate for a Cressid busily engaged in manipulating Diomede by keeping him in doubt. On fol. 102[r] Cressid's reception of the news of the projected interchange of hostages becomes a visual allusion, rather clumsily conceived, of the actual exchange of hostages because the figure supporting a swooning Cressid is labelled 'Anthenor' rather than Troilus.
[66] Alexander, *op. cit.*, 169.
[67] The recurrent battle scenes allow of stereotyped treatment — see e.g. fol. 114[r]. Even more obviously formulaic are the recurrent scenes of council which depict a king seated in an architectural framework and flanked by other seated or standing figures (fols 34[v], 38[v], 40[v], 138[r]). Fols 22[v]-25[r] are factotum pictures composed from a collocation of motifs that can be noted elsewhere in the manuscript. There is the distinctive motif of a boat, only the prow and foredeck of which can be seen since the stern is overlapped by a stylised, conical mountain. It appears on fol. 22[v] and is transcribed from folio to folio: see fols: 7[r]; 10[v] — the gesture of the small figure in the boat is very similar, as is the armed figure of Jason — 21[r]; 36[r]; 47[v] — the stern of the ship rather than the prow is visible — 74[v]; 157[v]; 158[v]; 161[r]; 162[r]; 164[v]. See also fols 31[v] and 57[v], a figure carrying a bale; the standing man in the prow

illustrations, while lacking in variety and vitality, are appropriate in a generalised way to the position of the text to which they purport to refer. He shows himself to be aware of English compositional types: the illustration which announces the beginning of Book IV translates the wounded Achilles into a white-bearded crowned king lying in bed, similar to depictions of Nebuchadnezzar's dream in *Confessio Amantis* manuscripts. He also recycles one of Abell's figure-types.[68] But general approximation to the text seems to have been all that was required.

It has, however, been shown that the system of production was flexible enough for the intervention of interested parties. Though Royal 18. D. ii is traditional enough in some respects, other aspects of the pictorial programme seem idiosyncratic. That Herbert took a personal interest in the production of the manuscript is perhaps indicated by the first page (see Pl. 4). One would expect a depiction of Lydgate presenting his book to Henry V; instead the composition is dominated by a king on his throne in the centre, flanked by three courtiers to the right and three to the left. The most unusual feature is the two kneeling figures in the foreground, the man on the left, the woman on the right. The male figure is in armour, wearing a surcoat emblazoned with the Herbert arms, and is evidently meant to represent Sir William Herbert; the woman wears the Devereux arms on her gown and mantle. The statement of ownership is reinforced by the rest of the decorative programme of the page: twining in angular loops round the bars of the border are either blue or red banderoles with the Herbert or Devereux mottoes; to the right of the first column are two shields which bear respectively the Herbert and Devereux arms.[69] The introduction of the figures of owner and wife into the actual miniature is evidence of Sir William Herbert's interest in the manuscript; the significance of the detail is difficult to reconstruct. Warner and Gilson suggest that the manuscript was commissioned by Herbert as a gift 'either to Henry VI before Herbert's definite adoption of the Yorkist cause (not later than 1457) or to Edward IV after his accession'.[70] In terms of the psychology of gift giving it would seem a prudent move to remind the king visually of the donor every time he perused his gift. There is, however, no sign of a book: Herbert and his wife kneel gazing up at the king with their hands raised as if in adoration. The pose is more appropriate for a devotional manuscript.[71] The illustration seems to represent an act of homage,

of a boat fols 10^v, 21^v, 22^v; the groom on fols 8^v and 18^v. For kneeling figures in a temple cf. fols 59^v and 115^r; for the stance of Ulysses on fol. 153^r cf. fol. 151^v; the grouping of three figures on fol. 155^v is identical to that of the three major figures on fol. 151^v.

[68] The figure of Venus in the frontispiece of Bodleian MS Fairfax 16, a collection of Chaucerian and Lydgatian pieces which was produced c.1450 and is thus roughly contemporary with our manuscript, reappears in one of the most complex miniatures in Eng. 1, the Judgement of Paris on fol. 42^r. The motif was rapidly incorporated into the clichés of Eng. 1. In most cases where a pagan idol on an altar is required, a simplified version of the Venus-type was supplied – fols 47^v, 50^r, 52^r, 115^r, 129^v, 149^v.

[69] For full description and detailed emblazoning see Warner and Gilson, *op. cit.*, 310.

[70] *loc. cit.*

[71] If we compare BL Royal MS 15. E. vi, a collection of romances, a present to Margaret of Anjou from John Talbot, 1st Earl of Shrewsbury, probably on the occasion of her marriage to Henry VI in 1445 (see Warner and Gilson, *op. cit.*, 177; for reproduction see vol. IV, plate 96), the difference is clear. The iconography centres round the actual act of presenting

Pl. 4   London, British Library Royal MS 18. D. ii fol. 6ʳ

an affirmation of loyalty, rather than to commemorate an act of presentation. The book remained in the Herbert family. It bears the record of the marriage of Herbert's daughter Maud (c.1476) to Henry Percy, 4th Earl of Northumberland, whose arms appear at the end of the *Siege of Thebes*.

The manuscript also remained incomplete; it is possible that activity ceased on the death of Herbert in 1469. Twelve miniatures are supplied for the *Troy Book* and the thirteen for *Thebes* — the only illustrative cycle provided for Lydgate's translation. Only five miniatures were executed in the fifteenth century, those at the beginning of each of the five books of the *Troy Book*.[72] The remainder are in two distinct styles, one being that of a sophisticated artist with Flemish affiliations. All the *Thebes* miniatures are in this style. These illustrations were probably added at about the same time that the extra texts were added to the original manuscript.[73] However, since all the miniatures take the form of framed pictures set within the column of the text, some form of illustration was envisaged at an early stage in the evolution of the manuscript so that the scribe could be instructed to leave blanks at the appropriate places. The location of all the pictures may thus be associated with Herbert, as may be the subject matter. Unusually, Royal 18. D. ii has a series of chapter-headings in red in the text in a contemporary script. A chapter-heading always occurs in conjunction with a miniature and it is often descriptive of the contents. On fol. 82^v the chapter-heading reads 'The grekys tentys and pavelones w^t stroke of thundure sodeynly wer cast oute of þe felde' above the miniature, and 'how the grekes had recouerede there pauilions' below it. The rubric beneath the illustration on fol. 74^r reads: 'How the Traytor Bysshop Calcas ymagined a large horse of brasse wherin was a M^l. knyghtes fainyng a sacrifice to be done to paullas'; that on fol. 75^r is: 'How the grekes had licens to breke the wall of Troy. to brynge in their Large stede of brasse to Offer vnto pallas in sacrifice. & how the knyghtes came oute in the nyght & betrayde þe citie'. That to fol. 87^r is briefer: 'Of the sorowe that Troilus made when Cressaide shulde depart', as is the heading on fol. 93^r: 'The lamentacyon of kynge priamus for the dethe of Ector'. The rubrics concerned with the death of Troilus on fol. 108^v are staunchly partisan: 'how worth [sic] Troylus was besett with .iij. thousand knyghtes. and how knyghtly. he defendid him'; 'how worthy Troylus. was cowardly slayn by Achilles'.

The rubrics relate precisely to the subject matter of the completed miniatures. It may be that when the later artists came to fill in the blank spaces left in the text for illustrations, they merely followed what looked to be directions provided

the book. In the foreground on the right, a kneeling figure presents a large volume with ornate clasps to a seated queen holding hands with a king. Furthermore, the decorative scheme of the page emphasises the arms of the recipient as well as of the donor.

[72] Both Bergen and Warner and Gilson divide the stints into two: in the words of Bergen, eight miniatures 'are English work of the third quarter of the 15th century'. This is inadequate as an account of the division of labour in the manuscript. Two distinct hands are involved in the '15th century work'. Only Fritz Saxl and Hans Meier, *Verzeichnis Astrologischer und Mythologischer Illustrierter Handschriften des Lateinischen Mittelalters, III Handschriften in Englischen Bibliotheken*, Warburg Institute (London, 1953), 216, share my opinion that the hand on fols 74^r, 75^r and 82^v is sixteenth-century.

[73] Warner and Gilson, *op. cit.*, 310.

by the chapter headings. None the less, the fifteenth-century rubrics, placed near spaces left in the text in the fifteenth century, do give some idea as to which sections of the text were marked out for special notice by the person who supervised the manuscript in the fifteenth century. Apart from the expected sequence at the beginning of each of the five books, all the miniatures are concentrated in the third and fourth books. The evidence of the additional illustrations suggests that a keen interest was taken in the story of Troilus, particularly in the circumstances of his death — this page is unusually lavishly provided with illustration — and in the events leading to the destruction of Troy. Hector, nominally the hero of the first half of the book, receives more cursory visual treatment than his star-crossed brother. One illustration is allocated to the grief at his death, but no depiction of his actual exploits occurs. The miniatures just mentioned all depict major events, especially if we suppose that the person behind the projected sequence was an admirer of *Troilus and Criseyde*. Slightly more puzzling is the evident interest in the fate of the Greek tents during a storm. Perhaps Herbert wished to luxuriate in the sight of the Greeks at a particularly low moment. Though the illustrations introductory to each book are spaced at regular intervals throughout the text, the additional pictures are placed far less evenly, and it seems plausible to assume that they reflect those incidents in the text that seemed to the man who commissioned the manuscript to be moments of high intensity. The standard sequence is used, but is elaborated in a particularly individual way.

In conclusion, I have attempted to indicate the uses that have been made and can be made, by literary historians, of secular manuscript illustration. Though the claims made must be severely limited, it is possible that miniatures offered a reading of a text through their choice of subject matter and position. It is possible, too, that they may reflect the predilections of the commissioner of the manuscript. The tradition of illustrations of the *Troy Book*, by and large, was to stress the formal division of the work into books. Manuscript detail suggests that a strong and authoritative sense of the work's structure prevailed throughout the production of manuscripts. The *Troy Book* was undoubtedly a prestigious work to be acquired by people of a certain social class. Issues of ostentatious display are undoubtedly pertinent to a discussion of *Troy Book* manuscripts and may in large measure account for the degree of standardisation to be found from copy to copy. Such an overview must be modified in the light of a manuscript like Royal 18. D. ii — an exception which indicates anew the inadequacy of generalised formulations.[74]

[74] I am grateful to the many people who gave assistance in the preparation of this article. I should like to thank the Master and Fellows of Trinity College, Cambridge, and the librarians and staff of the Cambridge University Library, the British Library, the John Rylands University Library, the Bodleian Library and the Pierpont Morgan Library for permission to consult manuscripts in their charge and the librarians of the Warburg and Courtauld Institutes for granting access to their photographic collections. Dr K. L. Scott generously gave of her time and scholarship in discussing Lydgate manuscripts with me; while my most abiding intellectual debt is to my teachers, Derek Pearsall and Elizabeth Salter. All former students of Professor Salter will continue to miss the scholarship, insight, and intellectual rigour, and unstinting enthusiasm which she brought to the supervision of their work.

BEGINNINGS AND ENDINGS: NARRATIVE-LINKING IN FIVE MANUSCRIPTS FROM THE FOURTEENTH AND FIFTEENTH CENTURIES AND THE PROBLEM OF TEXTUAL 'INTEGRITY'

C. W. Marx

The object of this paper is to discuss one type of problem that an editor may be faced with on examining the manuscript context of a text planned for a critical edition. It has frequently been observed in recent writing that critical editions, because they remove texts from manuscript contexts, tend to obscure issues such as audience, genre and relationships among texts within manuscripts;[1] it is this last issue which is the principal subject of this paper. A related problem concerns certain assumptions about the identification of texts that may lie behind entries in reference works such as the revised *Manual of the Writings in Middle English* and critical editions themselves. For example, a ME text may be a translation or paraphrase of a well known Latin text and the identification of the text in terms of its source may affect how or in what form the text is edited or how it is identified in reference works and bibliographies. In other words an identification by source may obscure or fail to recognise that a particular text may have been intended to relate in some important way to other texts in the manuscript(s) in which it is found, and indeed may form part of a larger narrative structure. Relationships of this kind among texts become apparent only from an examination of the manuscript context of those texts.

A text that provides a convenient starting point for this discussion is the ME prose translation of the *Gospel of Nicodemus* (afterwards, *GN*) found in Camb. Magdalene MS Pepys 2498 (P). This manuscript, written in one hand throughout, has been dated to the middle of the second half of the fourteenth century. It contains a large collection of ME prose texts on religious subjects, including the *Pepysian Gospel Harmony* and a text of the *Ancrene Riwle*; in the latest description of P the text of the ME translation of the *GN* is listed as the thirteenth item in the manuscript.[2] The revised *Manual of the Writings in Middle English* lists ten

---

[1] See, for instance, Derek Pearsall, *Old English and Middle English Poetry* (London, 1977), xi. The present paper owes much to the stimulating discussion of problems concerned with manuscript context, identification and affiliation by Elizabeth Salter in her essay, 'The Manuscripts of Nicholas Love's *Myrrour of the Blessed Lyf of Jesu Christ* and Related Texts', in *Middle English Prose: Essays on Bibliographical Problems*, ed. A. S. G. Edwards and Derek Pearsall (New York and London, 1981), 115-127.

[2] Cambridge, Magdalene College MS Pepys 2498, pp. 459, col. 2 – 463, col. 2; see M. R. James, *A Descriptive Catalogue of the Library of Samuel Pepys*, Part III, Mediaeval Manuscripts (London, 1923), 106-110, and A. Zettersten, ed., *The English Text of the Ancrene*

manuscripts, including P, which contain versions of ME prose translations of the *GN* but the text in P is not related to any other text in this list.[3] Since the publication of the revised *Manual* two other manuscript texts of the *GN* related to that in P have been identified. These texts occur in two fifteenth-century manuscripts, Leeds University Library MS Brotherton 501 (Br) of the mid-fifteenth century,[4] and Huntington Library MS HM 144 (Hh) of the last quarter of the fifteenth century.[5] Thus approximately one hundred years separate the earliest from the latest known manuscript text. The ME texts of the *GN* in P and Hh have been edited in an unpublished Ph.D. thesis by Jeanne Ferrary Drennan and Dr Drennan has shown that the source of the ME text is an AN translation of the *GN* which survives in at least two manuscripts, London, BL MS Royal 20. B. V (Rl) and BL MS Egerton 2781 (Eg).[6] Rl is a composite manuscript but the part containing the translation of the *GN* is of the fourteenth century and is a collection of religious writings including a thirteenth-century French translation of the New Testament and French translations of Latin hymns.[7] Eg, of fourteenth-century date, is of English provenance and contains mostly Latin material for private devotion; the translation of the *GN* is the last item in the manuscript, and this item and the one that precedes it are the only items in AN. Eg is lavishly decorated with miniatures, illuminated initials and borders.[8]

Thus there are at least five manuscripts which contain ME or AN texts of this version of the *GN*. In the description of Rl the text is said to be a paraphrase of part of the *GN*. The text is based on material from the latter part of the Latin *GN*, beginning in the latter part of what is chapter XII in modern editions of the text.[9] In the Latin text the episode which immediately precedes the first episode of this AN text is the imprisonment of Joseph of Aramathie. The AN text begins:

Riwle, EETS OS 274 (1976), ix-xxi.

[3] J. Burke Severs, ed., *A Manual of the Writings in Middle English, 1050-1500*, II (New Haven, 1970), 640-641.

[4] Leeds University Library MS Brotherton 501, ff.109v, 108r-v, 115r; the text is imperfect and the manuscript has been misbound; see K. W. Humphreys and J. Lightbown, 'Two manuscripts of the *Pricke of Conscience* in the Brotherton Collection, University of Leeds', *Leeds Studies in English and Kindred Languages*, 7 and 8 (1952), 29-38. I am grateful to Dr A. I. Doyle for drawing my attention to the text of the *GN* in this manuscript.

[5] San Marino, Henry Huntington Library MS HM 144, ff.47r-54v; J. M. Manly and E. Rickert, *The Text of the Canterbury Tales*, 8 vols (Chicago, 1940), I, 289-294.

[6] Jeanne Ferrary Drennan, A Short Middle English Prose Translation of the *Gospel of Nicodemus*, unpublished Ph.D. dissertation, University of Michigan (1980), and 'The Middle English *Gospel of Nicodemus*, Huntington Library MS HM 144', *Notes and Queries*, 225 (1980), 297-298. The two manuscripts containing the AN text of the *GN* are listed in A. E. Ford, ed., *L'Evangile de Nicodème: Les versions courtes en ancien français et en prose* (Geneva, 1973), 27.

[7] London, BL MS Royal 20. B. V, ff.153v, col.1 — 156r, col.1; Sir George F. Warner and Julius P. Gilson, *Catalogue of Western Manuscripts in the Old Royal and King's Collections*, II (London, 1921), 361-363.

[8] London, BL MS Egerton 2781, ff.173r-189v; *Catalogue of Additions to the Manuscripts in the British Museum in the years 1888-1893* (London, 1894), 473-474.

[9] L. F. K. Tischendorf, ed., *Evangelia Apocrypha*, 2nd edn (Leipzig, 1876), 333-416; chapter XII begins on p.365; see also, Jeanne Ferrary Drennan, 'The *Complaint of Our Lady* and *Gospel of Nicodemus* of MS Pepys 2498', *Manuscripta*, 24 (1980),164-170.

Ly noble & ly vaylant prince Nichodemus qi priuement feust desciple
Ihesu Crist pur pour des felons Iues nous conte en vn tretitz q'il fist de la
passion Ihesu Crist qe mesme le iour de la resurrexion les princes . . .[10]

This passage has no basis in the Latin text but is a preface to this translation or
paraphrase of the latter part of the *GN*, and it is this text which is the major
source for the ME texts of the *GN* found in P, Br and Hh.[11]

An examination of the contents of these five manuscripts shows that they
share one other text which in all five appears immediately before the text of the
GN. There is no suggestion for a title for this text in either Rl or Eg, but all three
manuscripts which contain the ME text have incipits or concluding remarks
which suggest a modern title, the *Complaint of Our Lady*.[12] The AN texts of the
Complaint in Rl and Eg contain an account of the passion of Christ narrated by
the Virgin. It begins with the entry into Jerusalem on Palm Sunday and includes
the episodes of the last supper, the betrayal, the trial, the crucifixion, deposition
and burial. The narrative concludes with an account of the resurrection and the
joys of the Virgin at this time. The ME texts have, in varying degrees, digressions
and embellishments of the narrative. This feature of the ME texts will be discussed
later, but it should be pointed out here that in the AN texts of the *Complaint* in
Rl and Eg the first person narrative of the Virgin is maintained throughout.

It seems in some way to be significant that these two texts should appear
together in five manuscripts and seem not to appear independently in any other
manuscripts. Even if there should come to light manuscripts containing one of
these texts independent of the other, the appearance of these two texts together
in these five manuscripts would raise a number of questions. Is it merely coincidence that the texts should appear in this way? Does this sequence of texts reflect
some design on the part of the original compiler of the sequence? Is the sequence
the work of a single author or translator who had some purpose in presenting
these two texts together? Was a design or intention recognised by later scribes
and compilers and by an English translator?

These questions cannot be answered conclusively, but some suggestions may
arise from an examination of the texts themselves and the way in which the texts
are presented and distinguished in the manuscripts. In general terms it can be
said that what we have in this sequence of two texts is an account of the passion
and an account of the resurrection, and in Eg the texts are distinguished in this
way: 'Cy finist la passioun. Et comencze la resurreccioun'.[13] In Rl there is no

[10] Rl, f.153v, col.1; see also Eg, f.173r-v. In all quotations from manuscripts contractions
have been silently expanded and punctuation has been modernised.
[11] Drennan, *Notes and Queries*, 225, pp.297-298 and *Manuscripta*, 24, pp.164-170.
[12] Rl, ff.147r, col. 2 − 153v, col.1; Eg, ff.131r-173r; P, pp.449, col.1 − 459, col. 2; Br,
ff.100r-v, 114r-v, 113r-v, 112r-v, 110r-v, 111r-v, 109r-v; Hh, ff.21r-43r and 45r-47r. The
AN text of the *Complaint* is printed from Rl with variant readings from Eg in F. J. Tanquerey,
Plaintes de La Vierge en Anglo-Français (Paris, 1921), 136-171. The three manuscripts containing ME texts are listed by Elizabeth Salter (1981), Appendix, 3 (A) (i), p.127. The title
the *Complaint of Our Lady* has been agreed on by Dr Drennan and myself for our joint
work on this text and the *GN*.   [13] Eg, f.173r.

rubric like this to separate the texts; however, the text of the *Complaint* in both Eg and Rl concludes with this passage:

> Vous q'auetz oy cel conte la beneceon mon douz fitz Ihesu Crist & la moye puyssetz auoyr. Et toux iceux qi apres l'escriuent, lisent ou oyent, heient mesme la beneceon & lour part en son regne qi oue son piere & fitz & seynt espirit vist & regne sanz fyn, Amen.[14]

The text of the *GN* then begins with the brief preface given above. These two passages establish the end of one text and the beginning of the other, and there is no indication of a link between the two texts. The preface to the AN *GN* given earlier suggests that the AN translator was aware that Nicodemus's treatise was a much more extensive text than the one he was presenting; he was aware that it also contained an account of the passion but he was interested primarily in the part of the treatise that contained an account of the resurrection. In other words, that this translation or paraphrase of the *GN* contains material from only the latter part of that text, that is from chapter XII onwards, is probably not due to the use of a corrupt text by the original compiler but rather the result of an intention to provide a more extensive account of the resurrection than appears in the first text and with this text to complement and extend the narrative of the first text. However, the preface marks a new beginning in the sequence and a change in narrative point of view from the intensely personal and emotional first person narrative of the Virgin to the third person narrative of the *GN*. Thus, if what was intended here was an extended account of the passion and resurrection, the narrative and the narrative linking are quite crude, one might even suggest awkward.

Might it be the case that the second text, based on the latter part of the *GN*, was appended to the first text by a compiler distinct from the author of the *Complaint*? This later compiler, who might be termed the compiler of the sequence, might have seen the opportunity to extend a passion narrative which already had some resurrection material by adding material from the *GN*; his aim might not have been to produce a single narrative with a consistent narrative point of view but to produce what might be called a 'loose narrative sequence' in which the integrity of the two texts would be preserved but through which would be presented an extended narrative of the passion and resurrection. This is one hypothesis suggested by the evidence, and it would seem that whether the text of the *GN* is posited as the work of a later compiler or as the work of the author of the *Complaint*, the abbreviated nature of the text of the *GN* can be most easily explained as the result of the intention to append to the *Complaint* a resurrection narrative.

The *Complaint* itself includes material dealing with the resurrection, amounting to approximately seven hundred and fifty words, which appears as part of the Virgin's narrative.[15] It might therefore be argued that the appending of the *GN*

---

[14] Rl, f.153v, col.1; see also Eg, f.173r, and Tanquerey, 171.
[15] Rl, ff.152v, col. 2 – 153v, col.1; Eg, ff.167r-173r; Tanquerey, 167-171.

to the *Complaint*, which also deals with events surrounding the resurrection, was the work of a later compiler rather than the work of the author of the *Complaint*. However, one feature of the resurrection material in the *Complaint* may have some bearing on the problem of separate or common 'authorship' of the two texts. After the Virgin's description of her sorrows at the burial of Christ and how she was lodged at the house of John the Apostle, her narrative turns to events of the next day and includes an account of the imprisonment of Joseph of Aramathie by the Jews. This passage of roughly three hundred and fifty words is for the most part based fairly closely on the early part of chapter XII of the Latin *GN*,[16] but the episode is presented here as part of the Virgin's narrative. Her narrative continues with descriptions of some of Christ's post-resurrection appearances, the first to the Virgin herself, and a brief account of about one hundred words of how Christ appeared to Joseph of Aramathie in prison and released him. This latter account is based on an episode in chapter XV of the Latin *GN* and some of the lines are clearly derived ultimately from the Latin text.[17] The Virgin's narrative closes with brief references to Christ's appearances to Mary Magdalene and to his disciples and the blessing on those who copy, read or hear the text. The two passages on the Virgin's narrative which are derived from the *GN* show that the author of the *Complaint* was thoroughly familiar with that text, so much so that he could select material and use it as it suited him. It is perhaps significant that the text of the *GN* which follows the *Complaint* begins with material which immediately follows that passage from chapter XII of the Latin *GN* incorporated into the Virgin's narrative, that is, the account of the imprisonment of Joseph.[18]

What does the presence in the *Complaint* of material derived from the *GN* suggest about the 'authorship' of the two AN texts and the compilation of the sequence? A number of hypotheses suggest themselves. It is possible that the author of the *Complaint* was also responsible for the AN text of the *GN*. The author of the *Complaint* certainly seems to have been very familiar with the *GN*, and that the narrative in the AN text of the *GN* begins at the point at which a passage from a fuller version of that text incorporated into the Virgin's narrative leaves off might suggest common authorship of the two texts. However, it might also be argued that the 'author' of the *GN* skilfully adapted his text to complement and extend the passion narrative. Other interpretations of the evidence are no doubt possible; the material in the *Complaint* derived from the *GN* might be interpolation. Dr Drennan argues tentatively that the 'author' of the sequence was working with a complete text of the *GN* and that he replaced chapters I-XI of the Latin text with the *Complaint* and used only material from chapter XII onwards, although he used some details from the earlier part of the text in the

---

16 Rl, ff.152v, col. 2 – 153r, col.1; Eg, ff.168r-170r; Tanquerey, 167-169; Tischendorf, 365-367.

17 Rl, f.153r, col. 2 – 153v, col. 1; Eg, ff.171v-172v; Tanquerey, 170; Tischendorf, 381-382.

18 An account of Joseph's release based on chapter XV is also found in the AN *GN*, but in this text the treatment is different from that in the *Complaint*; see Drennan, *Manuscripta*, 24, 168-169.

Complaint.[19] Hypotheses could be multiplied but what the evidence seems to suggest at least is that the two AN texts were intended by either the author of the *Complaint* or the compiler of the sequence as a loose narrative sequence covering the passion and resurrection.

It is not possible to discuss in detail here the evidence for establishing the textual history of this sequence, that is, the relationship between the texts in Rl and Eg, their relationship to the original AN text of the sequence and to the English translator's exemplar, and the relationships of P, Br and Hh to each other and to the original ME translation. However, some general comments on these issues can be made. The AN sequence of texts in neither Eg nor Rl is the exemplar of the ME translation; in some instances the ME text agrees with Eg against Rl and in others with Rl against Eg.[20] Of the three manuscripts which contain ME texts of this sequence the earliest is P and the texts in P and Br have a common ME original which seems to have contained a fairly close translation of the AN text. However, the texts in P and Br also show additions, omissions and embellishments, some of which are common to the texts in P and Br and some of which are unique. For example, the text of the *Complaint* in P contains a comment of roughly one hundred and fifty words on the episode of the salvation of the good thief which is clearly not meant as part of the Virgin's narrative. This passage does not however appear in Br or Hh, which might be taken to suggest that the passage is not the work of the translator but a later redactor.[21] However, a passage of roughly two hundred and fifty words describing events on the journey to Calvary and the meeting with Veronica which appears in the AN texts of the *Complaint* and in the ME texts in P and Hh has no counterpart in Br.[22] Thus Br's text may show evidence of the work of a redactor who removed certain details, or simply carelessness on the part of a scribe. At no stage do the texts seem to have been invulnerable to modification. The additions, omissions and embellishments may be accounted for in different ways; some may be the work of the translator or a later redactor, and some may have been present in the AN text of the sequence with which the translator was working. Neither P nor Br seems to contain the ME translation of the sequence in its original form. The special place of the texts in Hh in the textual history of the sequence is discussed below.

In Eg and Rl the scribes seem to have made little attempt to separate the two texts of the sequence by means of rubrics or incipits, although there is the brief rubric in Eg, 'Cy finist la passioun. Et comencze la resurreccioun'. In other words, in these two manuscripts the boundary between the first and second text is not

---

[19] Drennan, *Manuscripta*, 24, 166-170.

[20] Eg has been damaged; the text of the *Complaint* begins imperfectly (f.131r) due to the loss of a folio, and single folios are missing between folios 161 and 162 and folios 163 and 164.

[21] P, p.456, cols 1-2; this homiletic comment is ascribed to Augustine and parallels are found in a Latin sermon wrongly attributed to Augustine (*PL* 39, 2046).

[22] Rl, f.150v, cols 1-2; Eg, ff.153v-154v; P, pp.454, col. 2 − 455, col.1; Hh, ff.34v-35r; see also Tanquerey, 155-156.

readily apparent. In P, on the other hand, the two texts are carefully distinguished; the *Complaint* is prefaced by a rubricated couplet:

> Of oure lefdy Marie bigynneþ now here þe pleynt
> Þat of þe passion of hir son sche telde with hert feynt.
>
> (P, p.449, col. 1)

The text ends with a couplet:

> Þe passioun as oure lefdy seiþ of Ihesu endeþ here;
> In to þe blisse of heuen vs bringe it alle in fere.
>
> (P, p.459, col. 2)

Then follows the text of the *GN* which ends with the couplet:

> Of þe vprist of Crist as Nichodemus gan telle,
> Here now make ich ende; god schilde vs alle from helle.
>
> (P, p.463, col. 2)

This use of rubricated couplets to signal the beginnings and endings of texts is not unique to these two texts in P. The whole manuscript seems to have been carefully organised and couplets appear at the beginning of many of the prose texts. The couplets given above signal, in the same way as does the brief rubric in Eg, the main subjects of the two texts, that is, the passion and resurrection. These couplets also serve to isolate the two texts from each other; the scribe or compiler of P seems to have been in no doubt that these were two separate and distinct texts. And yet, either by chance or design, both the loose narrative sequence found in Eg and Rl and the integrity of each text have been preserved. The scribe or compiler of Br also seems to have recognised the integrity of each text; the two texts are separated by the following passage:

> Here endith the passion of Crist & the compassion of his modir, of the tellyng of the same modyr of Cryst. And now here begynnyth the epystyll of Nichodemus þe whyche tellyth of the resurreccion & of the assensyoun of Cryst.
>
> (Br, f.109v)

Here again the two texts are characterised and distinguished as narratives of the passion and resurrection. To a greater extent than is apparent in Eg and Rl, the scribes or compilers of P and Br seem to have sought to distinguish and preserve the integrity of each text. It might be argued that it was more by chance than design that these two texts survived together through the processes of translation and transmission. However, the survival of three manuscripts containing ME texts of the sequence seems to suggest more than this. It may suggest that the translator recognised something of the design or intention of the original compiler of the sequence and sought to preserve this in a ME translation; that is, the translator recognised that the two texts together presented a narrative of the passion and resurrection even though each text had its own integrity and its own beginning and ending. In the case of the scribes or compilers of P and Br it is not immediately clear if they too recognised a design in the sequence, but certainly the linking passage between the two texts in Br suggests that the two were meant to be read together.

The questions of textual integrity and the extent to which compilers and redactors were concerned to preserve this sequence of texts can be seen from a different point of view in Hh, a manuscript one hundred years later in date than P. It has already been mentioned that the ME texts of the sequence in P and Br contain some digressions and embellishments not found in the AN texts in Eg and Rl; nevertheless, the text of the *Complaint* in these two manuscripts remains substantially a narrative of the passion by the Virgin. In Hh the account of the passion is very much different. It is not clear if all the differences between the texts of the *Complaint* in P and Br and that in Hh are the result of the work of a single reviser, but the revisions have produced what can only be described as a distinct version of the *Complaint*. In this text the narrative is interrupted by digressions and commentaries on episodes and a reviser seems to have gone through the text removing many indications of first person narrative. A common variant reading in Hh is 'Crist Ihesu' where P and Br read 'my swete sone'. The effect of such revisions is the disruption and confusion of narrative point of view and a general lessening of the emotive character of the text. Something of the character of the text of the *Complaint* in Hh can be suggested by two examples. All five manuscript texts include the episode of Peter striking off the ear of the servant of the high priest and in all but Hh this incident is treated without comment; however, in Hh the episode is followed by this passage:

> Than seint Austyn mevith a questyun whi Crist Ihesu suffryd seint Petyr to smyte of Malchus ere radyr than ony othyr membyr þat longyd vnto hym, and he answeryth to þe same and sayeth, for two causis. One is þat euery prelate & curat of holy chirche hathe autorite & power to smyte his gostly childe on þe ere be þe sentence of excomunycate, to curse hym from al dyuyne seruyce þat he shal none here nor haue no parte of þe prayours þat is obstynat & rebellyth ageynst þe chirche. And another cause was þat it shewith þat he was no counnyng man of armys.
>
> (Hh, f.27r)[23]

This passage is typical of the sort of commentary on episodes that occurs throughout the text in Hh. The text also contains a wealth of legendary material: for example, the episode of the salvation of the good thief includes a passage of approximately five hundred words which relates the early history of the two thieves and their meeting with the child Jesus during the flight into Egypt.[24] Despite

[23] The question raised here finds a parallel in a text wrongly attributed to Augustine (*PL* 35, 2314) but the treatment of the question is somewhat different from that in Hh.
[24] Hh, ff.38r-39r; the legend appears in Aelred of Rievaulx's *De Institutione Inclusarum* (see *Aelredi Rievallensis Opera Omnia* I, ed., A. Hoste and C. H. Talbot, *CCCM* I (Turnholti, 1971), 664); this text was also known as the *De Vita Eremitica* and was sometimes attributed to Augustine (*PL* 32, 1451-1474; see 1466).

these additions and the piecemeal alterations in narrative point of view much of the material from the earlier version of the *Complaint* is preserved in this later version which is very much an eclectic text.

Although a reviser seems to have attempted to change the narrative point of view in certain areas of the text in Hh, the Virgin's first person narrative has been altered less in the episodes of the crucifixion, deposition and burial. Indeed, a reviser seems to have been concerned to develop and expand the text in this area, for additional material concerned with the sorrows of the Virgin has been incorporated into the episode of the burial. There are close verbal parallels between much of what has been added and another narrative of the Virgin which can be assigned the modern title, the *Lamentations of Mary*.[25] The verbal parallels between the *Lamentations* and this portion of the *Complaint* in Hh may indicate no more than the use of a common source. Nevertheless, it would seem that a reviser aimed to expand the presentation of the sorrows of the Virgin at the burial of Christ by incorporating material from another text. The narrative of the passion in Hh ends on an emotionally charged speech of the Virgin as she laments over the tomb of Christ and is led to the home of John the Apostle.

As was suggested earlier the text of the *Complaint* in Hh is a distinct version, one in which the emphasis has been, in part, shifted away from the Virgin's first person narrative of the events of the passion. Something of the character of this text is reflected in its heading in Hh:

> Here begynneth the stori of the blyssyd passion of Crist Ihesu and the grete soruis of his blissid modyr Marie.
>
> > (Hh, f. 21r)

This heading suggests that the text is not primarily a 'complaint of Mary' but an account of the passion in which, nevertheless, the subject of the sorrows of Mary has an important place.[26]

In this text in Hh there is no counterpart to the lengthy passage on the resurrection found in the texts of the *Complaint* in the earlier manuscripts.[27] Three blank pages separate this text from the next text which has the heading:

---

[25] Elizabeth Salter (1981), Appendix, 3 (A) (ii), p.127, lists four manuscripts containing texts of the *Lamentations*: C.U.L. MS Ii. 4. 9; Longleat MS 29; Bodley MS 596; BL MS Cotton Cleopatra D. VII. To this list may be added Westminster Diocesan Archives MS L. 45; I am grateful to Dr A. I. Doyle for drawing my attention to this manuscript. Rosemary Woolf refers to two early printed texts of the *Lamentations*, *STC*, 17535 and 17537 (*The English Religious Lyric in the Middle Ages* (Oxford, 1968), 361 and n.3 and 393 and n.2). *STC*, 17537 is a printing of the *Lamentations* by Wynkyn de Worde [1509-10?]; however *STC*, 17535 (revised *STC*, 14552) is not a text of the *Lamentations* but a prose meditation on the ten (*sic*) sorrows of the Virgin printed by R. Copland, 1522. This text is one of the 'Copland Tracts' in the Blairs College (Aberdeen) Collection, now on extended loan to the National Library of Scotland. The text in Bodley MS 596 was printed by C. Horstmann, 'Nachträge zu den Legenden', *Archiv*, 79 (1887), 454-459. The verbal parallels with the *Lamentations* appear on Hh, ff.42r-43r.

[26] The text has a running heading at the top of each folio: 'Passione' on the verso and 'Cristi' on the recto.

[27] See above, note 15.

Than aftir that Iesus was closyd in his sepulcre, ye shul here the stori of Ioseph of Aramathye and Nichodemus.

(Hh, f.45r)

This seems to signal the beginning of a new text. However, on examination the material on Hh, ff.45r-47r is found to correspond to that passage on the resurrection in the latter part of the *Complaint* as it is found in the earlier manuscripts, that is, the Virgin's account of the imprisonment of Joseph of Aramathie, some of Christ's post-resurrection appearances and his release of Joseph. As was mentioned earlier, portions of this part of the *Complaint* are based on passages in the *GN*. In this account in Hh in passages specifically concerned with Joseph of Aramathie the reading 'Crist Ihesu' appears where P and Br read 'my swete son'; elsewhere in this account phrases which indicate the Virgin's first person narrative have been retained. The conclusion of the *Complaint* found in the earlier manuscripts, namely the Virgin's blessing on all those who hear, read and copy the text, does not appear in Hh; however, apart from this, the latter part of the *Complaint* text as it is found in P and Br has been preserved almost intact, although in Hh it has been set apart from the passion text and given a separate heading. This account is followed by the text of the *GN* which has the heading: 'Now of the Resurrexion of Crist Ihesu I purpos sumwhat to telle' (Hh, f.47r). Here again the text of the *GN* is identified as an account of the resurrection.[28] In Hh the folios containing the material drawn from the latter part of the *Complaint* and the text of the *GN* are headed 'Ioseph' on the verso and 'Aramathe' on the recto. Although the text of the *GN* has the heading quoted above, it might be pointed out that this heading is less prominent than that on Hh, f.45r, and it seems likely that all the material from f.45r to f.54v of Hh makes up 'the stori of Ioseph of Aramathye and Nichodemus' (Hh, f.45r). In other words, a reviser seems to have established new textual boundaries in the sequence and separated material specifically concerned with the resurrection from that concerned with the passion.[29]

In Hh the loose narrative sequence of the passion and resurrection has been preserved although the texts within the sequence have been altered in a variety of ways. Although the main concern of this paper is with the manuscript history of the texts of the *Complaint* and the *GN*, it would seem that in Hh the loose narrative sequence is probably part of a larger sequence of texts. Following the conclusion of the text of the *GN* is a series of short texts dealing with the life of

[28] Dr Drennan (*Manuscripta*, 24, 167-170) discusses the character of this text of the *GN*.
[29] The material beginning on Hh, f.45r, that is, 'the stori of Ioseph of Aramathye and Nichodemus', begins on the first folio of what Manly and Rickert term a 'book' within the manuscript (Manly and Rickert, I, 290-292). This would help to explain the blank folios at the end of the *Complaint* text (Hh, ff.43v-44v). The *Complaint* text occupies the second book of Hh. It should be pointed out that Hh is written in one hand throughout, and it is probable that the scribe realised that not all the material in the loose narrative sequence could be fitted into this second book and chose to begin a new book with the resurrection material. In other words, the presence of three blank pages following the text of the *Complaint* does not undermine one argument of this paper, that the texts in Hh corresponding to the *Complaint* and *GN* in the earlier manuscripts were meant to be read together. See also Drennan, *Notes and Queries*, 225, p.297 and n.4.

Pontius Pilate (Hh, ff.54v-56r), the birth and lineage of the Virgin (Hh, ff.56v-57r), the life of Judas Iscariot (Hh, ff.57r-58r), lives of the apostles (Hh, ff.58r-59v), the life and martyrdom of John the Baptist (Hh, ff.59v-61v) and the siege and destruction of Jerusalem (Hh, ff.61v-64r).[30] Thus what Hh, ff.21r-64r seem to contain is a sequence of texts which presents an eclectic account of the major events of Christian history commencing with the passion of Christ and culminating with the destruction of Jerusalem. A sequence of texts such as this may find parallels in other medieval manuscripts and may reflect a tendency that is apparent in some Medieval manuscripts that contain texts of the *GN*, either Latin or vernacular, to append to the *GN* apocryphal, post-resurrection narratives which deal with events leading up to the destruction of Jerusalem.[31]

A study of the manuscript context of the *Complaint* in these five manuscripts seems to reveal an historical link with one vernacular version of the *GN*. As was mentioned at the beginning of this paper, the text of the *GN* in P is listed in the revised *Manual of the Writings in Middle English* as one among ten manuscript texts of various ME versions of the *GN*; no mention is made of the *Complaint*. The texts of the *GN* in Br and Hh were not known to the compilers of the revised *Manual* but one suspects that had they been known they would have been listed in the same way. A recent article in *Notes and Queries* on the text of the *GN* in Hh is entitled, 'The Middle English Prose Gospel of Nicodemus: A Newly Identified Version'.[32] On the other hand Dr Drennan has been concerned to stress the relationship between the *GN* and the *Complaint*.[33] In the catalogue descriptions of P and Br the texts of the *Complaint* and *GN* are listed as separate and distinct texts. In a way, of course, these are separate and distinct texts, but an examination of the five manuscripts in which versions of the *Complaint* and *GN* survive suggests that the two texts bear some historical relationship to each other. The precise nature of their relationship is not clear. It has been argued here that at an early stage the two texts were brought together with the intention of forming a loose narrative sequence. Whether later scribes, revisers and the English translator recognised this intention is not always evident. But, it would

---

[30] The material in these texts seems to have been drawn from the *Polychronicon*; the following correspondences may be noted (references are to *Polychronicon Ranulphi Higden*, ed., C. Babington and J. R. Lumby (Rolls Series, 1865-1866): life of Pontius Pilate, *Polychronicon*, IV, 364-369; the birth and lineage of the Virgin, *ibid.*, IV, 246-249 and 346-351; the life of Judas Iscariot, *ibid.*, IV, 352-357; lives of the apostles, *ibid.*, IV, 356-361, 388-391 and 402-413; the life and martyrdom of John the Baptist, *ibid.*, IV, 280-291 and 332-345 and V, 8-11; the siege and destruction of Jerusalem, *ibid.*, IV, 278-279, 424-431, 436-443 and 450-455. See also, Drennan, A Short Middle English Prose Translation of the *Gospel of Nicodemus*, 73-75.

[31] Latin texts of the *GN* are followed by the *Vindicta Salvatoris* (Tischendorf, 471-486) in Oxford, Bodleian Library MS Selden Supra 74 (*SC* 3462), s.xiii[2], ff.18v-31r, and Oxford, Bodleian Library MS Bodley 90 (*SC* 1887), s.xiii[2], ff.78r-90v. An account in ME prose of the imprisonment and release of Joseph of Aramathie after the destruction of Jerusalem follows a ME prose version of the *GN* in Worcester Cathedral MS F.172, f.12r.

[32] Phyllis Moe, in *Notes and Queries*, 224 (1979), 203-204.

[33] Drennan, *Notes and Queries*, 225, 297-298 and *Manuscripta*, 24, 164-170.

seem that an edition which presented the texts together would reflect what seems to have been the intention of the original compiler of the sequence and, at the very least, would reflect the manuscript history of these texts.[34]

[34] An edition by Jeanne Ferrary Drennan and C. W. Marx of these two texts is in preparation for Middle English Texts. I would like to thank Dr A. I. Doyle for much valuable information, and Prof. D. A. Pearsall and Dr O. S. Pickering for help and advice. Finally, I would like to acknowledge my debt and thanks to the late Prof. Elizabeth Salter, who first introduced me to this material.

THE COMPILER AT WORK
JOHN COLYNS AND BL MS HARLEY 2252

Carol M. Meale

Harley 2252 is perhaps one of the best known private collections dating from the late Middle Ages. It is usually classed as one of that amorphous group of MSS termed commonplace books,[1] and was compiled in the early years of the sixteenth century by a London mercer and bookseller, John Colyns.[2] It is possibly most famous for the fact that it contains unique copies of two romances, the 'B' version of *Ipomydon* and the stanzaic *Morte Arthur*,[3] which occupy nearly half of its 167 folios, and which are the only items in the MS not copied by Colyns himself, or under his direction. It also contains the unique MS copy of Skelton's *Speke, parrot*, and the most complete MS version of his *Colyn Cloute*. The rest of the contents of the MS appear, at first glance, to be very diverse, seeming to reflect a wide range of interests on the part of the owner. They include many items concerning civic and mercantile issues, such as an *Annals of London* (so called from the mayoral list which provides the basis of this particular form of historical record) and copies of acts passed on behalf of the mercantile community against foreign competition; lyrics of various types, ranging from the anti-feminist to the courtly and political; chronicles and pedigrees of the nobility; pious exempla, and such miscellaneous pieces, often found in commonplace books, as moral proverbs, tags and precepts, and medical recipes. Harley 2252 seems then, in its variety, to be an ideal subject for the study of the literary and professional interests of a middle-class reader at the beginning of the sixteenth century, and my aim in this paper is to give some indication of the various methods I have followed in the

---

[1] See the mentions of Harley in this context in the brief discussions by R. H. Robbins, *Secular Lyrics of the Fourteenth and Fifteenth Centuries* (Oxford, 1952), xviii-xx; Gisela Guddat-Figge, *A Catalogue of MSS Containing M. E. Romances* (Munich, 1976), 25-28 and A. G. Rigg, *A Glastonbury Miscellany* (Oxford, 1968), 24-26.

[2] Colyns states that he was a mercer in two of the three inscriptions of ownership in the MS, at the top of f.1v and the bottom of f.133v. The latter, the fullest in the volume, runs as follows:

> Thys Boke belongythe to John Colyns *mercer* of london dwellyng in the parysshe of our lady of wolchyrche hawe anexid the Stock*es* in þe pultre yn Anno domini 1517

For a summary of the evidence concerning Colyns' bookselling activities see the article by the present author, 'Wynkyn de Worde's Setting-Copy for *Ipomydon*' in *Studies in Bibliography*, 35 (1982), 156-171.

[3] Edited by Eugen Kölbing (Breslau, 1889) and P. F. Hissiger (The Hague, 1975) respectively. No edition has satisfactorily set either of the romances in the context of the manuscript.

attempt to document the literary, social and historical conditions which lay behind its compilation.

To begin with, I shall look at 'the compiler at work' in the most literal sense, by discussing the format of the MS and showing the stages by which it was assembled. The nucleus of Harley is formed by the two romances. These, on palaeographical and paper evidence, were produced as two independent booklets between 1460 and 1480.[4] *Ipomydon* occupies two quires of sixteen leaves (ff.54-85), and the *Morte Arthur* two of sixteen and one of twelve, plus an additional five bifolia (ff.86-133). Despite the fact that the paper used in the copying of the two works comes from different stocks, it is evident that they were produced in the same workshop, since the scribe who copied all but one side of a folio of *Ipomydon* also wrote out the first quire of the *Morte*.[5] The griminess of the outer leaves of these booklets suggests that the two romances were unbound for some time before Colyns acquired them, in or before 1517, as his inscription of ownership at the end of the *Morte*, on f.133v, states. The rest of the MS, ff.1-53 and 133*-167 is, but for the last four leaves, composed of paper from one stock.[6] The watermarks from these two further sets of paper suggest dates of manufacture around the last quarter of the fifteenth and the first decade of the sixteenth centuries respectively.[7] As is to be expected in an amateur compilation, the

---

[4] The hands of the two principal scribes are not sufficiently distinctive to enable close dating to be carried out, but there are three watermarks on the paper of these booklets. The first, a bull's head surmounted by a St Andrew's cross, occurs on ff.54-85, containing *Ipomydon*. Briquet's *Les Filigranes* (Jubilee edition, with introduction by Allan H. Stevenson, Amsterdam, 1968) shows a multitude of examples of this ubiquitous mark, but two in particular may be compared with that in Harley, no.15068, found at Bordeaux in 1462, and no.15073 from Sieger, 1465; however, a variety of similar-looking marks appear in this section of Briquet, all dating from the 1460s and 70s. In England this type of mark is found in some of the Paston Letters of 1444 to 1479 and in editions of Caxton dating from 1477, 1480, 1481, 1482 and 1486 (see Edward Heawood, 'Sources of Early English Paper Supply', *The Library*, 4th ser. 10 (1930), 282-307, no.18), and in documents dating from 1472 and 1477 (see Beazeley, *Tracings of Watermarks at Canterbury*, I (BL Additional MS 38637) nos.174, 190 and 192). The second mark, of the char or chariot, appearing on some of the paper on which the *Morte* is copied, bears some similarity to Briquet 3537, found in Palermo in 1465, but is closer to Beazeley no.177, found in a document dating from 1473. The third, which also appears in this section of the MS, is the crowned shield decorated with fleur-de-lis with pendant 't'. It is roughly similar to Briquet 1741 (Troyes 1470), and cf. Heawood no. 5, which he observes on paper used in the Paston Letters in 1475, 1477, 1477-78 and 1479, in various editions of Caxton, and in Lyndewode, Oxford, c.1478. Beazeley records nothing similar. It is important to stress that no definitive work on watermarks can be carried out without the use of beta-radiographs for comparative study, and the limitations of the majority of the existing source-books for marks (usually based on tracings) are summed up by Allan Stevenson on pp.17-18 of his introduction to *Les Filigranes*.

[5] The penultimate leaf of the romance, f.83v, is the work of an apparently contemporary scribe.

[6] There was an error in the original modern foliation of the MS whereby the leaf following f.133 was omitted from the count, but later marked as f.133*; this foliation therefore runs to f.166, although the total number of leaves is 167. For ease of reference in the present context, this earliest numbering is retained.

[7] The paper of ff.1-53 and 133*-162 has the mark of a hand emerging from a cuff with a stalked fleuron arising from the middle finger which is similar to Briquet's nos. 11421, 11423, 11428 and 11462, which are found in documents recorded at Troyes in 1483, Troyes 1486,

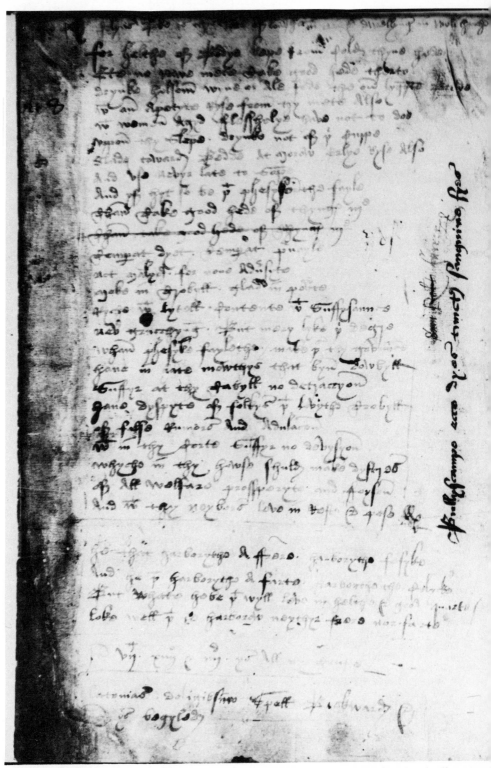

Plate 1 *BL MS Harley 2252, ff.1v-2r: the opening of Colyns' commonplace book, illustrating*
mark, at the top of ff.1v and 2r, respectively

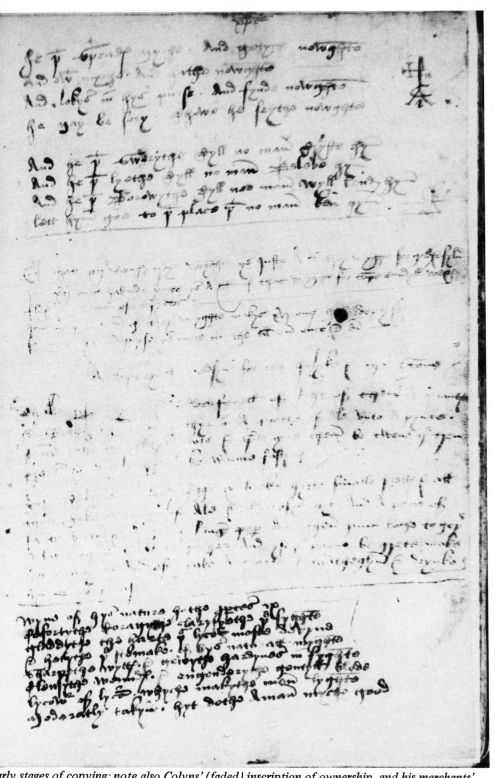

arly stages of copying; note also Colyns' (faded) inscription of ownership, and his merchants'

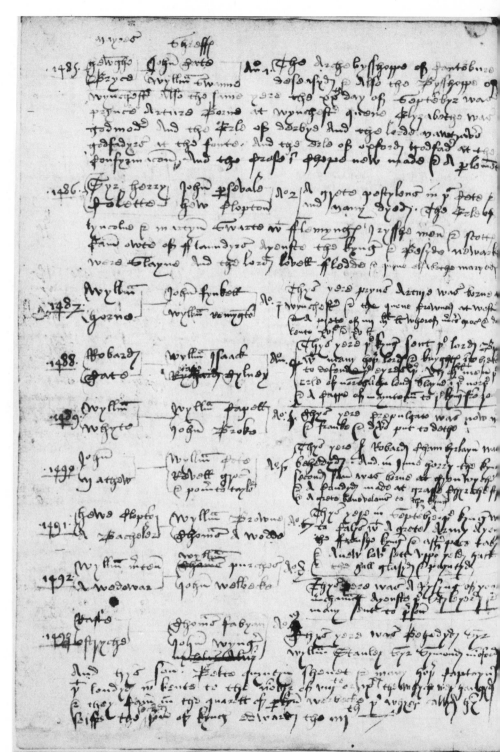

Plate 2 BL MS Harley 2252, ff. 6v-7r: part of the Annals of London, showing the change in in 1486

lay-out and the irregular sequence of copying after the end of Colyns' presumed exemplar,

The lamentacion of the kyng of Scottis

As y lay musyng my selfe a lone
In mynde noȝt stabyll but wandryng here & there
Accepting my frende dispysed me anon
And as the wede wont whystelyth in myn ere
Shortly conveyd I was I wyste not where
myn yȝe were closyd faste I cowde not see
I herd a man crye sore tremblyng for fere
miserere mei deus. et salua me

miserere mei deus after godys reporte
w[i] sorowfull syghes to no man here
for sorow and petye I began to resorte
the sore opprimitour made me sore aferde
Agayn I se openyd & I se opened I had a berd
I knowe not wherly who art shuld be
he cryed as he that byd stroked w[i] a swerd
miserere mei deus. et salua me

of Scotland he seyd late I was kyng
w[i] crowne on hed land septe in hande
In welthe and glorie I lackyd nothyng
In prosperyte man I tyllyd my londe
ordyr my realme I cowde w[i] awyȝte wand
now am I spiled from londe & prosperite
kyng w[i] owte realme lo now where I stond
miserere mei deus. et salua me

thus for my folye I fele I do smerte
sorow lowe & nature dothe me ... disese
of the vnkyndnes that I shulde take p[ar]te
Ayenste my brother & hys there ... [re]fuse
I repreposyd warre. hys frendys talse
thay dyd ... frensyp thyng for p[ar]lshe of the ...
... ordynaʒt affereou so dyd me abuse
miserere mei deus. et salua me

Colyns' hand, and on the recto, that of his collaborator

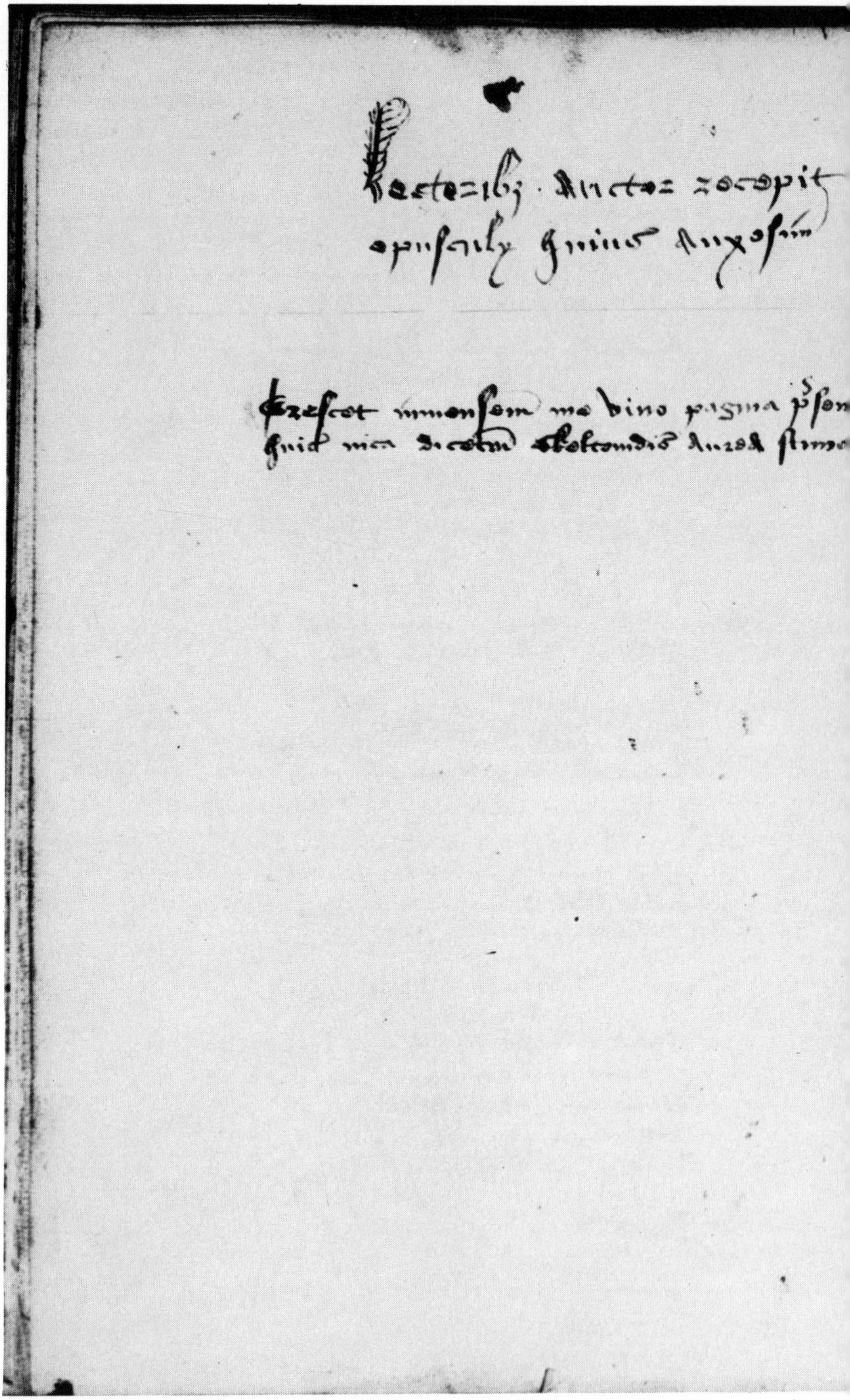

Lectoribus auctor recepit
opusculi huius auxesim

Crescet in immensum me vivo pagina p̄sen
Hinc mea dicetur Skeltonidis aurea fam

*Plate 4 BL MS Harley 2252, ff.133*v-134r: the epigraph to Skelton's* Speke, parrot, an

Lucas — My name ys parott a byrde of paradyse
By nature devysed of a wonderows kynde
Deyntely dyetyd with dyvers delycate spyce
Tyll Eufrates that flodde dryveth me in to ynde
Where men of that contre by fortune me fynde
And sende me to greate ladyes of estate
Then parot moste have an almon or a date

A cage curyowsly pardon with sylver pynne
properly payntyd to be my coverture
I myrrer of glasse that I may tote þerin
These maydens full merely with many dyvers flowr
Fresshely they dresse & make swete my bowr
with speke parott I pray yow full curteslye they sey
parrott ys a goodlye byrde & a prate popagay

Wythe my becke bente. And my lytell wanton iye
my fedders fresche as ys the emerawde grene
About my necke a cerculett lyke the ryche rubye
my lytyll legges my fete both fete & clene
I am a mynyon to wayte apon a quene
my propyr parott — my lytyll prate fole
With ladyes I lerne & go with them to scole

Heghe, ha, ha, parote ye can laughe prate
A parott hathe not dyned of all this long day
lyke Alexander lyke the who can say this fyrst parrott in wordes
was dysceyved the latyn in flode in paradyse
my dede and greate hony parott hath bene byse
as parott my prote dothe reporte of me
qui expedicit psitaco suum this

Solvyte faustse of prato parot þat berne
with wondes & prauolsyng my purpose aft my prate
audit meum to my owen parott ow plete apon
promate to Solvyte to spryngste my songe but lyps

gatherings of these sections of Harley are irregular. The first part of the MS is composed of four gatherings, 1, 2 and 4 being of sixteen leaves and 3 of four, apparently loose, leaves; at least one additional leaf may be missing here.[8] The last section of the MS, from f.133* onwards, shows a greater degree of irregularity; it again has four gatherings, the first of eighteen leaves (wanting one),[9] the second of six (again wanting one),[10] the third of eight and the fourth of four. Few of these gatherings are self-contained in the sense that a text ends on the last leaf of one and another begins on the first leaf of the next; indeed, only two conform to this pattern, the first and the last. With reference to the latter, ff.163-166, it has been noted that the paper is from a different stock, and in addition, each of the leaves is fairly dirty; these two factors together suggest that the sheets were lying around loose before Colyns used them. It is possible that some of the items linking the other gatherings were added as 'fillers' after copying on the rest of the leaves had been completed, but this does not often appear to have been the case, and there seem to be no grounds for thinking that the MS once existed in independent sections which were only bound together once filled.[11] This impression is strengthened by the fact that, apart from those on the final leaves, there are few signs of additional wear on the opening and closing folios of individual gatherings, which signs, if they could be perceived, would imply that they had remained separate for a time. Harley may be contrasted in this respect with a roughly contemporary commonplace book, Trinity College Cambridge O.2.53,

Namur 1530 and Cologne 1518-23. It is similar to no. 48 in Heawood, which he states to be found in the Paston Letters dating from c.1490-1500, and in editions of Caxton from 1483-86. The final mark, found on ff.163-166, is a gothic 'P' surmounted by a fleuron; this presents a problem of identification in that Briquet records a vast number of variants which appear on paper used from the 1460s to the middle of the sixteenth century. It is perhaps most like the group centreing around no. 8627, found at Bar-le-Duc from 1491-94. It bears some resemblance to Heawood's no. 62, and he notes its presence in various Paston Letters from 1472-1500 and in some of Caxton's books. There is nothing similar in Beazeley.

8 The first page of gathering 4, f.38r, is headed by a brief note on conducting a law-suit which begins rather abruptly with the words: 'ffor fayturys and penaltees to ffall And be . . .'; as the bottom half of the last page of gathering 3, f.37v, is blank after the completion of *The Brefe Cronekell of the Grete Turke*, it seems possible that a leaf is missing between ff.37 and 38.

9 There is a stub between ff.133* and 134 but there is no interruption in the text on these leaves (Skelton's *Speke, parrot*) and therefore no evidence to suggest that the gap was ever filled in the MS as it now stands.

10 The leaf between ff.154 and 155 was probably deliberately removed; the top of f.155r contains the concluding lines of a prose piece which run as follows:

> They sayd nothyng else savyng desyryng the pepyll to pray for them/& pater nosters
> 5 aves & iij^e Credys & Cry Apon Ihesu Cryste as hother before/god saue the Kyng.
> Amen

Since Wanley's MS description, *Catalogue of the Harleian MSS in the British Museum* (London, 1808), this piece has been taken to refer to various people executed during the reign of Henry VIII; if this supposition is correct, the reason for later censorship is self-evident.

11 For one such instance of a possible 'filler' see the indictment against 'Edmond grey clerke/parsone of the parysshe chyrche of Saynte benet gracechyrche/of london' for enforcing a bull of Pope Nicholas V concerning offerings to be made to the church within London; this begins half-way down f.32v, the last leaf of gathering 2, and finishes on f.33r, the first leaf of gathering 3.

assembled in Essex.[12] Here, signs of heavy wear and vestiges of the original sewing indicate that the MS once existed in independent units, although they do not constitute booklets in the sense in which we have come to understand the term.[13] The conclusion which can be drawn from all this evidence is that Colyns compiled his 'boke' by assembling a large stock of paper, probably all blank, around a core of two commercially-produced booklets, some time after 1517. He later consolidated the position of the romances within the format of the commonplace book by filling the blank leaves between them (ff.84v-85r) with odd items in verse and prose. At some later stage he added the last four bifolia. That he did, however, visualise the book as a single entity is emphasised by his inscriptions of ownership at the top of f.1v and the bottom of f.166r.[14]

On the question of assigning a more precise date to the composition of Harley, one or two clues are furnished by the manuscript itself. The first of these is provided by dated marginalia. Many folios are headed with variations on the phrase 'Ihesu mercy' and in two instances (ff.15v and 49r) these are accompanied by the date 1525. That work on the MS actually began around this date is further suggested by the manner in which the *Annals of London*, which start on f.3v, are copied. Several phases of compilation can be distinguished here. The neatness of the copying down to the year 1486 on f.6v suggests that Colyns used an exemplar thus far; after this date the appearance of the text is disordered, with notes being added at different times in different inks, and these are frequently inserted into such small spaces that they are difficult to read.[15] The next major

12 For a list of contents see M. R. James, *Catalogue of MSS in Trinity College Library* (Cambridge, 1902). The MS was owned and at least partially copied by members of the Ramston family of Essex. James mentions the names of various places in Kent (Wymelton, Bromley, Orpington) found in indentures, obligations etc., but seems to have overlooked the personal memoranda in the MS which deal with the Ramstons' holdings in Essex. Similarly, R. L. Greene in *The Early English Carols* (2nd edn Oxford, 1977), 326, only records the Kentish place-names, and also a note which mentions Worth Stratton, Cricklade (both in Wiltshire), Sevenhampton, Barnsted Manor and Grimsby. In fact, Roland Ramston, who seems to have been responsible for copying out accounts on ff.33r, 56v and 58r, was the resident of Chingford Hall, Essex, who made his will on 15 December 1549 (Essex County Record Office D/Aer 7/52). He left a wife Mary and children Robert, John, Thomas, Anthony and Elizabeth, all of whom are mentioned in the MS. His eldest son, Robert, was Yeoman of the Chamber to Edward VI, Mary and Elizabeth (see *V. C. H. Essex*, 5 (London, 1966) 104). I am grateful to Mr Victor Gray, County Archivist of Essex, for his help in pursuing these enquiries.
13 This structure is suggested by gathering 4 of the MS, ff.48-54, where the separate over-sewing of this quire still survives; the outer pages are noticeably grubby. The contents of this and conjoint gatherings are of a miscellaneous nature and there is no conscious ordering of items to form self-contained booklets.
14 That at the top of f.1v runs: 'John (C . . .) Colyns Boke is thys late of london (?mercer) & dwellyng in wolchyrche parsshe'; it is stained and partially cropped. That on f.166r reads 'John colyns bok(e)'. Colyns' merchant's mark appears with his signature on the latter leaf (it is also found on ff.2r and 133v).
15 Colyns' system in copying and compiling these *Annals* seems to have been as follows. Firstly he wrote out the year, names of mayors, and sheriffs in different columns, and then he went back filling in the record of events. Some confusion arose in the chronology as Colyns continued the compilation after the assumed ending of his exemplar, and this seems to have been the result of an imperfect understanding of the system of chronological compu-

phases of work seem to consist of the entries for 1487-1505, and 1506-1525, and it is this latter group which proves to be of considerable importance in establishing a chronology for the composition of the MS as a whole. The principal distinguishing feature of the entries for these years is the square brackets within which the names of the mayors are enclosed, and the resulting consistency of lay-out suggests compilation in one block. After 1525, a different ink is used, and entries seem to have been made in smaller retrospective batches, for example from 1526-1528, 1530-1531 and 1533-1535, with those for the other years down to 1539 being written up independently. The fact that the *Annals* are found so near the beginning of the MS lends weight to the idea that work was started on them fairly soon after the manuscript was assembled, and I think that it is therefore justifiable to assume that the process of compilation of Harley began not long before 1525.

The establishing of sequences of copying after this date again presents problems. The basis for judgements is provided by variations in the lay-out of items, in other words the number of lines to the page, whether the format was single or double column, etc. Observable changes in the ink and pens used can, on occasion, be used to lend corroborative evidence for the establishing of sequential copying, although of course no conclusions can be drawn solely from this source. The general method of analysis can be illustrated by reference to the opening folios of the MS. The first item on f. 2r, the eight-line 'rhymes on nowghte', appears to have been copied in direct sequence from those on f.1v, Lydgate's *Dietary* and various short riddles.[16] At some later date notes on troy weight and the 'spesyall medysin for the colyk and the stone' were added after the 'rhymes on nowghte', in an ink which has badly faded; at a still later date Colyns wrote out Lydgate's verses on the properties of wine, this time in an ink which has retained its colour. Now the phase of copying which this last piece represents carries over onto the next two folios, 2v and 3r, where two items, a lament for the death of the Duke of Buckingham in 1521, and the 'courtesy' poem, *The Proverbs of Good Counsell*, are copied in the same distinctively dark and unfaded ink.[17] These two poems give the impression of having been crammed into a severely limited space. For

tation in his source, which was based on regnal years. The situation became doubly complicated with the accession of Henry VII, since this monarch reckoned his reign from the eve of the battle of Bosworth in August 1485, and this overlapped with the normal yearly reckoning which ran from March to March. Hence Colyns has Henry dying in the correct regnal year, i.e. the 24th, but in the incorrect calendar year, i.e. 1508 instead of 1509. Other anomalies are striking; still following his source he notes the birth of Prince Arthur in I Henry VII (1485, in itself incorrect), then in the following year he records the marriage of Queen Elizabeth (this note seems to have been added at a considerably later date), and then in his continuation, he again records the birth of Arthur in the year 1487, 3 Henry VII.

[16] *Index* nos. for the rhymes and Lydgate's poem are 1163 and 824 respectively; see *Index to Middle English Verse* ed. C. Brown and R. H. Robbins (New York, 1943) and the *Supplement* ed. Robbins and Cutler (Lexington, 1963).

[17] *Index* no. for the verse on the properties of wine is 4175, and those for the other two poems, 158.9 and 432; the latter two poems are edited by F. J. Furnivall in *Ballads from MSS* II (London, 1868-73), 61-3, and *Queen Elizabethes Academy*, EETS ES 8 (1869), respectively.

example, each four-line stanza of the poem on Buckingham is copied in two lines, and the stanzas are written continuously, only being distinguished by strokes in the margin. The *Proverbs* are even more compressed in appearance; their eighty-four lines are compressed into double columns on f.3r, underneath the ending of the previous poem. When Colyns is copying in a more relaxed fashion, being free from the constraints of limited space, the number of lines to a page is only about thirty-two, so a count of numbers of lines to pages can give effective support to ideas on the order in which work was carried out. It becomes clear, from the example of these opening folios, that Colyns did not begin his compilation by copying items consecutively, page by page; rather, he seems to have begun on f.1v, carried on to the top of 2r, then gone onto f.3v, to begin the *Annals*. After this, having estimated the number of leaves he would need to keep the record up-to-date (and, judging from the space left after the last entry, he was not wildly over-optimistic as to his expected life-span), he began the next item, a list of the wards of London, on f.9r. At some point after this he returned to f.2r and filled in this and the following two leaves. This rather haphazard method of working is, of course, the kind we would expect to encounter in a commonplace book.

Indeed, if the whole of the MS is examined, it appears that from the beginning Colyns spaced his material at intervals all the way through. The last section, after the romances, opens with Skelton's *Speke, parrot*, which is notable for the spaciousness of its lay-out, and may therefore belong to the earliest stages of work. The Latin epigraph has a page to itself (f.133*) and the text proper begins on the next leaf (f.134r). Colyns evidently took some trouble over the presentation of this poem; it is on the whole copied tidily, the format is single column with the different types of verse-form distinctively set out, and it is one of the few items in the MS which are distinguished by an elementary form of rubrication.[18] Its appearance is in strong contrast to Skelton's other work, *Colyn Cloute*, which begins on f.147r in the same gathering. Here, apart from the copying being in double columns, there are approximately forty-five lines to the page, as opposed to around thirty-three in *Speke, parrot*. It is noticeable that the limitations of space seem to have had an adverse effect on Colyns' abilities as a copyist, since there are a comparatively large number of crossings out and corrections throughout the text.[19] The implication is that a period of some time separated his acquisition of the two poems. It is worth remarking at this point that the establishing of dates of copying for items within Harley has a more than local interest. *Speke, parrot*, for example, was not published until 1545[20] and so its presence in this one MS is of great importance in assessing the current status of Skelton as a poet and the circulation of his works during the 1520s when he was, for much of the

---

[18] Other short pieces which received this treatment can be found on ff.2r, 2v, and see also the *Crafte of Lymmyng*, ff.142r-146v; *Of the Cardnall Wolse*, ff.156r-156v, and the last few folios of the *Morte*.

[19] The overall appearance is not improved by the fact that Colyns was using an apparently slow-drying ink at this stage, and blotting from one page to another is not infrequent, e.g. on ff.150r, 151r.

[20] The edition was issued by Richard Kele (S.T.C. 22601).

time, in disgrace with the court.[21] The evidence of the Harley texts suggests firstly that Skelton's work went into manuscript circulation fairly quickly (*Speke, parrot* was not actually finished until the early part of 1522[22]) and secondly that his reputation was undiminished in certain circles; Colyns' exuberantly executed attributions to 'Skelton lawryat' ('or*ator* Reg*ius*' as he is also called at the end of *Speke, parrot*), make quite clear that the poet's supposedly rather subversive views on the Chancellor, Thomas Wolsey, had support from at least a section of the citizenry of London. This is a point I shall be returning to later, but I think it is worth emphasising that a close study of the physical make-up of MSS, as in a case such as this, can be of use when considering the broader issues of literary history.

Work continued on the MS well into the 1530s. The last entry in the *Annals* occurs for the year 1539, and Colyns died between then and the early part of 1541; administration of goods was granted to his wife, Alys, in July of that year.[23] Items which can definitely be assigned a late date of copying are relatively few, but such, for example, are the record of the Acts passed in the first of the 1534 sessions of the Reformation Parliament[24] and the two petitions to the King which immediately follow it.[25] These are found in the third gathering, as is *The Brefe Cronekell of the Grete Turke*, which probably also dates from this time. Colyns ascribes this piece to Thomas Gibson, who was active as a printer in London between 1535 and 1539 and, although there is no other record of this particular publication, there seems to be no valid reason to doubt Colyns' statement.[26] Of the items in the last section of the MS only one can, with any certainty, be said to belong to this late phase, and this is the allegorical poem in which Ann Boleyn bewails her fate.[27] She was tried and executed in May 1536, so the poem was presumably composed not long after this. Evidence of lay-out suggests that it was

[21] See Maurice Pollet, *John Skelton, Poet of Tudor England*, trans. John Warrington (London, 1971), Chapters VII-IX, and J. D. Mackie, *The Earlier Tudors, 1485-1558* (Oxford, 1952), 300-301.

[22] See *John Skelton: Poems*, selected and edited by Robert S. Kinsman (Oxford, 1969), 159-60. *Colyn Cloute* was in all likelihood finished by the autumn of 1523 (Kinsman, ed. cit., 180) and it was published by Thomas Godfray in 1530 (S.T.C. 22600), the year of Wolsey's downfall and death, and the year after Skelton himself died.

[23] The will is found in the probate register of the Commissary Court of London (Guildhall MS 9171/11 f.56r).

[24] This was the fifth session of the Reformation Parliament which lasted from 15 January to 30 March. A detailed discussion of the session can be found in Stanford E. Lehmberg, *The Reformation Parliament 1529-1536* (Cambridge, 1970), 182-199. The acts mentioned by Colyns are listed, but for one or two exceptions, in *Statutes of the Realm*, 25 Henry VIII.

[25] The first petition is on behalf of one John at Noke, a minister of the King's Chapel, for letters of presentation to the 'personage of B.' and for authority for the 'makyng & sealyng' of letters patent by the 'lorde Chaunceler of ynglond'. The second is a petition for pardon of murder, made on behalf of John Trevelyan of Somerset; the pardon was granted 24 Henry VII (see *Calendar of Patent Rolls, Henry VII*, Vol. 2, 1494-1509, 609). On these petitions see further p.103 and note 56 below.

[26] For details of Gibson's career see E. Gordon Duff et al., *Handlists of English Printers 1501-56* (London, The Bibliographical Society, 1917) and Duff, *A Century of the English Book Trade* (London, The Bibliographical Society, 1948).

[27] Edited by F. J. Furnivall, *Ballads from MSS*, I, 402-3.

an interpolation between a prose item, of which only the concluding lines remain at the top of f.155r,[28] and one of the many poems on Cardinal Wolsey in the MS, which begins on f.156r.

The example of the poem on Ann Boleyn conveniently highlights another aspect of the MS's compilation, that of the organisation of the material into subject groupings. Within the diversity of the contents of the whole, certain coherent blocks do emerge. For example, on ff.3v to 13v of the first gathering, the centre of interest seems to be the history and topography of London. This is reflected not only in the *Annals*, but also in the lists of the wards, parish churches, monasteries and hospitals of the City. On ff.14r-16v of the same gathering there are items of specific relevance to merchants,[29] while in the fourth gathering are copies of letters exchanged between James IV of Scotland and Henry VIII before the Battle of Flodden in 1513,[30] and two poems on the battle itself, *The Lamentation of the King of Scots* and *The Battle of Brampton*.[31] In the thirteenth gathering items on contemporary political topics are found, including the poems on Ann Boleyn and Wolsey already mentioned, and in the last, there are memoranda connected with the administration of Colyns' parish church of St Mary Woolchurch.[32] There seems, then, to have been some systematic attempt to group items on the same, or similar, themes together. But that it was not always possible to carry out this design is shown by the way in which the material on Ann Boleyn and Wolsey is positioned within the MS.

The allegory on Ann's downfall is followed by two poems on the Cardinal, *Of the Cardnall Wolse* on ff.156r-156v,[33] and 'Thomas, Thomas, all hayle' on ff.158r-159v.[34] These are separated by a long didactic poem, *Consilium domini in eternum manet*,[35] which, however, breaks off incomplete, appearing in full on ff.160r-161r. Of this group of four poems, *Of the Cardnall Wolse* seems to have been copied first; it is found on a new leaf, which also marks the beginning of

[28] See note 10 above.
[29] Many of these items are edited by George Schanz in *Englische Handelspolitik Gegen Ende des Mittalalters* (Leipzig, 1881), 591-94.
[30] Two of the three letters found in Harley were included by Edward Halle in *The vnion of the two noble and illustrious families of York and Lancaster* (in. off. R. Graftoni 1548) and by Raphael Holinshed in *The Chronicles of England, Scotlande and Irelande* etc. (1577).
[31] *Index* 366.8 and 2547.3. The latter entry is incorrect in stating that *The Battle of Brampton* is also found in Harley 293, Harley 367 and Additional 27879. The correct place in the *Index* for these MSS to be cited would be under 1011.5 which is *Scottish Field*, a poem associated with the house of Stanley; the three additional MSS cited under 2547.3 are in fact post-1544 versions of this poem. The two Harley poems were included in the 1587 edition of the *Mirror for Magistrates*; see the critical edition by Lily B. Campbell (Cambridge, 1938); a collation of the Harley texts against the printed edition is given in her Appendix D. See also Ian Baird, 'The Poems Called *Flodden Field'*, *Notes and Queries*, 28 (1981), 18.
[32] These are firstly, on ff.163r-165r, a record of the payments to be made for the tolling of bells and for burials in the parish, and secondly, on f.165r, a record of the payment to be made to the clerk for the performance of certain offices on St Anne's Eve and Day; they are both dated 17 Henry VIII. Colyns was one of ten elected 'Awdytors' who debated these matters.
[33] Edited by Furnivall, *Ballads from MSS*, I, 331-35.
[34] Edited by Furnivall, *Ballads from MSS*, I, 340ff.
[35] This is edited by R. H. Robbins in *Studia Neophilologica*, 26 (1954), 58-64.

gathering 13; the format is single column and there are five, seven-line stanzas to each page. There are two possibilities as to the course of events after this. Either Colyns could have left a leaf blank and copied out 'Thomas, Thomas' on f.158, afterwards returning to f.157 to copy *Consilium domini in eternum manet*, which attempt he abandoned when he saw that the space left was insufficient; or, he could have started to copy this poem immediately after completing *Of the Cardnall Wolse*, then broken off when he realised that he had another poem on Wolsey with which it would be more appropriate to follow the first one. Either way, a later date is suggested for 'Thomas, Thomas' by the fact that it is set out in double columns with between forty-two and forty-seven lines in each. The last addition to the group was the poem on Ann Boleyn on f.155. Colyns evidently took care in ensuring that he fitted this into the space available to him; it begins directly underneath the ending of the previous piece and is copied in double columns on f.155r, although it finishes in single column on f.155v (nevertheless, there are forty lines on this page as opposed to the thirty-five found on the opening leaf of *Of the Cardnall Wolse*). It is therefore clear that Colyns made some effort to fit material of a similar thematic nature into the same section of his 'boke', although this was not always possible, as the presence of two other poems on Wolsey in different parts of the MS shows; the first of these occurs in the second gathering, and the second, in the third.[36] What seems to have happened, then, is that when he started work he already had a certain amount of material on several topics which especially interested him, and he copied these at intervals throughout the manuscript. Beyond this, however, the form of the volume as it now stands was dictated by the pragmatic considerations of what was available to him to copy at any given time, and hence a blurring of distinctions gradually developed between the subject groupings and the other, more miscellaneous, texts which he acquired piecemeal.

Before looking in more detail at the contents of the MS, I want briefly to consider another feature of the physical characteristics which is of some interest. In the *Annals*, on f.4r, a hand which recurs throughout the MS makes its first appearance. The entries for the years 1412-16 and 1425-26 are the work of this second scribe (although Colyns made additions to the notes for 1415 and 1416). The two hands are quite distinct, as a comparison of individual letter-forms shows. Colyns, for instance, frequently does not use capitals, whereas the other scribe always does, and of the lower case letters, 's' and 'h' are particularly strongly differentiated; Colyns ends the latter with a loop, and his collaborator, with a hook. In more general terms, this second scribe writes in a more professional looking secretary script, his hand has a greater degree of angularity and more of a forward slope than Colyns', and he also makes a greater use of embellishment. This last feature is particularly noticeable in the copying of poetry. Colyns, for example, was responsible for f.43v, the opening page of *The Lamentation of the*

---

36 These are *The Ruyn of a Ream* on ff.25r-28r, and *The complaynte of northe to þe Cardinall wolsey* on ff.33v-34r (on which see further p.102 below). Both poems are edited by Furnivall, *Ballads from MSS*, I, 152-66 and 336-39.

King of Scots, and the second scribe took over the copying on f.44r; the different appearance of the two leaves is striking, with the initial letters of each stanza on the latter page being distinguished by flourishes extending well into the margin, and the ascenders of the first line being treated in a similar decorative fashion. The collaboration between the two men was extensive, and at some points in the MS they alternated their copying to a curious degree. For instance on f.48v the second scribe finished *The Battle of Brampton*, and Colyns then wrote out the title of the next piece, *The Composysyon of All offryngys with in the Cete of London*, and the first two lines; his collaborator then took over, in mid-sentence, and continued for the rest of this folio and the whole of the next one. Then half-way down the next leaf, f.49v, Colyns resumed copying, again in mid-sentence, and continued to the end of the item on f.50r. Whilst the presence of more than one hand in commonplace books is not rare (among the many examples are the 'Brome' MS and Trinity College Cambridge 0. 2. 53),[37] the degree of collaboration shown in Harley is unusual.[38] I cannot, unfortunately, make any convincing suggestions as to the identity of this collaborator; in the case of Trinity it is a possibility that some at least of the hands belonged to members of the same family, but we know from Colyns' will that his children had died young, so this cannot be the explanation here. The most that can be said is that Colyns had contacts with people who may well have had the kind of training which this second hand reveals; his father-in-law worked in the King's Exchequer,[39] and Colyns himself had business relations, which in all probability extended to friendship, with one of the ministers of the Chapel Royal, George Trevelyan (the son, incidentally, of John Trevelyan, one of the most unpopular of Suffolk's supporters during the reign of Henry VI).[40]

[37] On the Brome MS see in particular Norman Davis, *Non-Cycle Plays and Fragments*, EETS SS 1 (1970), lviii-lxx and the facsimile edition of the *Non-Cycle Plays and the Winchester Dialogues* with introduction by Norman Davis (University of Leeds School of English, 1979), 49-50. See also Lucy Toulmin Smith, *A Commonplace Book of the Fifteenth Century* (Trubner, 1886); Stanley J. Kahrl, 'The Brome Hall Commonplace Book', *Theatre Notebook*, 22 (1963), 157-161 and Thomas E. Marston, 'The Book of Brome', *Yale University Library Gazette*, 41 (1964), 141-45. As many as eight to ten hands may have been responsible for the copying of Trinity College 0. 2. 53, of which one can probably be identified as that of Roland Ramston, the owner of the MS; see note 12 above.

[38] There is one example of a scribe taking over from another in mid-sentence, although not in a commonplace book; this is in National Library of Scotland Advocates MS 19. 3. 1, where on f.91v a second scribe takes over from the first in the third word of the nineteenth line, and completes the rest of the poem ('Servis is no heritage'). These scribes can be identified as 'Recardum Heege' and 'Johannes Hawghton' respectively; see Phillipa Hardman, 'A Medieval "Library *in Parvo*"', *Medium Aevum*, 47 (1978), 264 and 266.

[39] There is a copy of a conveyance of a bakehouse in the parish of St Alban Wood Street, London, dated 8 July 10 Henry VIII, from John Colyns, mercer, and Alice, his wife, daughter of Edmund Bohun, late of the King's Exchequer, to three goldsmiths (Guildhall MS Hustings Roll 238 (54)). Edmund Bohun's will, in which he bequeathed his tenements in Wood Street to Alice, 'filia mea', is P. C. C. 6 Blamyr.

[40] Colyns is mentioned in a document together with George Trevelyan and three other men in the *Calendar of Close Rolls, Henry VII*, 2 (1500-1509), 955, iii. For pedigrees of the Trevelyan family see Lt.-Col. J. L. Vivian, *The Visitations of Cornwall* (Harleian Society, 9, 1874, and Exeter 1887); Burke's *Peerage* (London, 1970), under Trevelyan of Nettlecombe; and *The Trevelyan Papers*, ed. J. Payne Collier, Camden Society, 67 (1857).

To turn to the actual contents of the MS, despite their apparent heterogeneity, certain patterns governing Colyns' choice do emerge. Although Harley shares very few identical texts with other MSS, some of the shorter pieces are found elsewhere. These tend to be in the nature of proverbial tags, such as 'Kepe well x and flee from vii' (which appears in Richard Hill's commonplace book, Balliol 354)[41] or the longer moral guidelines in verse, such as the *precepts in -ly*, which appear in many commonplace books and other private compilations.[42] More general correspondences in taste can be observed between Harley and common-place books from different regions — treatises on the *Crafte of lymmyng*, for instance, are found in Harley and the mid-fifteenth-century MS Porkington 10, from the Welsh border country.[43] But the most striking similarities in taste can be seen in the group of MSS to which the term 'London collections' can be applied; these are Lansdowne 762 and Balliol 354, both roughly contemporary with Colyns' 'boke', and Egerton 1995 and ff.207-229 of the composite MS, Harley 541, which are slightly earlier.[44] The various compilers of these MSS share the interest in the history and topography of London which has been commented upon in Harley, and occasionally they also contain items of concern to merchants. Within this grouping Balliol and Lansdowne show some reliance on printed books for material; both for instance make use of the so-called *Chronicle* of Richard Arnold, a London haberdasher, which was published in ?1502 and 1521. This volume, which can be said to have institutionalised the commonplace book in printed form, contains, apart from the *Chronicle of London*, practical hints apparently designed to provide the average citizen with the means to overcome any crisis which might occur in the daily run of things, since the topics covered range from the removal of ink stains to the composition of petitions to the King.[45] The compilers of Lansdowne also drew extensively upon the *Boke of St Albans*, published first in 1486, and re-printed by de Worde ten years later.[46] Colyns

---

41 *Index* 1817; there are four MS versions, of which two are published by Robbins, *Secular Lyrics*, 253, 280; the Balliol text is edited by Roman Dyboski, *Songs, Carols and other Miscellaneous Pieces from the Balliol MS 354*, EETS ES 101 (1908), 140.

42 *Index* 2794.8; 3087; 3102; see also 317, 324, 799.

43 The texts are found in Harley ff.143r-147v, and Porkington ff.33r-52v, for which see Auvo Kurvinen, 'MS Porkington 10: Description with Extracts', *Neuphilologische Mitteilungen*, 54 (1953), 45. This version was edited by J. O. Halliwell, *Early English Miscellanies in Prose and Verse* (Warton Club, London, 1855), 72-91.

44 For the contents of these MSS see respectively: Henry Ellis, ed., *A Catalogue of the Lansdowne MSS in the British Museum* (London, 1819); Dyboski, op. cit. and R. A. B. Mynors, ed., *Catalogue of the MSS at Balliol College Oxford* (Oxford, 1963); *Catalogue of Additions to the MSS in the British Museum 1861-75*, II; Wanley, op. cit.

45 The ?1502 edition printed at ?Antwerp, is S.T.C. 782; that of 1521, printed by Peter Treveris at Southwark, S.T.C. 783. See also *The Customs of London, otherwise called Arnold's Chronicle*, ed. J. Douce (London, 1811).

46 S.T.C. 3308 and 3309 respectively. See also the facsimile of the 1486 edition with introduction by Rachel Hands (Oxford, 1975). The lyrics and proverbial sayings on f.16v of Lansdowne are all found in this book; see William Ringler, 'A Bibliography and First Line Index of English Verse Printed Through 1500' in *Papers of the Bibliographical Society of America*, 49, pp.153-80, nos.13, 71, 79, 88 and 89. The similarities in lay-out between the MS and the printed edition are such as to indicate a direct relationship between them.

similarly used printed books as a source for his MS but, except for the prose piece on the *Composysyon of All offryngys with in the Cete of London*, which he may have taken from Arnold, his choice seems to have been more eclectic, as is shown, for example, in his inclusion of the *Brefe Cronekell of the Grete Turke*. The comparatively wider range of the material he had available may, of course, have been due to his trading activities as a bookseller. This last point, on the differences which can be observed between Harley and other collections, is of some importance, for, once these general correspondences have been noted, the individual character of Colyns' MS achieves a clearer definition.

Whereas, for example, the literary taste of Richard Hill ran to both the popular lyric and aureate traditions, as reflected in his outstanding collection of songs and lyrics and the extracts from Gower's *Confessio Amantis*, that of Colyns seems to have been largely subsumed to his dominant interest in the world of practical affairs in which he lived. The extent to which his interests as a merchant, citizen of London and parishioner of St Mary Woolchurch are shown in his MS has been alluded to, but in addition to this, even the chronicles and pedigrees are explicitly directed towards supporting Henry VIII's position as a claimant to the French throne,[47] while the *Brefe Cronekell of the Grete Turke* has a strong contemporary relevance due to the incursions the Turks were making into Western Europe throughout the 1520s.[48] Apart from these examples, it is significant that the majority of items in Harley which can be described as 'literary' — except, that is, for the romances — bear some relation to current affairs. Of the twelve lyrics present, eight deal with contemporary national figures or events, and Colyns' interest in them can best be explained by reference to the social and political climate in which he lived. The Duke of Buckingham, for instance, who was executed in 1521, was not only an implacable enemy to Wolsey, but also commanded a strong measure of support from the inhabitants of London; after his death, his grave on Tower Hill became a centre of pilgrimage, much to the disquiet of the King, who complained that the people were 'reputyng hym as a saynte and a holy man'.[49] Equally, Colyns' evident antipathy to Wolsey himself was shared by many of his fellow citizens; the Cardinal's unpopularity stemmed both from the role he played in collecting taxes for Henry's foreign wars (which culminated in the Amicable Grant of 1525 — a demand for one sixth of the goods and incomes of the laity, and one third of the same from the clergy) and from his attitude to the governors of the City; on being appointed Chancellor in 1515 he

[47] E.g. the *Cronekell* on ff.51v-53v covering the years 876 to 1399, which was 'Compyled to Brynge/pepyll owte of dowte That haue not hard of/The Cronekellys. And of the lynyall dyssente vnto / The Crownus of Inglond ffraunce Castyll And of / legyons And vnto the dowchye of Normandy Sythe hyt/was Conqueryd'.

[48] The *Brefe Cronekell* extends down to the siege of Vienna in 1529; for comments on the strength of feeling in England against the Turks in the 1520s and 30s (especially after the formal peace made between France and the Emperor Sulieman in 1536), see Lehmberg, op. cit., 100 and Mackie, op. cit., 341 and passim.

[49] City of London Corporation Record Office, Repertory 5 fos. 199v, 204, quoted by Helen Miller in 'London and Parliament in the Reign of Henry VIII', *Bulletin of the Institute of Historical Research*, 35 (1962), 140.

had accused the aldermen of maladministration and illegal practices.[50] Against
this background, therefore, the popularity of Skelton's satires amongst this section
of society is perhaps not only explicable, but also predictable, and in this respect
it is significant that the only other MS copy of *Colyn Cloute*, a fragment of
eighteen lines, foretelling the downfall of Wolsey, is Lansdowne 762, another
London MS.[51] The record of the Acts passed in the 1534 session of the Reformation Parliament in Harley testifies to a more explicit and informed concern
with contemporary politics. A curious feature of this account is that Colyns
describes a meeting which took place between the King and Commons which is
documented from only one other source, a private letter.[52] It seems likely,
therefore, that since Colyns was not an M.P. himself, he must have known someone who was personally involved in the proceedings.

A clue which points this way can in fact be found elsewhere within the MS, in
one of the poems on Wolsey. The *complaynte of northe to þe Cardinall wolsey*
appears on ff.33v-34r, and is thought to be the work of Edward, 1st Baron North,
who was imprisoned for displeasing Wolsey and released on being pardoned in
January 1525.[53] The poem is in two parts, the first of which laments the 'fortune
vnstabyll' which has changed the poet's life, and which expresses regret on the
part of the author for the book he wrote which has caused him to be placed in
such straits; in his own words: 'makyng was my joy/and now ys my grevaunce',
but, regrettably, he gives no further details about his previous literary activities.
The second section has the air of a rather sycophantic eulogy of Wolsey designed
to reinstate the poet in his favour. It is interesting that North should apparently
have chosen literature as the medium for expressing political discontent because
he was actively involved in public affairs.[54] He was the son of a London merchant
who, after his education at St Paul's School and Cambridge, maintained his contacts with the business world of the City both through his marriages to daughters
of well established mercantile families, and through his tenure of posts within
both civic and national government. Among the positions which he held from
the 1520s onwards was the Clerkship of Parliament from 1531 to 1540, and he
would therefore have been in an ideal position to have provided Colyns with the
accurate information about the proceedings in 1534. His biographical details,
and the presence of those items in Harley with which he may have been connected

[50] For the Amicable Grant see *Letters and Papers, Foreign and Domestic, of the Reign of Henry VIII*, ed. J. S. Brewer, James Gairdner et al. (London, 1862-1901), IV. iii. 3089, and Mackie, op. cit., 304; and for Wolsey's antagonistic behaviour towards the City, Miller, art. cit., 140 and passim.
[51] Lines 462-480 appear on f.75r (old foliation) under the title 'The profecy of Skelton' with the date 1529. For the popular tradition underlying these lines see Kinsman, ed. cit., 188.
[52] A transcription of the Harley memorandum is printed by Lehmberg, op. cit., 193. The letter was from one John Rokewood to Lord Lisle (P.R.O. SP 3/7 f.18) and see also *Letters and Papers*, VII. 304.
[53] *Letters and Papers*, IV. i. 1049.
[54] For details of North's life see *D.N.B.* and G.E.C. *Complete Peerage*.

in some way, together suggest that he was the kind of man with whom Colyns is likely to have associated.[55]

This evidence of the coincidence between what may be termed Colyns' private and public interests as displayed in his manuscript is by no means unique; his connection with the Trevelyan family, for example, may have lain behind his inclusion of several other pieces.[56] It does, furthermore, suggest that for any study of a manuscript to be complete, some account must be taken of the historical and social circumstances under which it was produced. On a more exclusively literary level with regard to Harley, one of the most valuable conclusions to be drawn is that, despite the overwhelming impression of the contemporaneity of many of its contents, the literature found here in several respects echoes older medieval traditions. The antecedents of the laments of James IV, the Duke of Buckingham and Ann Boleyn, with their emphasis on the mutability of worldly fortune, can be found in such poems as the *Lamentation* of Eleanor Cobham, Duchess of Gloucester.[57] In addition, the poem on Ann Boleyn is semi-alliterative, and the form in which it is cast bears more than a passing resemblance to the *chanson d'aventure*, where the poet walks out on a spring morning and witnesses marvels, in this case an allegorical re-enactment of Ann's rise to fame and her subsequent decline. This would seem to indicate a degree of conservatism in the forms of literary composition, albeit minor, undertaken in the early sixteenth century, as well as in the tastes of a Londoner whom we can judge, from the evidence of his career and the other contents of his MS, to have been in a position to tap the mainstream of contemporary culture. I would therefore suggest that the value of a detailed study of a manuscript such as Harley 2252 lies in the fact that it provides evidence of a network of literary and historical associations which can assist in any reconstruction of the cultural background to what is, after all, a crucial phase in the history of English literature.

---

55 The literary interests of Edward North were continued by his sons; his eldest son Roger owned the Ellesmere MS (see J. M. Manly and Edith Rickert, *The Text of the Canterbury Tales*, I (Chicago and London, 1940), 153-54), and his other son Thomas was a renowned translator; possibly the most famous of his works was his translation of Plutarch's *Lives*. For details of both Roger and Thomas, see *D. N. B.*

56 For example the petition for pardon of murder on behalf of John Trevelyan, George's brother, mentioned in note 25 above, and the 'Grete myracle of A Knyghte/Callyd Syr Roger Wallysborow' on ff.50v-51v, which tells of the said knight's expedition to the Holy Land and his journey back to Cornwall with a relic; the Trevelyans were related to the Whalesburys by marriage; the mother of John and George was Elizabeth, daughter and heir of Thomas Whalesbury of Whalesbury in Cornwall. See the pedigrees above mentioned in note 40, also H. Jenner and T. Taylor, 'The Legend of the Holy Cross in Cornwall', *Journal of the Royal Institute of Cornwall*, 20 (1917-18), 295-309.

57 This poem appears in Balliol 354 and has been published by Dyboski, op. cit., 95-96.

LINGUISTIC FEATURES OF SOME FIFTEENTH-CENTURY MIDDLE ENGLISH MANUSCRIPTS [1]

Jeremy J. Smith

Recent research has drawn attention to the existence of a group of early fifteenth-century scribes, each occupied in producing comparatively large numbers of Middle English manuscripts. In this discussion, I want to touch not only on features of purely linguistic interest in these texts — such as the development of standard written English — but also to show how these features can in turn be exploited for our understanding of scribal attitudes to the text being copied.

I shall begin by looking at the problems presented by one of the most notorious manuscripts of the *Canterbury Tales*, British Library MS Harley 7334.[2] I have been highly selective in my choice of forms:

þay (((þei/þey))
wil/wol
eny (((ony)))
whil(e)s, but once, disturbing the metre
þerwhiles þat
not (nought/nouȝt) (((nat)))
hihe/hyhe/heyh
þurgh (((þorugh)))
oughne/owne
saugh
dede 'did'
gulty
fuyr
hield (sg.) 'held'

Fig. 1 Selected items from the text of The Pardoner's Prologue and Tale *as it appears in MS British Library Harley 7334*

These features are consistent with no one area of Middle English. In short, they form (to use the terminology of the neogrammarians) a *Mischsprache*. Recent

[1] The above paper could not have been read without the generous and extensive advice, help and encouragement of Professor M. L. Samuels. I am further indebted to Michael Benskin, Jeremy Griffiths, Anne Hudson, Angus McIntosh and Malcolm Parkes. I am grateful to Gloria Cigman for introducing my paper at the Conference, and to Derek Pearsall, not only for so kindly inviting me to give the talk but also for his help in preparing it for publication. Responsibility for opinions expressed, and for any errors, is mine.
[2] This MS was edited for the Chaucer Society by F. J. Furnivall (London, 1885). The brackets in the tables, up to a maximum of three, indicate relative frequency; the more brackets, the rarer the form.

studies — notably that of Michael Benskin and Margaret Laing in the *Festschrift* for Angus McIntosh[3] — have suggested that some such texts which, at first sight, might seem impossibly mixed, are in fact texts whose linguistic mixture is determined by factors other than random chance. Such texts exhibit a set of *layers* of language — layers which, theoretically at any rate, we ought to be able to separate.

And, indeed, closer examination of the forms I have noted in Harley 7334 suggests that some kind of pattern exists. *Nat, þurgh, saugh* suggest a layer of language very like the Hengwrt and Ellesmere manuscripts of the *Canterbury Tales*, manuscripts familiar to us from their employment as the base texts for so many editions. *þay, fuyr*, possibly *eny*, possibly *hield* suggest the South West Midlands. *oughne, dede, þerwhiles þat* (a metrically attested form in Gower's *Confessio Amantis*), again possibly *hield* suggest a Kentish area (*gulty*, essentially South Western, is also found in North West Kent); *hihe* would be something of a rogue form. The traditional approach to conflicting dialect features such as these is to compromise for a suggestion of provenance on some middling area; if some features are *x*, others *z*, then *y* suggests itself as the answer. But Harley 7334's widespread distribution of forms — some are alpha, others omega — makes such a compromise impossible. Evidently, we have here a 'layered' text.

By 'layered', I mean a text produced by a scribe who carries out a partial 'translation' of his exemplar, but who retains nevertheless certain forms from that exemplar. Harley 7334, then, appears to be a manuscript belonging to the second of the three categories distinguished by Professor Angus McIntosh back in 1963.[4] According to him, a scribe copying a Middle English text can, at any point in the process of copying, do one of three things:

(a) copy the spelling of his exemplar exactly;

(b) produce a mixture of exemplar-spellings and his own spellings;

(c) make a complete 'translation' into his own idiolect.

In a subsequent article on the dialects of MS Bodley 959,[5] Professor M. L. Samuels was able to show that there were *at least* three stages in the history of this text of the Wycliffite Bible:

(a) the earliest text must have included Northern forms;

(b) this text must have undergone a stage where the translation up to Judges 7.13 was 'breathed upon' by a Herefordshire scribe and thereafter by a Suffolk copyist;

(c) finally, it was copied by five scribes with varying degrees of translation into Central Midland dialects.

---

[3] Michael Benskin and Margaret Laing, 'Translations and *Mischsprachen* in Middle English manuscripts' in Michael Benskin and M. L. Samuels, eds, *So meny people longages and tonges: philological essays in Scots and mediaeval English presented to Angus McIntosh* (Edinburgh, 1981), 55-106.

[4] A. McIntosh, 'A New Approach to Middle English Dialectology', *English Studies*, 44 (1963), 1-11.

[5] M. L. Samuels, 'The Dialects of MS. Bodley 959', printed as an appendix to C. Lindberg, ed., *MS Bodley 959* (Stockholm, 1959-).

There is a methodology, therefore, for establishing the provenance of various layers in a manuscript, and for assigning those layers to a particular scribe. To take a hypothetical example:

In producing copies of one text, scribes X, Y and Z exhibit the following features:

X	*Y*	*Z*
Northern	Northern	Northern
SWM	East Anglian	Kentish

Fig. 2

In this situation, we can assume that the Northern elements found in all three manuscripts represent some archetypal or hyparchetypal layer in the text and that the second group of elements represents the peculiar contribution of each scribe (or his immediate predecessor, if that scribe is of McIntosh's first type).

Given the complexities of contamination in the Chaucer tradition, and the high degree of 'mixedness' displayed by Harley 7334, we might feel that such an approach, however attractive in theory, would be impossible in practice.

But, at this point, the palaeographers come to the rescue. In a recent article in the *Festschrift* for Neil Ker, Ian Doyle and Malcolm Parkes revealed the existence of a small group of scribes active at the beginning of the fifteenth century in copying manuscripts of (among other works) Chaucer and Gower.[6] They based their nomenclature for these scribes on MS Trinity College, Cambridge, R. 3. 2, a copy of Gower's *Confessio Amantis*, which was written by no less than five scribes: A, B, C, D and E. Scribes A and C are not yet known elsewhere. Scribe E is Thomas Hoccleve, poet and clerk of the Privy Seal. Scribe B wrote the 'Cecil' fragment of *Troilus and Criseyde* and both the Hengwrt and Ellesmere manuscripts of the *Canterbury Tales*. Scribe D, one of the most prolific copyists of his time, was active in eight Gowers, one Trevisa, a *Piers Plowman* (the Ilchester MS) and two manuscripts of the *Canterbury Tales* – one of which is Harley 7334. Given this mass of evidence, it should be possible to trace scribe D's activity from, as it were, the 'other end'. To reverse our hypothetical example:

Produced by a single scribe

Text X	*Text Y*	*Text Z*
Northernisms	South Westernisms	Kenticisms
E Anglianisms	E Anglianisms	E Anglianisms

Fig. 3

We can here postulate the East Anglian layer as our *scribe*'s contribution.

6 A. I. Doyle and M. B. Parkes, 'The production of copies of the *Canterbury Tales* and the *Confessio Amantis* in the early fifteenth century', in M. B. Parkes and A. G. Watson, eds, *Medieval Scribes, Manuscripts and Libraries: Essays presented to N. R. Ker* (London, 1978), 163-210.

D's Gowers are our opportunity. In a forthcoming article,[7] Michael Samuels and I establish the written language of Gower himself. We show that the idiosyncratic (linguistically speaking) set of forms found in the Fairfax and Stafford manuscripts of the *Confessio Amantis*, and in the Trentham MS of *In Praise of Peace*, can be localised to two smallish areas of South West Suffolk and North West Kent — areas with which Gower had close family connections. It is possible, therefore, to establish an archetypal corpus of forms to which all the corresponding forms of later scribes bear some relationship: they are retained, or they are modified, or they are replaced. We have a control for our study.

Figure 4 shows the kind of treatment to which D subjects Gower. British Library Egerton 1991 includes the following forms, compared with those found in Bodleian Library Fairfax 3:

Egerton 1991	*Fairfax 3*
eny (((any)))	eny
wol	wol
dede	dede
hield	hield
baþende (pres. part.)	baþende
þurgh	þurgh
aȝein	aȝein
þay (((þey)))	þei
seih/seigh (sihe in rhyme)	sih(e) throughout
berþ/bereþ (3 sg. pres.)	berþ
high	hih
kisse: Maistresse	kesse: Maistresse
oughne 'own' (adj.)	oghne
nought	noght
þough	þogh
distraught	distrawht
might	miht

Fig. 4   *Comparison of selected forms in Egerton 1991 with equivalent features in Fairfax 3*

Comparison and collation show that D reproduces Gower's language very closely, but that he does have certain consistent modifying tendencies. He prefers *þay*; an occasional *any* appears; when a back vowel is followed by *gh* in Fairfax, scribe D will introduce a *u* — *þough, oughne, nought*. Alongside *seigh* (*sih* accepted in rhyme) and *high*, *gh* is preferred in *night* and *might* in contrast to *niht* and *mihte* in Fairfax. Fairfax's *bot* is replaced by *but*. The Egerton MS has a preference for Old English $\underline{\bar{y}}$ to be reflected in *i* rather than in *e*. *ie* is rather less common in Egerton than in Fairfax — although it is still fairly frequent — as a representation of /e:/.

---

[7] M. L. Samuels and J. J. Smith, 'The language of Gower', *Neuphilologische Mitteilungen*, 92 (1981), 295-304.

Doubling of vowels to indicate length is very much more frequent in Egerton than in Fairfax.

D, then, reproduces some Gowerian features — such as the *-ende* endings in the present participle, some of the syncopated third person singular presents, and (albeit modified to take account of his own spelling rules) *oughne* — but he rejects others. Why is this?

The usual explanation in such cases is to use the phrase 'constrained variation'.[8] Yet another hypothetical example will illustrate this concept. Scribe X lives on an isogloss — a boundary for a dialect feature — between districts Y and Z (some, instead of *isogloss*, have preferred the term *band* in order to emphasise the woolly nature of such boundaries[9]). Scribe X is aware of both forms in Middle English for the word 'it' — *hit* and *it*.

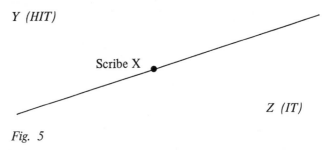

Y (HIT)

Scribe X

Z (IT)

Fig. 5

Scribe X's usual practice is to write a mixture of *hit* and *it*. On one occasion, however, he has to make a copy of a text produced wholly in district Y. The form in front of him is *hit* throughout. *Hit* is in his repertoire; *hit* is not foreign to him. So, whenever he sees *hit* he writes *hit*. *Hit* appears throughout; and, if this was all the evidence we had, we would assume that X came from district Y, without any contact with district Z. *Hit* is a *constrained variant*.[10]

The trouble with D is that the forms he uses to replace Gowerian features and the features he retains from Gower do not — still — form any consistent dialectal picture. *þay* and *oughne* are, for instance, widely separated dialectally; so are *seigh/seih* and *þerwhiles þat*, introduced (in the latter case) by scribe D into a Chaucer manuscript tradition which would not have had such a form. The features which form D's active repertoire of spellings — the forms he will use in any manuscript he produces — are just as mixed in dialectal provenance as the sum of the features in any individual manuscript.

The answer to the problem of scribe D is now, I hope, becoming clearer. A scribe's *repertoire* of spellings consists of two elements: his *active* repertoire — the forms he always uses, whatever he is copying — and his *passive* repertoire —

8 As by Benskin and Laing, op. cit.
9 See B. Sundby, *Studies in the Middle English Dialect Material of Worcestershire Records*, Norwegian Studies in English, 10 (Oslo, 1963).
10 For further discussion and maps, see M. L. Samuels, *Linguistic Evolution* (Cambridge, 1972), especially chapter 6, and also Benskin and Laing, op. cit.

the forms he will allow when faced with them in his exemplar but will otherwise prefer not to use. The best explanation for scribe D is that he has *learnt* some forms – like *oughne*, *þerwhiles þat* – when faced with them in his exemplars of Gower. He reproduces them; they are part of his passive repertoire. Copied repeatedly, however, they move into his active repertoire; and, when D turns to copying Chaucer – a text whose tradition never included them – there they will appear, spoiling the metre and confusing us dialectally.

What happens in D's other Gowers? I have taken two other manuscripts, Corpus Christi College, Oxford, B.67 and Bodley 294, as representative:

Corpus B.67	*Egerton 1991*	*Bodley 294*	*Fairfax 3*
eny	eny (((any)))	eny	eny
wol	wol	wol	wol
dede	dede	dede	dede
hield	hield	hield	hield
heih	high	high	hih
baþing, walkende	baþende, walkende	baþend, walkend(e)	baþende, walkende
bereþ, etc.	berþ/bereþ	berþ	berþ
þorgh, þorugh, þurgh	þurgh	þurgh	þurgh
seih (sihe in rhyme)	seih/seigh (sihe in rhyme)	seih/seigh (sihe in rhyme)	sih(e)
kisse: Maistresse	kisse: Maistresse	kesse: Maistresse	kesse: Maistresse
owen	oughne	oughne	oghne

Fig. 6   Comparison of selected forms in Corpus B.67, Egerton 1991, and Bodley 294. Equivalent features in Fairfax 3 included for ease of reference. Examples are drawn from parallel passages in Book III of the Confessio Amantis.

There is, evidently, some sort of progression here. With a few local eddies ('any'), Gower-features are being progressively reflected in the sequence Corpus – Egerton –Bodley, although modified by certain features which seem to be chronologically conditioned. These chronological changes appear in all three manuscripts – doubling of vowels to indicate length, use of *but*, the rule by which back vowels plus *gh* require an intervening *u* to be inserted. Otherwise, in all three cases, the archetypal features of Gower's poem, as represented by the language of the Fairfax manuscript, are clearly marked; so it is unlikely that the exemplar from which the scribe is working is to blame. The 'purging' is always in the one direction: the non-Gowerian features are being steadily expunged. In effect, the nature of the scribe's repertoire is changing under the influence of the manuscripts he is copying.

And, since scribe D copies more Gower than anything else, it is Gower who influences him more than the other texts with which he comes into contact. The forms which he gradually purges from his copying of Gower — *heih, þay, any* and so on — suggest that D's own origins are to be sought in the South West Midlands, although it is possible that they represent an earlier learning process, when he copied Trevisa and the Ilchester manuscript of *Piers Plowman*. Occasional *vche* in the Corpus manuscript of the *Canterbury Tales* suggests that Trevisa — with *eche* forms in the most reliable manuscripts — was not the source for these SWM forms. North Worcestershire might be a good suggestion, although the characteristic features of that area are not strongly marked.[11] Given the origin of the C-texts of *Piers Plowman* in the SWM,[12] it is appropriate that D should start his copying career by producing such a text. Certainly, an origin in the Northern part of the SWM would explain D's tolerance of *sih* in rhyme alongside *seih/seigh* within the line — *sih* would be a minor constrained variant in the Northern part of the SWM[13] — while objecting to Gower's *kesse: maistresse* rhyme so obviously that he spoils it. (By Bodley 294, he seems to have swallowed his objections!) A SWM origin, too, explains some of the oddities which Furnivall noted years ago in the Harleian manuscript — the rounded vowels in *fuyr* 'fire', the occasional *-us, -ud*.

In the fifteenth century, it was more common for reasonably educated men to write some form of their own regional dialect, simply 'purging the grosser provincialisms' (to use Norman Davis' phrase).[14] The Pastons, in fact, are the obvious examples of this, with the stay-at-homes using *x-, qu-* and so on (characteristic Norfolk features), while the travelled element in the family use more common, less 'provincial' forms. Standard written English seems to have evolved in just this way. As E. J. Dobson put it, 'the educated language of late fourteenth-century London (was) a mixed dialect, an amalgam of elements drawn from all parts of the country . . .'[15] D's writing reflects this state of affairs. Through his production, we can trace the education of a scribe, an orthographic *Bildungsroman*.

When a dialectologist localises a text, a very frequent response is: 'but the manuscript was never in that part of the world at all!' The answer to that is the obvious one: scribes move about, and they take their forms with them. For instance, Wykes, one of the Paston amanuenses, is a good witness for Devonshire! This jump in perception is important when we discuss the production of commercial books like D's. Eilert Ekwall long ago showed how immigration to the capital in the late fourteenth century took place.[16] Seeking their fortunes (the

---

11 A *streng*-North Worcestershire text is Leeds, Brotherton 500, a MS of the *Prick of Conscience*. But it should be noted that a precise localisation for the putative original dialect of scribe D is still being sought.

12 See M. L. Samuels, 'Some Applications of Middle English Dialectology', *English Studies*, 44 (1963), 81-94.

13 ibid., for a map of the various Middle English forms for Modern English 'saw' (pret. sg.).

14 N. Davis, 'A Paston Hand', *RES*, NS 3 (1952), 209-21, and cf. *Proceedings of the British Academy*, 40 (1954), 122-31. Note *xall* 'shall', *qwat* 'what' in Clement Paston's letters.

15 E. J. Dobson, 'Early Modern Standard English', *Transactions of the Philological Society*, (1955), 34-35.

16 E. Ekwall, *Studies on the Population of Medieval London* (Stockholm, 1956), and *Two Early London Subsidy Rolls* (Lund, 1951).

Dick Whittington story), men came up from the country and made those fortunes; or, they came up from the country and lost whatever money they had. This demographic fact has a significance for the history of written standard English. When men rose in social standing, they ceased to write: it was a menial occupation. When men sank in social standing, they ceased to write: they did not know how to. The middling sort of folk in the capital seem to have been only first- or second-generation Londoners, no doubt retaining many of their 'country habits'. What happened when an aristocrat, for instance, was unexpectedly forced to write is shown in the writings of Edmund de la Pole, Duke of Suffolk, author of some of the oddest spellings of the fifteenth century.[17]

This is a probable explanation for why so many of the manuscripts of the *Canterbury Tales*, in particular, are either wholly 'dialectal' (as against 'standardised', 'purged') or display a strong dialectal colouring. The tensions which the unsettled linguistic state of the country bred are well illustrated by scribe D, who steers a wavering path between the Scylla of demand for generally comprehensible (i.e. 'purged', non-provincial) texts and the Charybdis of his own dialectal inclinations. Scribe D is important as a reflection of the growth of a written standard English during the early fifteenth century – a reflection which can be based on more than simple impressionism.

The textual implications of such studies as I have been outlining are considerable. We are not yet in that fortunate position where we can afford to neglect any source of information which might suggest relationships between manuscripts. In a recent paper,[18] Jeremy Griffiths outlined the complexities involved with the 'evolving exemplars' of the Chaucer and Gower traditions. Although linguistic evidence needs to be carefully treated, it can supply some of the answers. There is nothing particularly new or revolutionary about this; for instance, Atkins at the beginning of this century was noting the distribution of *eo* spellings in the Cotton manuscript of the *Owl and the Nightingale* and deducing valuable textual information therefrom.[19] But the resources of the Edinburgh Middle English Dialect Survey give us many more tools for the job.[20] A study of manuscripts of the *Confessio Amantis* and *Canterbury Tales* in which I am at present involved shows that a large proportion of these copies are 'layered' texts. Changes in the underlying stratum or strata of these manuscripts, therefore, can be detected; and we have another tool to trace the shifting relationships of these complex, contaminated traditions.

The close attention to detail required in such cases can be seen if we turn to the relationship between D's two Chaucer manuscripts, Harley 7334 and Corpus

[17] See A. Kihlbom, *A Contribution to the Study of Fifteenth Century English* (Uppsala, 1926).
[18] There is a synopsis in G. Cigman, ed., *Medieval Sermon Studies Symposium, Report* (1980), 11-12.
[19] J. W. H. Atkins, ed., *The Owl and the Nightingale* (Cambridge, 1922).
[20] See, for instance, A. McIntosh, 'The textual transmission of the alliterative *Morte Arthure*', in N. Davis and C. L. Wrenn, eds, *English and Medieval Studies presented to J. R. R. Tolkien* (London, 1962), 231-40.

Christi College, Oxford, 198.[21] With the Corpus manuscript, D has done his usual job, although there are fewer Gowerisms than in Harley, suggesting that it was copied when Gower manuscripts were not at the forefront of his mind.

In comparison with Harley, however, there are a number of distinctive features, among them *lijf*, *wijf* rather than *lif*, *wif*, *yet* rather than *ʒit*, a higher proportion of *wil* to *wol*. These suggest the East Central Midlands, stretching into parts of East Anglia; and the presence of some East Anglian exemplar in the evolution of the Corpus manuscript is dramatically confirmed by the presence of *drynclyng* at line A 2456 (*Knight's Tale*) — a form of very restricted provenance.

But this is not all there is to be found in the Harley and Corpus manuscripts. Old English *a* + lengthening group is reflected variously in these two manuscripts as *a* and *o*. The reflex in *a* is traditionally considered vaguely Northern (Scots *lang*, Modern English 'long'). Preliminary studies and collations have shown that these forms are distributed in pockets in the two manuscripts. Moreover, these pockets do not coincide. It is as if an exemplar with 'Northernisms' lies behind different parts of these manuscripts. Given sufficient time and resources, it should be possible to trace the ebb and flow of the 'evolving exemplars' in the manuscript tradition of the *Canterbury Tales*.

This is something for the future. What of the literary implications of such study? Although I would not want to press this at this stage, it strikes me that one of the most interesting things about this topic is the light it throws on readers' attitudes to Chaucer and Gower in the fifteenth century. In the Royal manuscript of Gower (British Library, Royal 18. C. xxii), a rather pedantic corrector went through the manuscript, adding little marginalia whenever he came across a 'Gowerian' dialectalism of which he disapproved. We know that his activity was contemporary with the production of the manuscript because, at one point, the decorator had painted over part of one of these scribblings.[22] The corrector's dislike of these forms, however, did not catch on; it seems to have been traditional for copyists of Gower to retain, as far as possible given the pressures acting upon them, many of the fairly idiosyncratic features found in the repertoire of the Fairfax and Stafford manuscripts. D's variation in his Gowers is much less than in his Chaucers, which show all the signs of 'negligence and rape' which the angered poet ascribed to Adam Scriveyn. It is possible that this state of affairs can tell us something about the literary standing of the two authors: Gower, with those fixed idiosyncratic spellings throughout the manuscript tradition of his English works, a respected monument; Chaucer, with his unfinished poem ravaged by scribal intervention, a living poet. But that is really another matter altogether.

---

[21] The Corpus MS was edited for the Chaucer Society by F. J. Furnivall (London, 1868).
[22] I am indebted to Mr Griffiths, who noticed how the decorator had painted over the correction.

THE COMPILER IN ACTION: ROBERT THORNTON AND THE 'THORNTON ROMANCES' IN LINCOLN CATHEDRAL MS 91

John J. Thompson

The figure of Robert Thornton is an important one in any discussion of late medieval vernacular book production. It is now generally accepted that this fifteenth-century Yorkshire scribe wrote two MSS, the Lincoln Thornton MS (Lincoln Cathedral MS 91) and the London Thornton MS (British Library MS Additional 31042).[1] Both MSS are well known to scholars but it is the Lincoln MS, with its larger and more varied range of items, which is commonly referred to as 'the Thornton MS'. Since 1975 it is as *The Thornton MS* that the Lincoln MS has been made accessible to modern scholars in a facsimile edition. However, and surprisingly, the actual terms in which we should consider the relationship between the items in the Lincoln MS miscellany and in the London MS miscellany remain obscure.[2] Of course clarification of these terms is vital before a detailed analysis of Thornton's scribal activities can take place, and it is as a preliminary to my discussion of these activities elsewhere in greater detail that, in this short paper, I want to once again draw attention to the 'Thornton Romances' in the Lincoln MS. In particular I want to examine how these items in Thornton's MS provide us with evidence of Thornton the 'compiler' in action.[3] By examining some of

---

[1] The contents of both MSS have been described many times, often as part of the introductions to modern editions. However, for a general description of each MS see the relevant library catalogues: R. M. Woolley, *Catalogue of the Manuscripts of Lincoln Cathedral Chapter Library* (London, 1927), 51-61; and *Catalogue of Additions to the Manuscripts in the British Museum in the Years 1876-1881* (London, 1882), 148-51. A revised list of contents and a more detailed description of the MSS can be found in D. S. Brewer and A. E. Owen, *The Thornton Manuscript* (London, the Scolar Press, 1975, revised edn, repr. 1978), vii-xx; and Karen Stern, 'The London "Thornton" Miscellany: A new description of British Museum Additional Manuscript 31042', in *Scriptorium*, 30 (1976), 26-37, 201-18. Most of the MS evidence I discuss in this paper can be conveniently found in the Scolar facsimile edition; however I am also grateful to the Dean and Chapter of Lincoln Cathedral and to Miss Joan Williams of the Cathedral Library for permission to examine the Lincoln Thornton MS itself. Thanks are also due to Dr A. J. Minnis for reading an early draft of this paper and offering many helpful suggestions.

[2] In this context however see D. S. Brewer's brief comments in the Introduction to the Scolar Facsimile, p.ix, and also E. G. Stanley's review of the facsimile in *Notes and Queries*, 25 (1978), 165-8.

[3] In their recent work both Malcolm B. Parkes and Alastair J. Minnis have shown that the idea of *compilatio* belongs in its purest form to the realms of medieval literary theory. See for example, Parkes' 'The influence of the concepts of *Ordinatio* and *Compilatio* on the Development of the Book', in *Essays Presented to R. W. Hunt*, ed. J. J. G. Alexander and M. T. Gibson (Oxford, 1976), 115-41; and Minnis' 'Late-medieval discussions of *Compilatio* and the rôle of the *Compilator*', in *Beiträge zur Geschichte der deutschen Sprache und*

the problems which the present condition of the Lincoln MS forces us as readers to face, I want to suggest something of the conditions under which Thornton received and copied his exemplars and so compiled his collection.

In the past this codicological approach has been largely neglected. This is despite the fact that, traditionally, Thornton's reputation as an important collector of literary texts rests mainly on his 'romance' narratives, and furthermore rests largely on his ordering of a sequence of these items in the Lincoln MS. Research into the activities of Robert Thornton has tended to take this latter fact for granted, and has concentrated instead on the socio-literary milieu in which our scribe worked. We have moved from the tentative attempts of J. O. Halliwell in 1844 to identify the scribe as Robert Thornton of East Newton, to the well known work of Margaret S. Ogden who, in 1938, put flesh on the bones of Halliwell's candidate. Most recently, in 1979, the figure of Robert Thornton has been filled out by George R. Keiser's examination of a wide range of historical evidence in late medieval Yorkshire documents.[4] From his study Keiser concludes that many religious narratives, but also a wide variety of 'romance items', were actually in circulation in mid-fifteenth-century Yorkshire at the time when Thornton, a member of the minor gentry, was copying his texts. Despite the inevitable generalisation imposed upon him by the nature of this historical evidence, Keiser makes strong claims for what he sees as the clear-sighted way in which Thornton compiled his miscellany. Due mainly to the tripartite structure of the Lincoln MS he argues that, 'when Thornton began work for this book, he did so with a plan of organisation that indicated complete confidence in his ability to acquire other materials, both narrative and devotional for his volume' (p.179). Closer analysis of the MS evidence in Thornton's book can, I believe, establish an even more precise and more accurate description of Thornton's compiling activities.

Fig. 1 gives a preliminary indication of the way in which the physical structure of Thornton's book can be related to the contents of this obviously composite MS. Seen in this way the Lincoln MS breaks down into three main sections: the 'Thornton Romances' (gatherings A-K); a miscellany of religious and devotional items (gatherings L-P); and the *Liber de Diversis Medicinis*, a medical 'compilation' within Thornton's larger compilation (gatherings Q-R).[5] When we now examine the internal structure of Thornton's romance unit closely we can begin to recon-

Literatur, 101 (1979), 385-421. In this paper I use the term 'compiler' in a less specialised sense to describe Thornton's activities as a scribe working consciously, although not always consistently, to impose his own system of order on the diverse material he was inheriting and copying from his exemplars.
[4] References here are to J. O. Halliwell, ed., *The Thornton Romances*, Camden Society, 30 (London, 1844, repr. 1970); M. S. Ogden, ed., *Liber de Diversis Medicinis*, EETS, OS 207 (1938, repr. 1969); and George R. Keiser, 'Lincoln Cathedral Library MS 91: Life and Milieu of the Scribe', in *Studies in Bibliography*, 32 (1979), 158-79. Despite the evident popularity of the name 'Thornton' in late medieval Yorkshire, Keiser limits unnecessary speculation by citing both the name and geographical designation given in the public records.
[5] For a discussion of the self-contained and 'tailor-made' nature of Thornton's medical unit in the Lincoln MS see further my note on 'Textual *Lacunae* and the Importance of Manuscript Evidence: Robert Thornton's Copy of the *Liber de Diversis Medicinis*', *Transactions of the Cambridge Bibliographical Society*, 8 (1982), 270-75.

Gathering	Folios	Item	Description
A-C	1r-49r	The prose *Life of Alexander*	Copied as prose; commences abruptly as a fragment
	49v	Pen trials and a birth record	'Filler' item
	50r-50v	Prognostications on the amount of thunder in the months	'Filler' item copied by a later hand
	51r	Blank	
	51v-52r	*Lamentacio peccatoris* (prologue of 'the adulterous Falmouth squire')	Copied in double columns as 'Filler' item by a later hand
	52v	Ink sketches of knights	
	(Following f.52 at least eight leaves have been cancelled)		
D-K	53r-98v	*He[re] begynnes Morte Arthure*	Alliterative long lines Copied in single columns
	98v-109r	*Here Bygynnes the Romance off Octovyane*	12 line tail-rhyme stanzas Copied in double columns
	109r-114v	*Here begynnes the Romance Off Sir ysambrace*	12 line tail-rhyme stanzas Copied in double columns
	114v-122v	*Here bygynnes þe Romance off Dyoclicyane* (the 'Earl of Toulous') . . .	12 line tail-rhyme stanzas Copied in double columns
	122v-129v	*Vita Sancti Christofori* . . .	Rhyming couplets Copied in double columns
	130r-138r	*Sir degreuante*	16 line tail-rhyme stanzas Copied in double columns
	138v-147r	*Incipit Sir Eglamour of artasse*	12 line tail-rhyme stanzas Copied in double columns
	147r-148r	*De miraculo beate marie*	12 line tail-rhyme stanzas Copied in double columns
	148r-149r	*Lyarde*	Rhyming couplets Copied mainly in double columns
	149v-153v	*Tomas Off Ersseldoune*	Verse quatrains Copied in double columns
	154r-161r	*Here Bygynnes The Awentyrs off Arthure At the Terne Wathelyn*	Alliterating 13 line stanzas Copied in single columns
	161r-176r	*Here Bygynnes The Romance Off Sir Perecyuell* (sic) *of Gales*	16 line tail-rhyme stanzas Copied in double columns
	176r-178v	Latin prayers, medical charms	Copied partly in double columns and partly as prose
	(Following f.178 at least one leaf has been cancelled)		
L-P	179-279	A large miscellany of religious and devotional items in verse and prose. This section is headed by the *Previte off the Passioune* in prose.	
Q-R	280-321	*Hic incipit liber de diuersis medicinis*	

Fig. 1 The contents of the Lincoln Thornton Miscellany

struct at least some of the earlier production stages through which Thornton's romance items seem to have had to pass before they settled in their present MS context.

The first item in Thornton's book is a copy of the ME prose *Life of Alexander*. This acephalous and fragmentary item survives only in Thornton's MS. Keiser speculates that Thornton probably copied this 'romance biography' of one of the Nine Worthy as a companion piece for the *Morte Arthure* but *after* he had completed the Lincoln miscellany and as he was starting work on the London miscellany.[6] From purely literary evidence this certainly sounds plausible. Thornton may have been aware of the well known concept of the Nine Worthy since the *Morte Arthure* itself contains a vision of the Nine (ll.3278-455); moreover, in the London Thornton MS, the *Parlement of the Thre Ages* also contains a lengthy description of the Worthy (ll.300-583).[7] Indeed it may even be significant that two other romance narratives, dealing with episodes involving figures in the court of Charlemagne, another Worthy, also appear in the London MS.[8] However the physical evidence in Thornton's books provides us with important indications that we must balance our impressions of what may be Thornton's general literary interests here with an awareness of the practical exigencies which his methods of book compiling imply.

When we discuss the probable relationship between Thornton's copy of the prose *Alexander* and the alliterative *Morte* we should also take into account the way in which Thornton used the intervening leaves which separate the two romances in the MS. Thornton finished copying his Alexander item on f.49r of gathering C and the Arthurian item begins on f.53r in D. Following f.52, at least eight of the intervening leaves in C were removed before the modern foliation was added; indeed we can tell that it was Thornton himself who removed these leaves because the catchword on f.52v for f.53 was added in the scribe's hand. However the additional and originally blank leaves at the end of C were left intact and some of this blank space was eventually occupied by 'filler' items. So the only attempt which Thornton seems to have made to preface the *Morte Arthure* with this 'Alexander unit' seems to be to have added several ink sketches of knights in armour on the last surviving leaf in C. These were possibly, but not certainly, inspired by the general chivalric content of the neighbouring Arthurian item. What is clear however is that Thornton's juxtaposition of these two romances on

---

[6] Keiser writes: 'the *Alexander* interested Thornton but did not have a place in [the London Thornton MS] ... It would however serve nicely as a companion piece to the *Morte Arthure* which like the Alexander, told the story of the conquests by and the death of one of the Nine Worthies' (pp.177-8).

[7] Line references are to E. Brock, ed., *Morte Arthure*, EETS, OS 8 (new edn 1871, repr. 1904); and to M. Y. Offord, ed., *The Parlement of the Thre Ages*, EETS, OS 246 (1959).

[8] These are the *Sege of Melayne* (ff.66v-79v) and the *Romance of Duke Rowland and Sir Otuel of Spayne* (ff.82r-94r). Both items survive as unique copies in Thornton's MS and both were edited by S. J. Herrtage in *The English Charlemagne Romances II*, EETS, ES 35 (1880). Recently *Melayne* has been edited and discussed by Maldwyn Mills in *Six Middle English Romances*, Everyman's Library, 90 (1973).

the theme of the Nine Worthy was achieved indirectly, and even then only in the most rudimentary way.

Inevitably we have to draw certain conclusions from the present state of Thornton's MS. Firstly, if Thornton or anyone else had really wanted to juxtapose these romances, they must have already added the 'filler' items on the blank leaves which were left in C before the Arthurian text was finally prefaced with the Alexander item. If this had not been the case then surely Thornton (or a later reader) would have removed all, and not just some, of the blank leaves which remained in C after the prose *Alexander* had been copied? F.49v would then have been the last remaining leaf in C and this folio, and not f.52v, could have been filled with the ink drawings to complete the juxtaposition. Instead the blank leaves seem to have been removed as Thornton required them for some other purpose and those which remained were partly filled up with little regard to the fact that the very existence of these leaves interrupts what the modern reader suspects may be a deliberately created thematic grouping. So although we cannot, for the moment, retrieve the exact chronology in which Thornton copied the Alexander text and the other items in his romance unit, we have, in gathering C, a good preliminary indication of the haphazard way in which some items were added by Thornton to his collection. We must always suspect that Thornton's ability to decide on the order in which items appear in either of his MSS was restricted by the piecemeal way in which he received his various exemplars.

Gatherings D-P form the central core of the Lincoln miscellany. The two main units in this section of the MS are headed by the alliterative *Morte Arthure* and the *Previte of the Passioune*. In his well known article, 'The textual transmission of the alliterative *Morte Arthure*', Professor Angus McIntosh has concluded that both these texts form a linguistically distinct grouping in the Lincoln MS.[9] On the basis of this evidence McIntosh argues that Thornton's source for these two items was probably the work of a single scribe. Thornton would appear to have copied the *Morte* in gatherings D, E and F, and then he turned to a new gathering (L) in order to copy the *Previte*, presumably from the same exemplar. Superficially, if these were indeed the first texts which Thornton copied for his collection, then this would suggest that Thornton did begin work with a 'plan of organisation', or at least with a sense of the eventual shape of his completed miscellany. However an even closer examination of the MS evidence can qualify quite seriously our use of a term like 'plan of organisation'.

Thornton's practice in gatherings D, E, F and then L merely suggests that, at the time when the one exemplar was available to him, Thornton copied the *Morte* in one set of gatherings and the *Previte* into another, independent gathering. Thus, when he completed his copy of the alliterative item, ff.99r-102v in F originally remained blank. If we bear in mind the existence of Thornton's 'Alexander unit' then this 'Arthurian unit' is the second occasion where we have noticed that Thornton copied a lengthy romance text concerning one of the Nine Worthy onto

---

[9] McIntosh's article can be found in *English and Medieval Studies Presented to J. R. R. Tolkien*, ed. N. Davis and C. L. Wrenn (London, 1962), 231-40.

an originally independent set of gatherings. At the moment we can only assume that Thornton's reason for then copying the shorter *Previte* text onto the opening folios of a new gathering was because at this point he was uncertain how he was eventually going to arrange his material. Moreover he obviously did not want to lose the opportunity of obtaining a copy of this important devotional item while the exemplar he was using was still available. So, by copying the *Previte* onto another independent gathering, Thornton had the advantage of *not* actually committing himself to any specific plan of organisation. The order in which he would eventually have to group his texts remained optional for as long as he continued to copy his items into independent gatherings.

So we can now identify two smaller MS units within Thornton's collection of romances: an Alexander unit, and an originally independent Arthurian unit. However, if we take the existence of these units as an indication that Thornton once toyed with the idea of copying a sequence of romance biographies on the Nine Worthy theme, then that scheme, if it ever existed, was obviously thwarted by the way in which Thornton received his other exemplars. We might expect, for example, that Thornton's Charlemagne texts would have been added by Thornton after the Arthurian material to continue a thematic sequence in the Lincoln MS. Instead we find that the blank leaves following the alliterative *Morte* were eventually filled with the romance of *Octavian*; Thornton's Charlemagne texts ended up in the London MS. Nevertheless it is of some consolation here that the *incipit* of *Octavian* does indicate that Thornton was generally aware that he was grouping 'romances' together (see fig. 1). Equally of course I believe that it is vital to take account of the probable time lapse between the point when Thornton copied the *Morte* and the point when he came back to the unfilled gathering and added *Octavian*. That time lapse is perhaps indicated in the Lincoln MS by the sudden change in the way in which each text is presented. On f.98v the nineteen remaining lines of the *Morte* are copied in single columns onto a carefully prepared writing space. However, when Thornton came to copy the shorter lines of *Octavian*, he took the trouble to adjust the ruling on his page so as to allow the romance to be copied in double columns.

Thornton's presentation of *Octavian* and most of the remaining 'romance' items using this double column format is hardly unusual. Indeed in most cases we can assume that this practical and economical method of layout was inherited from Thornton's exemplars. *Octavian* is followed in gathering G by *Sir Ysumbras* and this romance is in turn followed by the *Erl of Toulous*. Like *Octavian* the *incipits* for these items provide some justification for assuming that Thornton himself understood the relevance of grouping these tail-rhyme items as 'romances'. As modern readers of Thornton's MS, however, we have a greater degree of difficulty in accounting for the inclusion of the next item, the *Vita Sancti Christofori*, in this sequence of 'romance adventures'. Thornton's lengthy *incipit* for this text does not specifically refer to this saint's life as a 'romance' but instead states that, 'to þe heryng or þe [red] yng of þe whilke storye langes [gr] ete mede & it be done with deuocione'. Nevertheless the text which then follows does deal with the secular adventures of the saint as ferryman and it is possible perhaps that Thornton himself may have considered the edifying life of St Christopher as particularly appropriate material for inclusion in his sequence of romance narratives. If this was the case however Thornton was obviously not as interested in adding the adventures of St John to the same section of his MS. His copy of *Sayne John þe euangelist* seems to be an equally attractive saint's life, yet it appears on ff.231r-233v in the middle of the religious section of the Lincoln MS. Because of this obvious inconsistency we must also admit the likelihood that Thornton was just as interested in filling up the remaining blank space in gathering G as he was in exercising a degree of medieval 'literary discrimination' when he commenced copying the *Vita Sancti Christofori* on f.122v.[10]

The *Vita* is completed in gathering H and is followed by two more orthodox 'Thornton Romances' written in tail-rhyme stanzas. These are *Sir Degrevant* and *Sir Eglamour*. Thus the items in the Lincoln MS from *Octavian* to *Sir Eglamour* form a continuous sequence of six items which have all been copied in double columns. Here the purely physical evidence in Thornton's book provides us with no reliable indication of whether Thornton copied this sequence from a single source or from a variety of different exemplars. Similar short sequences of romances also occur in other medieval miscellanies, so Thornton's importance as a compiler of these texts may have been minimal, especially if we assume that clusters of ME romances occasionally circulated independently of other vernacular items, perhaps even in booklet form.[11] Fortunately however the actual MS evidence in the remainder of Thornton's romance unit is much more helpful in indicating Thornton's personal role in the compilation of his texts.

To the modern reader at least, the juxtaposition of the remaining items in gatherings I and K of Thornton's romance unit is puzzling. Thornton completed his copy of *Sir Eglamour* in the opening five folios of I. This text is followed by the items, *De Miraculo Beate Marie*, *Lyarde*, and *Thomas of Erceldoune*. It is these items which cause problems for the literary critic looking for evidence of

10 For a more optimistic discussion of the present MS context of this saint's life among Thornton's 'romances' see James Owen Daly, 'This World and the Next: Social and Religious Ideologies in the Romances of the Thornton Manuscript' (Diss. University of Oregon, 1977). Using a mainly literary-critical approach, Daly argues that all Thornton's 'romances', but in particular the *Vita Sancti Christofori*, articulate a pious lay ideology where spiritual and religious significance is found not only in the chivalric way of life, but also in more mundane secular activities. More generally Derek Pearsall and John Burrow among others have of course argued that the ME saint's life and the ME romance often share similar stylistic and thematic features. See, for example, Pearsall's comments on 'romance style' in *Old English and Middle English Poetry* (London, 1977) or Burrow's recent comments in *Medieval Writers and their Work* (Oxford, 1982).

11 Miss P. R. Robinson has already suggested that Thornton may have copied *Octavian*, *Sir Isumbras* and the *Erl of Toulous* from a single booklet exemplar. See her contribution to the recent Scolar Press facsimile edition of *Cambridge University Library MS Ff. 2. 38*, introduced by Frances McSparran and P. R. Robinson (London, 1979), xvi. MS Ff. 2. 38 is of course interesting in its own right as an example of another 'organised' late medieval miscellany. For a general descriptive survey of the variety of extant medieval MSS which contain ME romances, see Gisela Guddat-Figge's useful *Catalogue of Manuscripts Containing ME Romances* (Munich, 1976).

a discriminating intelligence at work in Thornton's organisation of his romance sequence. We are forced to question Thornton's motives when we realise he has placed a text telling of a miracle of the Virgin, a satirical text ostensibly about an old grey horse, and a text containing a series of political prophecies, in what we have up until now considered a 'romance unit' in Thornton's MS. Of course the most obvious reason for this peculiar combination of texts seems to be that there is no other context in Thornton's MS which would have been any more appropriate for these items. *Thomas of Erceldoune*'s prophecies, in particular, seem to share and perhaps even to borrow directly from the vocabulary, themes and preoccupations of other ME romances, so, in this case at least, the context of *Thomas* in Thornton's collection is not all that surprising.[12] We have to stretch the literary evidence even further, however, if we are to make a case for *De Miraculo* being another of these unorthodox 'Thornton romances'. Nevertheless this particular Marian text does tell of the conversion of a wicked knight, and it does tell this 'knightly' tale in the same twelve line stanza form as some of Thornton's other tail-rhyme romances. In this sense then we can probably accommodate *De Miraculo* within a marginally acceptable definition of a 'Thornton romance'. It is stretching our impressions of Thornton's literary sensibility a little too far however to present a similar justification for his inclusion of *Lyarde* in this sequence.[13]

Lyarde is quite simply the most obscene, and, to the intelligent and pious late medieval reader, must have seemed the most controversial item which Thornton copied in his entire collection. This satirical anti-mendicant poem contains no 'romance' features whatsoever but instead castigates the friars for their lechery. When dealing with this text we are, in fact, a world removed from the ME romance. Moreover it is hard to see any element of deliberate device in the positioning of this item among Thornton's romances. We should ask ourselves where Thornton could have obtained such material in the first place, and then, having presumably read the text, why he proceeded to copy it into his collection. We can in fact begin to find answers to these questions simply by reference to the MS evidence in Thornton's book. In this context the presentation of *Lyarde* in the Lincoln MS is very important. It is our first major indication of the problems which Thornton had to face when he imposed his double column format too rigorously on the items he was copying. Thus on f.148r Thornton had to crush the opening, metrically longer lines of *Lyarde* into the available remaining space in the second column of that page. The result is that every line of text badly overruns the frame-ruling

---

[12] In this context see further E. B. Lyle's '*The Turk and Gawain* as a source of *Thomas of Erceldoune*', in *Forum for Modern Language Studies*, 6 (1970), 98-102.

[13] Both *De Miraculo Beate Marie* and *Lyarde* are available in nineteenth-century editions. For *De Miraculo* see C. Horstmann, ed., *Altenglische Legenden, Neue Folge* (Heilbronn, 1881), 503-4; for *Lyarde* see T. Wright and J. O. Halliwell, eds, *Reliquiae Antiquae*, II (1843), 280-2. Apart from these editions both texts have suffered considerable neglect. However in *Politics and Poetry in the Fifteenth Century* (London, 1971), 245, John Scattergood gives some brief indication of the anti-fraternal literary traditions to which *Lyarde* properly belongs. *Lyarde* has recently been re-edited and discussed by Jason Reakes in his '*Lyarde* and Goliard', in *NM*, 83 (1982), 34-41.

which Thornton had originally drawn for this page. On f.148v the situation gets even worse. Thornton persisted in copying *Lyarde* in double columns even though this means that the long lines of this item often merge on the page. Eventually, and much to the reader's relief, Thornton abandoned the ruling which he had previously prepared on f.149r, he forgot any ideas he had about imposing a double column format on this text, and he commenced copying *Lyarde* in single columns. Thus visually, as well as thematically and stylistically, *Lyarde* does not fit its present context in the Lincoln MS.

The changes in the presentation of the remaining, more orthodox, romances in Thornton's collection suggest that they too have certain important distinguishing features. *The Awentyrs of Arthure*, written in a complex thirteen line stanza form, is the first item in Thornton's romance sequence since the alliterative *Morte* which Thornton has copied using a single column format.[14] The *Awentyrs* is followed immediately, on f.161r, by the final romance item in the Thornton sequence, *Sir Perceval*. Thornton used the same double column format for copying *Sir Perceval* as he used for all his tail-rhyme romances. However the abrupt change of format from single to double columns on f.161r is visually quite striking. As the modern reader turns the pages of the Scolar Facsimile his attention is caught by the way in which this change of format means that the *Awentyrs* is both stylistically and visually isolated from its immediate MS context. Admittedly however this visual isolation is, by itself, an insignificant detail. Again Thornton probably inherited the single column format from his exemplar. Nevertheless it assumes some greater importance when we remember that the only other occasion where we have noted a similar change of layout occurring in Thornton's romance collection was on f.98v. There, of course, the change marked the end of the alliterative *Morte* and the beginning of *Octavian*. So we should bear in mind that the juxtaposition of such stylistically different romances as the *Awentyrs* and *Sir Perceval* may well reflect a similar change in Thornton's exemplar. Moreover, when we look more closely at the items in gatherings I and K as a whole, we are once again made very aware of the probable time lapse between the point when Thornton originally copied some of his romance items, and the later date when he returned to partly filled gatherings and added more 'romance' items.

We have already noticed how Thornton copied some of his material, but particularly material on the Nine Worthy, onto originally independent gatherings. We might therefore expect, if it were possible, that the *Awentyrs*, as another Arthurian item, would also have been copied onto an originally independent gathering. Like the Alexander unit and like the other Arthurian unit, this gathering may have only been absorbed into Thornton's larger collection

---

[14] See Ralph Hanna III, ed., *The Awentyrs of Arthure at the Terne Wathelyn* (Manchester, 1974). Hanna's introduction contains a discussion of the many and complex stylistic and textual problems which are raised by the *Awentyrs*. For an analysis of the important literary affiliations of the *Awentyrs* with other poetry written in the thirteen line stanza see Thorlac Turville-Petre's '"Summer Sunday", "De Tribus Regibus Mortuis", and "The Awntyrs off Arthure": Three Poems in the Thirteen-Line Stanza', in *RES*, NS, 25 (1974), 1-14.

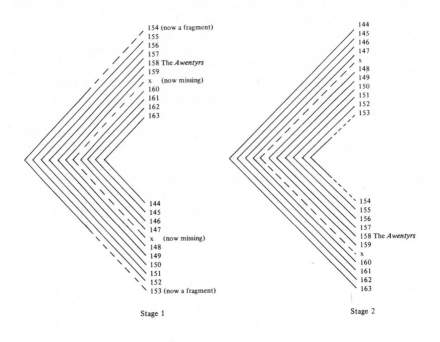

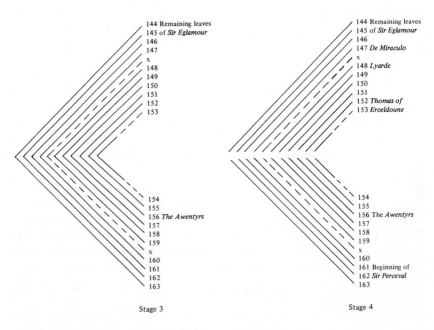

Fig. 2   Thornton's compiling activity in gathering I

at a later date. Using this as a working hypothesis then we can actually reconstruct the chronology in which Thornton appears to have copied the items in gathering I (see fig. 2). In stage 1 Thornton copied his text of the *Awentyrs* onto ff.154r-161r. I suggest that these were originally the opening nine folios of I and, if this was the case, it meant that Thornton was left with just over half of the gathering remaining blank. The gathering stayed that way until eventually Thornton needed extra paper on which to complete his copy of *Sir Eglamour*. Presumably faced with a shortage of paper, and with more than half of I remaining blank and the other half already containing a romance, Thornton simply had to refold his paper (stage 2) so that ff.153-154 no longer formed the outer bifolium of the gathering but instead became the central bifolium. Thornton then copied the remainder of *Sir Eglamour* into I (stage 3) and, at an even later stage, used the limited space available on ff.147r-153v to copy *De Miraculo beate Marie*, *Lyarde*, and finally *Thomas of Erceldoune*. Similarly at some time Thornton filled the blanks on ff.161r-163v with the opening few folios of *Sir Perceval* (stage 4).

Some supplementary MS evidence confirms the plausibility of this reconstruction of Thornton's unorthodox compiling methods. The grubby appearance of ff.153v and 154r is certainly grubby enough to suggest that these leaves were for a time the worn outer leaves of a gathering which was rearranged as well as incorporated into Thornton's larger collection. Moreover, if the present physical condition of I is significant, and I believe that it is, then the present state of I can best be explained by Thornton's peculiar use of paper in that gathering. When A. E. B. Owen examined the unbound Lincoln MS he found that damage to most of the gatherings elsewhere in Thornton's book was confined to the outer leaves, many of which had become detached from their conjugates. Quire I is unique in that *all* its leaves had become detached and the whole quire is now made up of singletons (see stage 4). This unusually complete deterioration of gathering I might possibly have been prompted by the folding, and then refolding, of the paper in I which would have had to take place for Thornton to rearrange the gathering. Inevitably Thornton's action would have weakened the paper along its folds (gutters) and presumably this contributed towards the particularly fragmentary state of the unbound gathering.

Finally, and regardless of this latter speculation, it was probably because the order of Thornton's quires was subject to some adaptation and change that Thornton added a note on the last leaf of I (f.163v). The note originally read, 'here is ix quayers' but this was subsequently cancelled by a single ink stroke. Quires A-I do form nine quires, so presumably I was for a time the last quire in Thornton's romance unit, the prose *Alexander* was the first romance item, and the *Awentyrs* was the last. Ff.161v-163v were originally blank. It was only when gatherings A-I had been assembled in their present order that Thornton came back to his romance unit and added *Sir Perceval* as a final romance item. *Sir Perceval* fills the remainder of I and most of K and Thornton then had ten 'romance quires'. His earlier note on f.163v was no longer valid and consequently he cancelled it. The remainder of K remained blank for a while but eventually Thornton appears to have removed what was probably a blank leaf following f.178. On the final leaves in K he added devotional 'filler' items in the remaining available space. This action completed Thornton's gradual compilation of his 'romance unit'.

SOME MEDIEVAL ENGLISH MANUSCRIPTS IN THE NORTH-EAST MIDLANDS

Thorlac Turville-Petre

It is still true that in most cases Middle English literature exists within only the haziest of contexts. The most notorious example is that of the *Gawain* group of poems — written by whom, for whom, exactly where, and with what in mind? On the other hand, when we come to Chaucer, we have at least a name, a portrait even, a man with a job or series of jobs, who lived and worked in a setting we know something about, but we have less certain knowledge of what sort of audience he could count on. Perhaps it was not the courtly circle so much as the civil servants, lawyers, administrators, men of his own class and background, who formed the nucleus of the audience for whom Chaucer wrote.

In the fifteenth century there is more evidence to go on, with writers such as Lydgate and others, patronised by great lords who left records of their purchase and ownership of fine manuscripts, so that we can build up a rather patchy picture of the social context of literature among the higher echelons of society. Good work has been done in this field, but less attention has been paid to a close study of a limited provincial area in order to illuminate the relationship between literature and society within that area. I would want to know, first of all, the social make-up of that area: where were the main centres of population? What was the presence of the church? Were there large monasteries that might act as reservoirs or even springs of literary culture, as libraries and centres of scribal activity? Were there professional urban scribes and even bookshops? In the rural areas, who owned the manors, who were the important landowners and the local administrators? Having built up a picture of a particular society, we could, ideally, tie this in with the literature of the area. Was there a specifically local literary culture? What relationship did this bear to the metropolitan cultures, and the worlds of French romances and Latin learning? Or was the culture not local at all; did local readers rely on a national literary culture, the work of Chaucer, Gower, Lydgate and others?

In order to give some examples of an approach that might prove fruitful, I have concentrated on Nottinghamshire and the adjacent areas of south-east Derbyshire and north Leicestershire. The work I envisage would be a long-term project, and I am not in any sense offering the results of it now. Instead, I point out a few small pieces of the jigsaw, which may one day find their appropriate place in a more complete picture of medieval literature in the north-east Midlands. I want to show the kind of evidence we might look for, and the sort of use that might be made of it.

The most obvious way to start this work would, I suppose, be to base oneself on dialect evidence, and analyse manuscripts that appear to come from the east Midlands, which is a fairly well-defined dialect area in any case, and will become more so with the publication of the Middle English Dialect Atlas. There are a number of crucial difficulties with this approach, however, for manuscripts that seem to be from an area may have less significant connection with that area than at first sight appears. First of all, the dialect evidence itself presents so many problems, especially when there are layers of scribes to a greater or lesser extent translating the work of their exemplars into their own dialect. Secondly, there is no necessity to suppose that a scribe worked in his native area, or wrote for those who lived in the immediately surrounding region. Thirdly, manuscripts from elsewhere may have been commissioned or bought or inherited by local readers, so that they *became* the manuscripts located in that new area, just as much as manuscripts written by local scribes in the local dialect for a local audience.

There are other ways in which manuscripts can be more firmly located. These may be demonstrated by looking at two manuscripts in some detail, Middleton MS 01 and Advocates MS 19. 3. 1, and also by investigating the manuscripts owned by one man from the area, Thomas Chaworth of Wiverton in Nottinghamshire.

Nottingham University Library holds an interesting collection of medieval manuscripts, the majority of them deposited by Lord Middleton, formerly of Wollaton Hall, Nottingham. One day Alan Cameron of the Manuscripts Department showed me a roll of two leaves of parchment sewn together, very crumpled and stained. It was most uninviting at first glance — a Commission for the construction of sewers, in the wapentakes of Bingham and Newark in Nottinghamshire, the Commission dated 1394, the Return 1395. But on the back of the second sheet, mainly indecipherable at first glance, were some lines of English verse.

There turned out to be ninety-one lines of verse there, a poem written in alliterative verse with end-rhyme. The lines described the life and death of a certain John Berkeley, from Wymondham in Leicestershire, not far from Melton Mowbray.[1] It took many hours to make out what the poem said, and even with the help of ultra-violet light some parts of it are still illegible to me. But the story it tells is as follows.

A group of noble lords gather together for a hunt, full of joy and excitement. However, there is an undercurrent of sadness since one of their number is no longer with them. The poet himself is in deep grief for the death of this noble knight. All thoughts and expressions of joy are far from him now, though in the past he was full of lightheartedness. Like the proverbial grasshopper, he made merry while the gardens were green, but now the frost has come and he is joyless. He depended on his departed lord, and he will never rejoice again. He goes on to tell of the virtues of his lord: he was trusted by his fellow-gentry, and respected by all those round him; his name was Sir John of Berkeley. He was a man of right and reason, a generous householder who entertained in the grandest fashion

---

[1] The poem is published and discussed in my article, 'The Lament for Sir John Berkeley', *Speculum*, 57 (1982), 332-9, where full references to Berkeley's life-records are given.

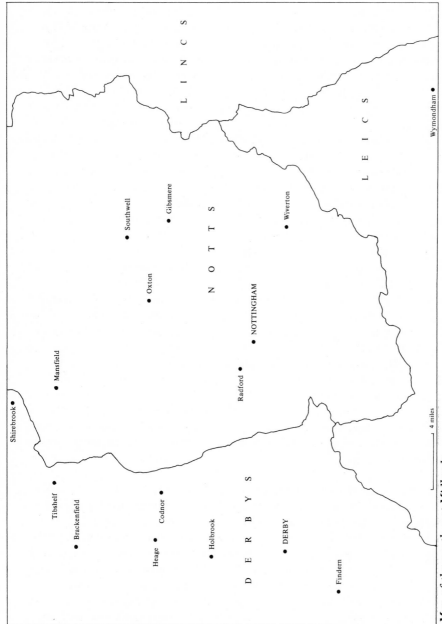

Map of the north-east Midlands

all who came to Wymondham with food and jollity, song and 'daliance of damisels to driue away þo day', and the reading of romances. He was generous to all; his foresters loved him and followed him loyally, and were rewarded with green outfits and presents of deer.

One sad Wednesday, however, Berkeley left Wymondham and travelled across the sea to Brittany to defend that dukedom against the French, and a noble company of knights with bacenets rode with him. He was a skilled tactician in the fighting there, and was trusted by those lords to whom he was attached. But the English king soon recalled his forces, and Brittany was left undefended against its French attackers. On the way home, Berkeley was suddenly afflicted with sickness, and as he lay dying he called for pen and parchment, and wrote a letter to be taken back to his beloved wife at Wymondham.

Now although John Berkeley was not a man of any national importance, there are enough historical records of him to supply the necessary background to the poem. The basic sources are the usual materials at the Public Record Office, but in the case of Berkeley these are supplemented by a record of great value, the Berkeley Cartulary, drawn up for the Berkeleys of Wymondham in the fifteenth century (BL MS Harley 265).

The Berkeleys were a cadet branch of the illustrious Gloucestershire family. At the beginning of the fourteenth century, Thomas, younger son of the first Lord Berkeley, married a daughter of John Hamelin of Wymondham. The next three generations of Wymondham Berkeleys were all named John, which has confused genealogists trying to distinguish between them. John I died before 1356; his son John II is the one that we are concerned with; his son John III died in about 1413.

John II was married to Joan when in 1368 he was granted manors in Leicestershire including Wymondham. He stood as mainpernor in 1370, he sat on a Commission of the Peace in Leicestershire in the same year, and also collected a subsidy there for the French wars. All these were local offices, but in 1372 he represented Leicestershire in Parliament. In 1374 he sat on a Commission in Nottinghamshire, and had by this time remarried, since the Cartulary records dealings over a manor at Oakley between John and his wife Elizabeth on the one hand, and their children on the other.

In November 1374 John Berkeley prepared to go and fight abroad. He is listed as one of those who were to accompany Edmund, Earl of March, on an expedition 'ad partes transmarinas'. This, which was the expedition to Brittany, was very much delayed, and in fact it did not sail until April 1375.[2] Perhaps in the meantime John had given up hope of the expedition ever getting going at all, because in December 1374 he was pricked as sheriff of Warwickshire and Leicestershire, though two weeks later there appears a request for his discharge as sheriff.

So they sailed in April 1375, but after only three months the English forces withdrew following the Truce of Bruges between the English and the French.

[2] See M. Jones, *Ducal Brittany 1364-1399* (Oxford, 1970), 76-80.

John Berkeley appears no more in the records, and the poem explains why.

The interest of the Berkeley *Lament* for the sort of project I am envisaging is this. First of all we have a manuscript that can be assigned to a definite location and date: the deed relates to Nottinghamshire and has always remained in that county, and the date of the deed is 1395. Secondly we have a poem that can similarly be assigned to a location and given a date: it was written by somebody who knew John Berkeley and Wymondham, presumably in the year of Berkeley's death in 1375 or shortly after. It was, we may be sure, composed for those who knew Berkeley and the local area.

Given these factors, we can draw several conclusions. The first is that somebody who moved in the same circles as the Berkeley household, indeed was almost certainly from that household, was a competent, if by no means an outstanding poet. I had thought earlier that the author's name might be Turner; at any rate Turner is named as the man who carried the letter to Berkeley's wife after his lord's death. It is perhaps possible, however, that it was Elizabeth Berkeley herself who wrote in such passionate terms about the love she had for her lord, and about the misery she felt at his loss. This would find a humbler and later parallel in Margery Brews' Valentine poem to John Paston in 1477.[3]

The second conclusion we can draw is that the poet was a conscious stylist, who had considerable knowledge of English poetic traditions. The verse is accentual alliterative verse in rhyming couplets. That is to say, it is not rhymed verse in a regular metre with additional alliteration, but is essentially the alliterative long-line with additional end-rhyme. Unrhymed alliterative verse is in the main associated with the west Midlands, but alliterative verse with rhyme is found also further east and north. The poems that are most obviously comparable to the Berkeley *Lament* are the stanzaic alliterative poems on political subjects by the mid-fourteenth-century poet Laurence Minot, who probably came from Lincolnshire. We might also compare some of the lyrics of the Yorkshire school of Richard Rolle and his followers, such as the poem 'My Truest Treasure', written in ornate quatrains:

> My trewest tresowre sa trayturly was taken,
> Sa bytterly bondyn wyth bytand bandes,
> How sone of þi seruandes was þou forsaken
> And lathly for my lufe hurld with þair handes.[4]

Perhaps it was upon works such as these that the author of the Berkeley poem based his style. However, some of the unrhymed alliterative poems may also have been known in the east Midlands; for instance Professor McIntosh has argued that the Thornton text of the alliterative *Morte Arthure* was derived from north-east Midland copies.[5]

---

3 *Paston Letters and Papers*, ed. N. Davis, part i (Oxford, 1971), 662.
4 *Religious Lyrics of the XIVth Century*, ed. C. Brown (revised G. V. Smithers, Oxford, 1957), 94-5.
5 See A. McIntosh, 'The Textual Transmission of the Alliterative *Morte Arthure*', in *English and Medieval Studies Presented to J. R. R. Tolkien*, ed. N. Davis and C. L. Wrenn (London,

In other respects, too, the poem impresses itself as one written by an author who was well acquainted with the conventions of medieval poetry. The description of the hunt with which the poem opens is an effective use of a well-established convention. In this poem, the hunt is the expression of courtly joy and lively activity, of the entertainment of an elegant society that has been diminished by the death of one of its members. It acts both as a social setting and as a contrast to the misery and isolation of the bereaved poet. There are some similarities, I think, in the use of the hunt in *The Book of the Duchess*, where the expression of the noble pleasures of life highlights the contrast with the life-denying misery of the Black Knight; similarities, too, in the contrasts in *Sir Gawain and the Green Knight* between the energetic hunting scenes and the mental agility in the bedroom. There are also a number of poems — Audelay's *The Three Dead Kings*, *Summer Sunday*, *The Awntyrs off Arthure* and several of the 'chansons d'aventure' — where a hunting scene acts as an introduction to a much more sober encounter or reflection.[6]

A few lines further on in the Berkeley *Lament* comes the effective simile drawn from the Aesopic fable of the grasshopper and the ant:

It was winter-time; the ants' store of grain had got wet and they were laying it out to dry. A hungry cicada asked them to give it something to eat. 'Why did you not gather food in the summer, like us?' they said. 'I hadn't time,' it replied; 'I was busy making sweet music.'[7]

This is retold as follows in the Berkeley *Lament*:

> Yore I bourded broode with birdes all aboute;
> I dar not with hem deele for drede ne for doute;
> Bot as a gresshop is gladd whil gardins ben grene,
> He thinkes o no tempest þat turnes him to tene,
> He mas him miri whils he may, of mischef has no mynde,
> So is he combred with colde, suche is þat caytifs kinde;
> He falle[s] and he fades in a fel frost,
> And for he loues noo labour, his life has he loste.
> Soo hit fares be a fole when his frendes founde[n];
> He is abated of his bost, in bale is he bounden,
> He leued him on his lord when he was olife,
> Nou it rewes him, bi my thrift, for throng he mai not thrife;
> And for þe lof þat I haue lost, list me neuer be light.   (15-27)

This shows an easy familiarity with Aesop's fables — they were, after all, a school text — and also an understanding of how a simile *works*: the poet wishes to say that once he (or she) was thoughtlessly glad, now he is miserable with a misery that will never lift.

1962), 231-40.
[6] See T. Turville-Petre, 'Three Poems in the Thirteen-Line Stanza', *Review of English Studies*, new ser. 25 (1974), 1-14.
[7] *Fables of Aesop*, translated S. A. Handford (Harmondsworth, 1964), 142.

The account that follows this, of Berkeley's knightly qualities, with particular stress on his open-handedness, creates a picture of the ideal figure of the romances, whose hallmark is *largesse*, as in *Sir Isumbras*:

> Menstralles he hadde in his halle,
> And yafe hem robes of ryche palle,
> Sylver, golde and fee;
> Of curtesye he was kynge,
> His gentylnesse hadde non endyng,
> I[n] worlde was none so fre.   (25-30)[8]

In *Sir Launfal*:

> He gaf gyftys largelyche,
> Gold and syluer and clodes ryche
> To squyer and to kny3t.
> For his largesse and hys bounté
> Þe kynges stuward made was he.   (28-32)[9]

There is an even closer parallel from *Sir Amadace*. When Amadace asks how the dead knight spent his money, his widow replies:

> Sir, on gentilmen and officers,
> On grete lordus that was his perus:
> Wold giffe hom giftes gay.
> Riche festus wold he make,
> And pore men for Goddus sake
> He fed hom evyriche day.   (148-56)[10]

The point that this demonstrates is that the poet was steeped in traditions of literature, and to be more precise, English secular literature. Where did the author acquire this familiarity? The poem itself gives a clue — though it is the sort of clue that must be regarded with circumspection — when it describes the reading of romances as one of the household diversions 'to driue away þo day'. Now the reading of romance is so much a feature of the courtly romance-world itself that any literary description of a noble household might be expected to include it. Nevertheless, if the Middle English romances were not written for this sort of entertainment, then what were they for? Though we have no idea of what sort of books the Berkeley household possessed, we can I think be sure that it did possess romances and other works from which an amateur poet of some skill could have learned how to put a poem together, how to use conventions and imagery, and in what terms to portray ideal knightly qualities. The Berkeleys' romances may have been in French at this date, but there were by this time

[8] *Sir Isumbras*, ed. M. Mills, *Six Middle English Romances* (London, 1973).
[9] *Sir Launfal*, ed. A. J. Bliss (London, 1960).
[10] *Sir Amadace*, ed. M. Mills, op. cit.

English romances, such as *Sir Isumbras*, which were composed or at least copied in this general area of the country.

If the Berkeley's did own English books, however, these books would not necessarily have been copied in the north-east Midlands, or have contained works that were composed there. An instructive case from rather later, but from much the same region, is that of Sir Thomas Chaworth. He was a man of considerable wealth, who owned land in many counties, but the centre of his activities was in Nottinghamshire, and his main residence was at Wiverton. He held administrative offices of very much the same kind as John Berkeley; Justice of the Peace for Nottinghamshire from 1401, sheriff at various times from 1403 to 1424, and M.P. for Nottinghamshire over a period of forty years, from 1406-1446.[11] What we have for Chaworth, which we lack for Berkeley, is his will, proved in 1458, and this is very detailed indeed.[12] In it he bequeaths a number of his books. Several of these are religious books for the chapel or the chamber: 'the best Mes boke, another olde Messe boke with a boke of Placebo and Dirige liggyng in his seid closed at the chapell, in the which ar titled of olde tyme the obitts of the auncetors as welle of the faders of the said Sir Thomas as of his moder, the lesce Antiphoner of iiij, a Graile, a Manuell, a litel Portose, the which the saide Sir Thomas toke with hym alway when he rode', and so on. But there are English books as well: he bequeaths 'a boke of Englissh þe which is called Policonicon' (there is also a Latin *Policronicon*), 'a newe boke of Inglisse þe which begynnyth with þe lyffe of Seynt Albon and Amphiabell and other mony dyvers lyfeʒ and thynges in þe same boke, and unto my cosyn Richard Willughby squyer an Englisse boke called Grace de Dieu', and 'an Englissh booke called Orilogium Sapienciae'. There are in fact at least three of Chaworth's books still in existence, all with his arms illuminated on them, though none of them appears to be mentioned in the will. One is a copy of John Trevisa's translation of Bartholomeus, *On the Properties of Things*; this manuscript was sold by Lord Middleton of Wollaton Hall, Nottinghamshire, in 1925, and is now Columbia University MS Plimpton 263.[13] The second is a copy of Lydgate's *Troy Book* (BL MS Cotton Augustus A. iv; see Pl. 1). The third is the enormous and magnificent Wollaton Antiphonal,[14] reputedly bought for ten marks by the administrators of the goods of William Husse, rector of Wollaton from 1448-60, and donated by them to Wollaton Parish Church, from where it was recently taken into the care of Nottingham University Library (see Pl. 2). This is hardly the 'lesce Antiphoner of iiij', for it is an unusually heavy and bulky book. The Trevisa and the Lydgate link up with two books in

---

[11] This information is taken from J. C. Wedgwood, *History of Parliament: Biographies of the Members of the Commons House 1439-1509* (London, 1936), 175-6.

[12] The will is printed in *Testamenta Eboracensia*, part ii (Surtees Society, 30, 1855), 220-29.

[13] On this manuscript generally see R. W. Mitchner, 'Wynkyn de Worde's Use of the Plimpton Manuscript of *De Proprietatibus Rerum*', *The Library*, 5th ser. 6 (1951-2), 7-18. The folio with Chaworth's arms is illustrated in G. A. Plimpton, *The Education of Chaucer* (Oxford, 1935), plate 5. The manuscript is lot 371 (illustrated) in the sale catalogue of Christie, Manson and Woods, 16 June, 1925.

[14] See A. du B. Hill, 'The Wollaton Antiphonale', *Transactions of the Thoroton Society*, 36 (1932), 42-50.

the will; the English 'Policonicon' is presumably Trevisa's translation made for Sir Thomas Berkeley,[15] and the 'newe' *Life of St Albon and St Amphabell* must be Lydgate's version,[16] rather than the version from the *South English Legendary*. The *Orilogium Sapienciae* is an English prose translation of the Latin devotional work by Suso, and *Grace de Dieu* is the prose translation of Deguileville's *Pelerinage*.[17]

The extant manuscripts owned by Chaworth are professional and costly productions, probably made in London. They have no association in style or in literary content with the north-east Midlands. If it were not for the fact that we know they were made for Chaworth, there would be no reason to suspect they had anything to do with the area I am interested in. Chaworth subscribed to the latest in fashionable literature, and probably bought his books in London. He could afford to. Perhaps he also had volumes made by local scribes including works by local authors; if so, they were not worth mentioning in the will. Perhaps, though this is pure speculation, the Berkeley poem was copied for him. After all, he was sheriff of Nottingham at the right time to have access to Nottinghamshire deeds at the sheriff's office, and furthermore, the Berkeley poem and several of Chaworth's books came into the hands of cousins, the Willoughbys, later the Barons Middleton, of Wollaton Hall.

In the case of Chaworth, as in the case of Berkeley, we are looking at men of very much the same social standing, the gentry, who lived in style, who indeed travelled to London, but whose chief preoccupations were with local affairs, and whose reputations were local and not national ones. I shall go on to examine another case of a local family and their literary involvements, this time from the second half of the fifteenth century.

I want to deal in some detail with the provenance of NLS Advocates MS 19.3.1. In describing this late fifteenth-century manuscript, I am basing myself on a very thorough account of its make-up and contents by Dr Hardman.[18] She explains that this large manuscript of 216 folios is made up of nine booklets, and that these were originally separate, as shown by the wear of the outer leaves of each booklet, though the folio numbering of the first forty folios is early, so that it probably was not long before at least some of the booklets were gathered

---

15 The Willoughby family of Wollaton Hall owned a fine copy of Trevisa's *Polychronicon*, but it seems that this did not come into their possession until the sixteenth century, before which it was in Hertfordshire and Somerset. See Sotheby's sale catalogue for 8 December, 1981, lot 80 (illustrated on p. 84).
16 A manuscript that begins with Lydgate's *Lives of St Albon and St Amphabell*, followed by 'other mony dyvers lyfeȝ and thynges', is Huntington MS HM 140, and it has been suggested that this may have been the manuscript mentioned in Chaworth's will (see J. M. Manly and E. Rickert, *The Text of the Canterbury Tales*, vol. i (Chicago, 1940), 433-8 and 609). However, Dr A. I. Doyle has informed me that the paper appears to be too late to allow this identification.
17 *The Pilgrimage of the Lyfe of the Manhode* is entitled *Grace Dieu* in one manuscript (Melbourne State Library of Victoria, MS *096/G94). *The Pylgremage of the Sowle* also has this title; in BL MS Egerton 615 it is entitled *Grace de Dieu*, as in Chaworth's will. (I am indebted to Dr Avril Henry and Dr Doyle for this information.)
18 P. Hardman, 'A Medieval "Library in Parvo"', *Medium Aevum*, 47 (1978), 262-73.

Mighty mars that wyth
thy sterne hyght. In armys
haſt the power & ye myзt
And named art frō eſt til
omdent. The myзhty lorde
the god armypotent.

Plate 1 BL MS Cotton Augustus A. iv, fol. 1ʳ. Lydgate presents his Troy Book
to Henry V. Below this are the arms of Sir Thomas Chaworth and his wife

Plate 2 A page from the Wollaton Antiphonal (58.5cm x 39cm) showing the Nativity and the arms of Sir Thomas Chaworth and his wife

into one volume. In discussing the manuscript as a whole, there is obviously a danger that what I say is applicable to one part of it, one booklet only, though in fact I think that in this particular case the danger is more apparent than real.

Before the manuscript was bought by the Advocates Library, it was in the hands of the Sherbrooke family of Oxton, in Nottinghamshire. Dr Hardman has given an account of the sale of the manuscript in the early years of the last century, when Sir Walter Scott, acting on behalf of the Advocates Library, bought it from Mrs Sherbrooke.[19]

The manuscript was certainly in the hands of the family from the time of the Reformation, because it contains the signature of Cuthbert Sherbrooke. He was the rector of Rockland in Norfolk in 1537, and he owned a large collection of books, most of which were dispersed in sales at Sotheby's in 1887 and 1912. *The Nottingham Guardian Literary Supplement* for 2 January, 1912, has a head-line reporting 'A Notts. Literary Find'. The article relates that 'the vicar of the parish, the Rev. W. Laycock, obtained permission to go through the books in the library [at Oxton Hall] at his leisure. While so doing his curiosity was aroused by a locked and forgotten cupboard therein, which he proceeded to investigate, with the consent of Capt. Sherbrooke, the owner of Oxton Hall, who was aware that it contained some old books which had not been looked at for a very long while. Its contents proved to be between forty and fifty volumes . . . The bulk of them contain the very distinctive, not to say flourishing, signature of "Cuthbert Sherbrooke".' These books must have been sent off to the auctioneers almost as soon as they were discovered, and most of them fetched paltry sums. The present Mrs Sherbrooke kindly lent me her copy of Sotheby's sale catalogue for 27 June, 1912, with the prices in the margin — total £75. 18s. 0d. A volume that failed to sell and is still in the hands of the family is a thirteenth-century Bible, in which Cuthbert signs himself as rector of Rockland in the Norwich diocese in 1537, a living in the presentation of the Premonstratensian Canons at Langley, an abbey which was suppressed in 1536.[20] Evidently the Bible came originally from Langley, as is shown by a document on the last folio concerning William Cyrlew, abbot of Langley in 1500-1502.[21] Cuthbert Sherbrooke, wise man that he was, took the Bible into his own hands at the Dissolution, and from him it passed into the Sherbrooke family collection, together with many other books of his, one of which may have been the early fourteenth-century Sherbrooke Missal, now MS 15536E in the National Library of Wales, which is described as probably of East Anglian origin.

Many of Cuthbert's manuscripts and incunabula were probably obtained in East Anglia where he was priest. The Advocates manuscript, however, was from the Midlands. The scribes have left a few blank pages at the ends of the booklets, and these have been filled with miscellaneous notes and jottings, one of which,

19 P. Hardman, 'A Note on some "Lost" Manuscripts', *The Library*, 5th ser. 30 (1975), 245-7.
20 See *The Victoria History of the County of Norfolk*, vol. ii (London, 1906), 418-21; and *Valor Ecclesiasticus*, vol. iii (1817), 304.
21 On the Bible see N. R. Ker, *Medieval Libraries of Great Britain* (London, 1964), 108.

on fol. 173v, in a hand which is probably late fifteenth century, lists expenses incurred on a visit to Gibsmere, a few miles from Southwell in Nottinghamshire:

> Memorandum þat þes bene þe parcelle þat I hawfe spend: þe ferst when I went to Gybbysmere, iiiid. Item for seynyng brede, iid. Item for schowyng of þe horse when I went to my lord harsbechope [at Southwell], iid. . . . Item for makyn of þe birne walle toward þe cyrche yard, viiid.

and so on.

The Sherbrookes moved to Oxton in 1551. Before that they had lived in Tibshelf in Derbyshire, near the Nottinghamshire border.[22] They took their name from Shirebrook, again in Derbyshire on the border with Nottinghamshire, only a few miles north of Tibshelf. I have found no record of their holdings there, but another signature in the Advocates manuscript is 'Michaell Sherbrooke off Shyrbroke' (fol. 148v).

So far the evidence shows clearly that the Sherbrookes owned the manuscript in the first half of the sixteenth century, while the family was still living at Tibshelf or Shirebrook. It does not indicate, though, where it was made and for whom. I believe that the evidence suggests that it was made in the north-east Midlands for a local family, possibly the Sherbrookes themselves.

The evidence for locating the manuscript in the north-east Midlands is two-fold. Firstly, the name of the main scribe is Richard Heege. He contributed to every one of the booklets, and he was the chief scribe of all but one of them, the sixth, which he wrote in conjunction with John Hawghton, who also contributed to the eighth booklet. Other short pieces are written by a number of unsigned hands, generally to fill up a page or to complete a booklet. Heege signs his name also as Heeg and as Hyheg. Without doubt he took his name from the Derbyshire village of Heage, which in the fifteenth century was spelt in just these ways.[23] It lies a few miles south of Tibshelf.

This on its own means nothing. A scribe or his forebears can move around the country as easily as anyone else. Nevertheless, we have Sherbrooke of Shirebrook, and Heege of Heage, which is at least suggestive. What appears to me to clinch the evidence that this manuscript was made for a north-east Midland audience is a burlesque poem on fol. 10v; we might title it *The Battle of Brackonwet*:

> The mone in þe mornyng merely rose
> When þe sonne & þe sevon sterrs softely wer leyd
> In a slommuryng of slepe, for-slokond with ale.
> A hoswyfe of Holbrucke owt hornus blu
> For all þo pekke was for-bedon paryng of chese;
> Þo reyncus of Radforde wer redy at a nonswer
> For to expond þe spavens of þe spade halfe.
> Tom þe teplar tryde in þe gospell

---

22 See K. S. S. Train, *Twenty Nottinghamshire Families* (Nottingham, 1969), 24.
23 See K. Cameron, *The Place-Names of Derbyshire*, part iii (Cambridge, 1959), 565-6.

> What schuld fall of þe fournes in þe frosty murnyng.
> At þe batell of Brakonwet þer as þe beyre justyd
> Sym saer & þe swynkote þei wer sworne breder.
> Þe hare & harþeston hurtuld to-geydur
> Whyle þe hombulbe hod was hacked alto cloutus.
> Þer schalmo[l] þe scheldrake & schepe trumpyd,
> Hogge with his hornepype hyod hym be-lyve
> & dansyd on þe downghyll whyle all þei dey lastyd
> With Magot & Margory & Malyn hur sysstur.
> Þe prest in to þe place pryce for to wynne.
> Kene men of Combur comen be-lyve
> For to mot[e] of mychewhat more þen a lytyll,
> How Reynall & Robyn Hod runnon at þe gleyve.[24]

There are three identifiable places here: Holbrook (1.4), Radford (1.6), and 'Brakonwet' (1.10), that is Brackenthwaite, a place now named Brackenfield. These are all in west Nottinghamshire and east Derbyshire within a radius of about eight miles. Near the end of the poem is another place-name, 'Combur', or perhaps 'Conibur' (1.19). Possibly this is an error for Codnor, which lies just at the centre of the radius of the other villages mentioned, but it is more likely a lost village.

This poem only makes any sort of sense — and there is not much of that — as a local production for a local audience. What the poet is doing is burlesquing the ancient heroes of traditional alliterative chronicle-poems and the far-away battle-fields of romance, transmuting them into housewives, innkeepers, jousting bears and dancing pigs fighting it out in the local villages. The mention of Robin Hood is interesting in a poem so closely associated with the Nottingham area, particularly as he is here linked with 'Reynall', Reynolde Grenelefe, a companion of Robin not otherwise named before the sixteenth century.[25]

However, the main point is that only a local audience would appreciate the allusions to the places. The poem is written at the end of the first booklet, which consists entirely of burlesques: the first item is *The Hunting of the Hare*, a jolly poem about foolish villagers getting into a terrible tangle over a hare-hunt; the second item is a mock-sermon in prose, where the jokes are extraordinarily laboured, and on the last folio, in Heege's hand like the rest of the booklet, is *The Battle of Brakonwet*. Evidently Heege felt it would nicely fill the space and round off the booklet of comic pieces, but it is difficult to imagine him including it unless he knew his readers would understand the local allusions.

The possibilities are, then, firstly that Heege copied out this booklet for his own pleasure and that of his circle of friends, or secondly that he did it on com-

---

[24] Previously printed, with some inaccuracies, by T. Wright and J. O. Halliwell, *Reliquiae Antiquae*, vol. i (London, 1841), 84, together with lines from *Sir Gowther*, incorrectly taken to be part of the alliterative poem.

[25] See R. B. Dobson and J. Taylor, *Rymes of Robyn Hood* (London, 1976), 4 and 90. This poem is not noticed by the authors.

mission for a local family, such as the Sherbrookes, who wanted a small and varied collection of literary material to entertain and instruct them. Possibly Heege and John Hawghton (the minor scribe) were household servants of one of the local families, like those who acted also as amanuenses for the Pastons.

Looked at from this point of view, the contents of the booklets are very interesting. The range of material is so wide as to suggest that this may have formed not part of the library, but more or less the complete library, of a smallish provincial household. The contents seem to cater for the complete needs of a family: spiritual, practical, and recreational.

The first booklet, as has been shown, consists of comedy and burlesque. The second, fourth and fifth each contain as their principal item a romance of a moral and didactic cast – *Sir Gowther*, *Sir Isumbras* and *Sir Amadas*. We can imagine the less pious members of the family being attracted by these items, and perhaps then being drawn in to sample the great mass of devotional and didactic writings in the other booklets. There are lives of those to be emulated, the prose *Life of St Katherine* and long extracts from Lydgate's *Life of our Lady*. There are examples to be shunned, *The Vision of Tundale* and *The Lamentations of the Sinner*. For the unsophisticated worshipper there is *The Lay Folk's Mass Book* giving simple guidance on following Mass, and there are a great number of prayers of homage and repentance in the form of carols and short devotional verses. In addition to this there is much practical advice scattered throughout the booklets. Considerable space is given to instructing children in table-manners in *Stans Puer ad Mensam* and *The Little Children's Book* – 'pyke not þyne eyris nor þi neysetyrlys', 'pyke not þi teþe wyth þy knyfe', 'Nor spitt þu not ouer þe tabull'. There are the terms appropriate to carving game, prognostications of the weather in each month, forms of how to begin letters, a picture of a Guidonian hand to give basic guidance on musical notation, medical advice against the cholic, against bleeding, against a 'malaundre', which is a sore on a horse's knee, as well as a great range of conventional wisdom expressed in maxims, proverbs and precepts. In short, all that a respectable, but perhaps not very sophisticated, household could want is contained in these booklets. The impression that this *was* the library is perhaps reinforced by the mass of jottings that fill every available space, the Gibsmere accounts already mentioned, copies of indulgences, a later song, a short Italian-English glossary, and scribbles of all sorts, more or less legible. The impression given is that there was not a great deal of paper lying about to take these notes, so that the hand with the pen inevitably took up the paper that was conveniently within reach – MS Advocates 19. 3. 1.

My suggestion is, then, that the Sherbrookes or a neighbouring family of similar status owned this manuscript from the beginning. I have not been able to find out anything about the Sherbrookes in the late fifteenth century. The Sherbrooke records are in the Nottinghamshire Record Office, but they start in the sixteenth century when the family had risen to some local prominence and acquired a fair amount of land. There is no information about them in the Derbyshire Record Office. It is certain that in the fifteenth century they never attained the same importance or standing as Sir Thomas Chaworth did; they did not hold local offices, and so they were a family considerably lower down the social scale from the Chaworths.

Interesting work has been done on another large manuscript from much the same area — the Findern anthology (CUL MS Ff. 1. 6), owned from the mid-fifteenth century by the Findern family, who lived in south Derbyshire, much of the time at Findern itself.[26] There are similarities and differences between the Findern and the Advocates manuscripts. The Findern anthology appears also originally to have been made up in booklets that were kept separate for some time, and here too a large number of scribes contributed to the collection, some of whom were possibly professionals or household servants, but others were certainly members of the family or of a circle of local friends. The Findern anthology, too, was used for jottings, though these are much fewer and of more weight than many of those in the Advocates manuscript. Professor Robbins suggests that the Findern anthology was used as a repository of record; that the memorandum of money spent on a journey into Leicestershire and the inventory of the bedding at Findern were noted there precisely because they were items that might need to be referred to at some later date. The main differences between the Findern and the Advocates manuscripts, though, are in content. Instead of the very varied miscellany of everything a decent household needs to know, the Findern anthology's contents are almost entirely secular poetry, much of it by well-known authors, Chaucer, Gower and Lydgate, together with some shorter love-lyrics, not recorded in other manuscripts, added by the minor scribal hands. The Finderns wanted an anthology of polite literature; the compilers of the Advocates manuscript had the humbler aim of building up a compendium for the instruction and occasional amusement of the family.

I have dealt in some detail with two manuscripts from the north-east Midlands, the Middleton and the Advocates manuscripts, and I have discussed the manuscripts of two other families from the area. We have thus seen something of the literary tastes of four local families, the Berkeleys, the Chaworths, the Sherbrookes and the Finderns. It is interesting that only two of the works in these manuscripts are unquestionably local products — the Berkeley *Lament* and *The Battle of Brakonwet*. Much more comes from further afield — the works of named authors such as Trevisa, Chaucer, Gower and Lydgate. To some extent, certainly, these families drew on national literary tastes. This may not represent the general picture in this area. By and large, these are some of the important families of the district, and presumably there was a whole stratum of more popular literature that has not been considered here: songs and tales, Robin Hood ballads and so on. I have not looked at the literary tastes and activities of the clergy. The picture of literature in the north-east Midlands needs to be filled out a great deal more. That task may turn out to be impossible, but I hope that by concentrated work

---

[26] A facsimile of the manuscript has been published, with an introduction by R. Beadle and A. E. B. Owen (London, 1977). For detailed discussion see R. H. Robbins, 'The Findern Anthology', *PMLA*, 69 (1954), 610-42.

on one geographical area, employing a range of other people's expertise — dialectology, palaeography, genealogy, local history, and so on — it will prove possible to begin to make links between the important families, to build up a more detailed picture of a local community, to recognise products of the same scribes, to identify local authors by their work if not by name, to see if there were schools of writers, and to find out about the activities of the monasteries and other centres of learning. This project, if it is to get anywhere at all, should aim at setting medieval literature much more securely and illuminatingly within its local context.

RETROSPECT AND PROSPECT

A. I. Doyle

The York conference from which the foregoing papers come was, so far as I know, only the second devoted to Middle English studies to be held in the British Isles, the first having been that concerning the proposed Index of Middle English Prose held at Emmanuel College, Cambridge, in 1978.[1] Although the specific focus at York was on manuscripts rather than authors, texts or language, the attendance had to be limited for convenience to sixty. That so many came, and more would have done if it had been possible, indicates how far investigation of the manuscript context has come to be felt the most promising way to advance our knowledge of Middle English literature, and this feeling was also reflected in the proportion of younger scholars attending. It is notable that nearly all the papers were given by people whom I hope I may describe (since it emphasises the freshness of their approach) as comparative beginners, and that most of them were products of the Centre for Medieval Studies at York itself, a well-justified expression of its influence in promoting research in this direction over the last fifteen years.

When I gave the opening talk (not printed here because it was already promised for publication in a volume edited by another former York student)[2] I said I wondered if I had been invited to open the batting as one of the longer-toothed practitioners or at least one of the first post-Second World War generation. At the time I started research on the origins and circulation of certain kinds of later Middle English literature in 1945 there were decidedly fewer models of method and sources of information, while some of the best had not been long available or much used, because of the war: Manly and Rickert[3] (Chicago, 1940), Ker[4] (London, 1941), Brown and Robbins[5] (New York, 1943), to which I would add Robbins' Ph.D. thesis[6] (Cambridge, England, 1938). There is not uncommonly a time-lag before scholars realise the potentialities for further advance from a major work of learning, as if the subject were exhausted by it, and some of these and other long-standing tools have begun to be utilised widely only in quite recent

---

[1] Of which the papers were published in *Middle English Prose: Essays on Bibliographical Problems*, edited by A. S. G. Edwards and Derek Pearsall (New York, 1981).
[2] *Middle English Alliterative Poetry and its Literary Background*, ed. David Lawton (Cambridge, 1982) 88-100, 142-7.
[3] J. M. Manly and Edith Rickert, *The Text of the Canterbury Tales*.
[4] N. R. Ker, *Medieval Libraries of Great Britain*.
[5] C. F. Brown and R. H. Robbins, *The Index of Middle English Verse*.
[6] On the medieval English lyric, much of which has appeared in his subsequent publications. I should also mention perhaps H. S. Bennett, 'The production and dissemination of vernacular manuscripts in the fifteenth century', *The Library*, 5th ser., vol. 1 (1946-47), 167-78.

years. The existence of a thorough-seeming description of a manuscript, and even more one of a group of manuscripts, and increasingly of a complete facsimile, is liable to make anyone assume (although one may have learned the lesson more than once already) that there is nothing to be discovered by looking at the original. However meticulous previous inspectors may have been, different people carry different things in their heads and in their hands, and can so make different connections, especially with new techniques (e.g. in paper-history) to aid them.

When I gave the Special Lectures in Palaeography at King's College, London, in 1965 on 'Later Middle English Manuscripts' they were concerned in part with what had been done and in part with what had not, and consequently with the directions in which and the methods by which our knowledge could be advanced. The lapse of years since (in a career not concerned primarily with medieval manuscripts or literature) and the great growth of interest in the field has entailed repeated revision of an intended book based on those lectures, the aim of which is to give an account of the situation as up-to-date as possible in order to help newcomers. The extent and quality of relevant new work, as exemplified in the present volume, and now the universal contraction of academic prospects, together make the case for the completion of such a book arguable.[7] It is not however entirely impossible for such studies to be pursued outside the ordinary framework of university English teaching and it is to be hoped that the present essays are not the last we shall hear from some of the authors. I am not the only person present at the York conference who was rewarded to hear how the hopes of 1965 are being carried into effect, for Professor Julian Brown, who was also there and had invited me to give the London lectures, went out of his way to say so.

In 1965 I was already able to give a leading place to the methodology and early results of the Edinburgh Middle English Dialect Survey, which had commenced in 1953 but which established language specialists elsewhere for long were unduly wary about, despite a series of demonstrative articles by Professors McIntosh and Samuels, assisted subsequently by Dr Michael Benskin.[8] In the meantime individual editors from various countries have not been loath to make use of their help, and a new respect for the evidential value of the exact spelling of every copy of a text has converged with growing consciousness of the benefits of precise codicological and palaeographical analysis of each manuscript. I could cite Dr G. S. Ivy's explications of codicology in English before the term itself was invented or imported,[9] and I had the advantage of knowing the outlines of Mr Malcolm Parkes'

---

[7] The scope and approach would not be the same as either Beverly Boyd's *Chaucer and the Medieval Book* (San Marino, 1973) or Charles Moorman's *Editing the Middle English Manuscript* (Jackson, 1975), although they would obviously overlap.
[8] Commencing with Angus McIntosh, 'The analysis of written Middle English', *Transactions of the Philological Society* (1956), 26-55.
[9] In his unpublished London Ph.D. thesis (1953), *The Make-up of Middle English Verse Manuscripts*, especially those at Trintiy College, Cambridge, and 'The bibliography of the manuscript book' in *The English Library before 1700*, ed. F. Wormald and C. E. Wright (London, 1958), 32-65. 'Codicologie' is thought to have been first used by A. Dain, *Les Manuscrits* (Paris, 1949), though in a more restricted sense than subsequently employed by others, as here, for the archaeology of the book.

book on *English Cursive Book Hands* before it was published (1969), since when
the elements of his classification have been picked up by more people than have
grasped the significance of their presence in the practice of particular scribes.
Although palaeography in the stricter sense does not loom large in the present
volume, its assistance is everywhere presumed, and Jeremy Smith's paper epit-
omises the promising development of the Dialect Survey's reach, beyond the
publication of its Atlas, in illuminating some of the most important choices in
the copying of a vernacular text, paralleled by those of a more purely graphic
character.[10] It incidentally offers part of an answer to the assumptions about
spelling consistency made in a more recent challenge to the identity of the copyist
of the Hengwrt and Ellesmere manuscripts of the *Canterbury Tales*.[11]

Pamela Robinson's and Jeremy Griffiths' papers to the conference (both substantially printed elsewhere)[12] also concerned the relations of actual copies to
hypothetical exemplars, with regard to physical structure and stages of growth
of a codex or a work. Both afford warnings, implicit and explicit, against ignoring
the individuality of antecedent circumstances affecting textual history. The
contributions by Julia Boffey, Thorlac Turville Petre and Carol Meale pursue
some of the paths opened by Brown, Greene and Robbins in defining the codicological and social contexts of (mostly) shorter poems, exemplifying too the happier
interaction between literary and historical considerations which has spread in the
last twenty years or so. John Thompson shows what can be construed about the
process of compilation of another, even-better known volume than Harley 2252,
Lincoln Cathedral 91, of less obvious incremental construction, of which our
comprehension can be helped by the availability of a complete facsimile. The
flow of published facsimiles in recent years, not only of whole manuscripts but
also of single pages, ought in time to encourage more extensive and exact comparative teaching or learning of how varied our matter is, beyond the limited
number and range of specimens in text-books, although what is now published is
not always well-chosen.[13]

Carl Marx and Kate Harris, though the one presents an instance of greater
textual persistence and the other of more variation, both evoke the question
whether the actual scribe or someone behind him (or her) is responsible for
modifications found only in a single copy — until another copy of the same is
found and the problem put back a stage or more. In the circumstances of medieval

[10] See the articles by M. Benskin and M. Laing and myself in *So Meny People Longages and Tonges: Philological Essays in Scots and Mediaeval English presented to Angus McIntosh* (Edinburgh, 1981).
[11] R. V. Ramsey, 'The Hengwrt and Ellesmere manuscripts of the *Canterbury Tales*: different scribes', *Studies in Bibliography*, 35 (1982), 133-54. Professor M. L. Samuels has a direct reply forthcoming.
[12] The former as 'The *Booklet*: a Self-Contained Unit in Composite Manuscripts', *Codicologica*, iii, edited by A. Gruijs and J. P. Gumbert, Litterae Textuales (Leiden, 1980), and the latter as part of the Introduction to the facsimile of St John's College, Cambridge, MS L. 1, to be published by the University of Oklahoma Press as part of the *Variorum Chaucer* project.
[13] A smaller area than a single page would sometimes be more useful in showing details nearer actual size, and particularly where changes of hand etc. occur.

manuscript descent what was one person's individual adaptation for the purposes of his anticipated readers might be accepted willy-nilly by subsequent copyists, or further altered by others. It is not easy to be sure where we can pin down the interpretative intention of particular changes or additions, in consequence. Similar considerations apply to the providing of pictures, and the details of imitation and innovation, which Lesley Lawton discusses judiciously, with regard to one of the groups of vernacular books which were, until not long ago, neglected by art historians, before the latter became more concerned with the exhaustiveness of their evidence and the codicological dimension.[14]

Despite the ground-work by Macaulay and Bergen, the study of the manuscripts of Gower's and Lydgate's longer works, of their writing and decoration together with their textual relationships, had also been surprisingly neglected, as I tried to indicate in my London lectures of 1965 and the Lyell lectures at Oxford in 1967. Anthony Edwards has since done something to remedy this neglect of Lydgate and here outlines the room for further progress, while others have Gower again in hand.[15] Manly and the two Rickerts in their survey of the manuscripts of the *Canterbury Tales*, although it awaits more palaeographical development, offered valuable clues for copies of Gower, Lydgate and other authors as well as of Chaucer. There is now appearing a landscape of, on the one hand, overlapping work by scribes and decorators probably for the metropolitan book-trade and, on the other, of more self-contained circles of craftsmen based on one locality or special-ising in one type of text, such as the Lydgate manuscripts probably from Suffolk. In contrast with those anonymous associations we have the ambiguous position of John Shirley, from his words, products and milieu more an amateur impresario than a commercial entrepreneur, it seems to me, although a new discovery could make it clearer. There is a temptation to jump the slow steps we need to take if we are to build up a firm reconstruction of the rôles of different kinds of compiler, editor and copyist in producing Middle English manuscripts in various places at various times and for various purposes.[16]

The integration of our knowledge of medieval literature with the understanding of its contemporaneous conditions is the goal towards which most of the contri-butions to the York conference tended. It is of course not accidental that academic attention has swung to this area of interest when the number of texts as yet unedited is becoming steadily fewer, though the recovery of additional copies and the employment of improved techniques will justify the re-editing of some, with benefits for the sort of study represented here, which is characterised by such healthy cross-fertilisation. It is impossible to pursue manuscript studies nowadays satisfactorily in individual isolation, for one cannot find all one ought

[14] Dr J. J. G. Alexander and Dr K. L. Scott have led the way with English manuscripts of the later middle ages.

[15] Mr Griffiths, Miss Harris and Professor Pearsall.

[16] A more recent treatment of the subject by Cheryl Greenberg, 'John Shirley and the English book trade', *The Library*, 6th ser. vol. 4 (1982), 369-80, ignores the indispensability of first-hand investigation and of caution in historical assumptions.

A. I. Doyle

to know by oneself and one ought not to keep all one knows to oneself; the jig-saw puzzle we are all working on is so big that it may need the help of every eye to try to fit a piece in it. The growing pace of its visible improvement by this collaboration must encourage us to persist with our methods, whether we can meet in person for the purpose or only by other means of communication.